IF NOT CRITICAL

IF NOT
CRITICAL

ERIC GRIFFITHS

Edited by

FREYA JOHNSTON

OXFORD
UNIVERSITY PRESS

OXFORD
UNIVERSITY PRESS

Great Clarendon Street, Oxford, OX2 6DP,
United Kingdom

Oxford University Press is a department of the University of Oxford.
It furthers the University's objective of excellence in research, scholarship,
and education by publishing worldwide. Oxford is a registered trade mark of
Oxford University Press in the UK and in certain other countries

© Freya Johnston 2018

The moral rights of the author have been asserted

First Edition published in 2018

Impression: 7

Published in the United States of America by Oxford University Press
198 Madison Avenue, New York, NY 10016, United States of America

British Library Cataloguing in Publication Data
Data available

Library of Congress Control Number: 2017949308

ISBN 978-0-19-880529-8

Printed and bound in Great Britain by Clays Ltd, Elcograf S.p.A.

For Mark Godowski

Acknowledgements

For their help in preparing and commenting on this book, many thanks to Colin Burrow, Robert Douglas-Fairhurst, Alistair Jones, Ruth Mackenzie, Daniel McCann, Jeff New, Jacqueline Norton, Seamus Perry, Adrian Poole, Christopher Ricks, and Jenny Polak.

For permission to reprint extracts from the works of W. H. Auden, Samuel Beckett, John Berryman, T. S. Eliot, and Ezra Pound, I am grateful to Curtis Brown, Faber & Faber, and New Directions Publishing Corp.

I am also grateful to my colleagues in the Oxford English Faculty for their support. Jemma Stewart's efficiency and resourcefulness brought this book to completion.

Freya Johnston

Contents

Note on texts and editions

References to the Bible are to the King James Version.

References to Shakespeare, unless otherwise stated, are to the First Folio (1623) and are given by act, scene, and line number (in the system of through-line numbering, counting all printed lines continuously from first to last).

All translations, unless otherwise stated, are by Eric Griffiths; footnote references have also been provided to scholarly editions and translations of texts cited in the lectures.

Some entries in the *Oxford English Dictionary* have been revised and altered in the online edition since the lectures in this book were written; all definitions have been left in the form in which they originally appeared in Eric Griffiths' work.

Introduction

True critics, like true poets, have a way of writing about things before they happen to them, so that their words take on the cast of intimations or apprehensions.[1] Before his speaking voice was cut off by a stroke, Eric Griffiths had spent decades thinking about the sound of words. In *The Printed Voice of Victorian Poetry* (1989), he wrote:

> Print does not give conclusive evidence of a voice; this raises doubts about what we hear in writing but also gives an essential pleasure of reading, for as we meet the demands a text makes on us for our voices, we are engaged in an activity of imagination which is delicately and thoroughly reciprocal.[2]

This book, 'evidence of a voice' and of its absence, started life as hundreds of lectures, here represented by a selection of ten, and as the verses and translations from French, German, and Italian that Eric Griffiths wrote in his spare time, read out, and gave to his friends. Hearing his critical and creative voice in print is now the only way to hear it in something like full flow. Of William Empson's public readings John Wain recalled 'a very wide range of sheer volume'; he 'shouted' some passages 'like a Neapolitan stevedore, laryngitically croaking others'. There were moments of shouting and croaking in Eric Griffiths' lectures, too, marinated as they were in cigarettes, watered-down whisky, coffee, and milk. His public voice was fast, sardonic, protesting, and exact. Reading texts aloud with smaller groups

---

[1] T. S. Eliot remarked to William Empson 'that the test of a true poet is that he writes about experiences before they have happened to him'; Empson 'felt I had once passed this test, though I forget now in which poem'. William Empson, 'Donne the Space Man', *Kenyon Review* 19 (1957), 337–99 (p. 398).

[2] Eric Griffiths, *The Printed Voice of Victorian Poetry* (Oxford: Clarendon Press, 1989), 13.

of people, he adopted like Empson 'a much quieter style', though 'the curious angularity of rhythm' and the upturned eyes, a tribal characteristic of Cambridge English, were typically still part of the show.[3]

The title of this book comes from one of Eric's favourite dramatic characters, Iago—'I am nothing, if not Criticall'[4]—and the pieces of writing collected here are, like Iago, full of provocation, experience, and advice: on how to read, think, watch films, make a list, brush your hair, and put on a jumper (not necessarily in that order). Like A. E. Housman, Eric Griffiths was well aware that 'Poems very seldom consist of poetry and nothing else; and pleasure can be derived also from their other ingredients'[5]; he registered, time and again, the ways in which literature is touched by and gestures towards a world beyond itself, and that such ways were 'at best oblique and stylized' ('Lists'). Crammed into his writing are decades of reading in several languages and across most genres and literary periods. He did not remotely speak as if to a group of specialists in the academy; as a result, his work is not sequestered but original, open, and surprising. It has both the comedy and the virtue of 'observational patience and careful statement' ('Lists'), and it is shot through with the exhilaration of discovery, immediately responsive to the details of what it is describing.

Eric has always loved to read, to argue, and to tease; his prose toys with characters and texts and their audiences, but it also looks the horrors and miseries of real life as well as careless and ill-founded critical orthodoxies in the face. As a critic, he is richly alert to human fallibility, backsliding, and contradiction, and relentless in his pursuit of those who do not or will not acknowledge such lapses and oddities or who knowingly put them, in writing, to one side. His work gathers up 'hints of unrecounted lives', as he describes them in 'A rehearsal of *Hamlet*', echoing Wordsworth's 'little, nameless, unremembered acts / Of kindness and of love'.[6] It points towards what might have been left out of an account of literature—perhaps especially towards those who cannot read what is written about them, and those whose

---

[3] John Haffenden, *William Empson: Against the Christians* (Oxford: Oxford University Press, 2006), 353, 458.

[4] *Othello*, II.i.892.

[5] A. E. Housman, *The Name and Nature of Poetry* (Cambridge: Cambridge University Press, 1933), 34.

[6] 'Lines Written a Few Miles above Tintern Abbey', l. 35, *Lyrical Ballads* (1798), in *William Wordsworth: 21st-Century Oxford Authors*, ed. Stephen Gill (Oxford: Oxford University Press, 2010), 50.

existence is suggested by rather than included in a text. Eric Griffiths pursues the blind spots not only of other people's arguments, but of the whole business of criticism in general, with what he calls its 'over-concentration on a narrow range of examples…such over-concentration warps our thinking' ('Beasts'). Implicit and explicit throughout his work is the argument that 'an appropriately wide range of instances is essential to making progress in conceptualization'; that what we need, in order to do better thinking, is 'a keener attention to a greater variety of examples' ('Beasts'). The following chapters show how such attentiveness might work in practice. Take the handling of theorists who assert the absolute centrality of laughter to comedy, in reply to which Eric Griffiths inquires after 'all those other expressions of a comic sense': 'the snigger? the wry smile? the twinkle? the gloating cackle? the insult? the raised eyebrow? the limp wrist? and particularly, that intriguing and central comic abstention from expression, the poker-face?' ('Beasts').

All these 'expressions' and more punctuated his lectures, which were brilliant performances; they demonstrated criticism in action. He rehearsed his disagreements both mildly and heatedly, verbally and physically, but without enforcing his views on the audience. He often confessed quite openly that such differences as he had with other writers would need to be left unsettled—not just by him, but by the limits of what criticism as a discipline might achieve. One thing it could reasonably and usefully attempt, as Eric showed over and over again, was to check us in our assumptions. It might also help to revivify something lost or gone cold:

The most practical form which criticism can take is performance, reading aloud, whether theatrically or not, for when we read aloud we put ourselves in the world of those whose beliefs may be other than our own, if only for the time the reading lasts. To read out something written down is to try to bring something to life, to give birth in the moment of giving voice, or to try to bring something back to life, a form of resurrection, as Hamlet making jokes of Yorick's mouth tries to put back in that mouth the jokes that Yorick himself might have made had he been there to make them.[7]

The terms in which he describes this live performance of imaginative identification echo Samuel Johnson—a critic who, like William Empson

---

[7] Eric Griffiths, Practical Criticism 8: 'A girl can't go on laughing all the time' (unpublished lecture).

and like Eric's friend and doctoral supervisor Christopher Ricks, shapes the writings included in *If Not Critical*. Eric's work is in perpetual communication, agreement, and disagreement with theirs, as with a continuous human tradition from which he drew his own ways of reading and interpreting literature. Johnson, discussing biography, suggests that:

All joy or sorrow for the happiness or calamities of others is produced by an act of the imagination, that realises the event however fictitious, or approximates it however remote, by placing us, for a time, in the condition of him whose fortunes we contemplate; so that we feel, while the deception lasts, whatever motions would be excited by the same good or evil happening to ourselves.[8]

Eric Griffiths' lectures are, apart from anything else, fragments of autobiography—they include joyous digs and swipes at his own name, his school, friends, family, cats, students, college, faculty, and colleagues. That it mattered to him that such jokes were accurate is evident in the corrections he made to drafts of his work. He also celebrated the hard-won achievement, exemplified in Kafka's Josef K., of finding nothing special about yourself; of gaining a vantage-point on your own experience as that of someone among countless others, a view that tries not to privilege your own case. His writing has a nimble sense of perspective that is at once self-affirming and self-denying; revelling in its ability to clock details and their implications, it also knows that while we laugh at things and people that have gone out of date, we should be conscious that we ourselves are becoming outdated, passing through, and going off; that we will one day, and probably quite soon, turn into the butt of a joke ourselves. The forms of comedy and tragedy which he set out to chart arise from the 'clash of the human being—soaked to the bone in life in time—and the divine judgement—ever there, immobile, on the look-out, impending' ('Timing'). Towards the end of this book, Christian theology is called 'simply literary criticism' ('Godforsakenness'): as a Catholic, Eric Griffiths offers in his work 'honest amplitude about the varieties of religious experience' and bears witness to 'the intermittences of devotion' ('*Inferno* 32 and 33').

---

[8] Samuel Johnson, *Rambler*, no. 60 (1750), in *The Yale Edition of the Works of Samuel Johnson* (New Haven and London: Yale University Press, 1958–), vol. 3: *The Rambler*, ed. W. J. Bate and Albrecht B. Strauss (1969), 318–19.

His lectures often discuss turning and conversion, and they test out some basic, vital principles concerning evidence, faith, and reason, whether in the realm of the believer or the non-believer.

There are plenty of things to object to in this book. The writing can be scornful, rude, and slangy; it includes glancing references to soap operas, jibes at other critics, and disdain for politicians. Some of the jokes are, inevitably, dated. But I have not taken it as part of my editorial remit to delete them; aside from the addition of references and the omission of some Cambridge-specific material, directed at students and about examinations, the lectures have been left as they were written and originally delivered. Eric Griffiths never gathered up his unpublished work for revision into published form, but the task of editing it has been made a lot easier than it might have been by the fact that he usually typed out every single word of what he was going to say. The lectures were delivered fast, 'so conceptual gaps do not become obvious', as he once said (very quickly) on his way to an auditorium. The speed at which they were given is obvious from how long they are: on average, around 8,500 words; nearly all the sentences and many of the quotations in them are pretty long, too. I guess that most of us who lecture to students, week by week and for the standard fifty minutes, would aim for a script of no more than 7,000 words. But Eric didn't mind keeping those who wanted to stay in the room for up to ninety minutes (his *Hamlet* lectures, as he pointed out in the first of the series, were like the play itself a bit too long). Timing was central, and is indeed the subject of several pieces included here; the crafty lulls and rushes built into his delivery were part of the arresting effect. He laughed incredulously when reading a comment on one student feedback form that answered 'yes' in response to the question whether his lecture series had facilitated note-taking. Yet he only very rarely stumbled over his words; one startling instance, in his F. W. Bateson lecture in Oxford on 'The Disappointment of Christina G. Rossetti' (1997), was a reference to 'the elephants of criticism' rather than 'the elements of criticism'—such a happy infelicity as to make even Eric pause before resuming the usual verbal canter.[9]

---

[9] The lecture was later published as 'The Disappointment of Christina G. Rossetti', *Essays in Criticism* 47: 2 (1997), 107–42. That text has 'elements of a unified theory' (p. 110), but not 'elements of criticism'. I have included here my recollection of the text as it was spoken, since it may differ from the text as published; it is at least equally possible that my memory is at fault.

His lectures started countless thoughts without unfolding them, suggesting to his mostly undergraduate audience dozens of ways forward with stubborn or apparently unpromising material. He showed them both in his lectures and in his translations how to imagine the difference it would make if a story or poem or shopping-list were written or arranged otherwise, or in another language, or within the context of an entirely different set of conventions, and how to value such acts of imagining. His writing is rich in explica-tion and implication. What would a poem sound like if it presented itself in another form? What would it mean if one word were replaced by a similar one? Would the joke be lost? Might there also be a gain? Such suggestions, often made in passing, triggered whole books by his students, many of whom now teach English in schools and universities. Eric Griffiths' work was and is generous; what remains on paper hints at his resourcefulness and prodigality as a supervisor. He could also be a frightening teacher, as is suggested by these agile, clear-sighted pieces of work; when he comments on the 'co-occurrence of laughter and fear' in Rabelais, having noted coolly that 'people wet themselves in terror as well as in laughter' ('Beasts'), he is talk-ing partly about a mixed mood that he enjoyed creating in his rooms. Empson summed up the influence of T. S. Eliot as 'perhaps not unlike an east wind'.[10] He might have been describing the atmos-phere of Cambridge indoors and out, at least as I recall it—chilly, bracing, and hard on the nerves.

'If we have superseded the past, we too will be overtaken in our turn' ('Beasts'): Eric often said that he wanted his students to outsmart him, and would wryly lament the fact that no one had yet managed it. Although, most of the time, he loved teaching, he was also bored and frustrated by students and their non-stop questions: a miniature black-board propped up on his mantelpiece protested 'How the fuck should I know?' These writings are a prompt to vigilance, to prize the vitality and particularity of literature and not to flatten it out into something more comfortable and less advertent than he had found it to be. Like his friend the art critic Tom Lubbock, whose laughter is mentioned at the start of 'Beasts', Eric pursued as his calling 'the discipline of observation',[11] and the following chapters work by deft and watchful accumulation. Each judgement feels earned but not laborious.

---

[10] William Empson, 'The Style of the Master' (1948), in *Argufying: Essays on Literature and Culture*, ed. John Haffenden (London: Chatto & Windus, 1987), 361–3 (p. 361).

[11] Tom Lubbock, *English Graphic* (London: Francis Lincoln), 47.

In Eric Griffiths' prose, 'thinking *happens*' ('A rehearsal of *Hamlet*'). Reading through it again, it seems to me to be predominantly about comedy and forbearance—perhaps, in fact, about the comedy of forbearance, which is another way to describe the experience of teaching and of being taught. Or, as he puts it in 'Beasts', this book is about 'the test and the pleasure of examples'.

Freya Johnston
St Anne's College, Oxford

I

Lists

A long time ago, the term 'literature' just meant 'reading-matter' or 'learning', so you could say 'she's a woman of great literature' and mean she was very widely read in, say, history and theology and the law. The term shrank, in the century or so after Dr Johnson (who still used it in the old sense), until it ended up as the slimmed-down version represented nowadays in the 'literature' department of bookshops, where you find only fictions, poems, plays, and perhaps even only rather arty fictions, like Booker Prize Winners, rather than books anyone might read for pleasure such as thrillers. Of course, literaturists who exist on a diet of literature alone have a restricted notion of how language operates and what can be inferred about the world from particular instances of language use, just as someone who lived exclusively on strawberry jam would probably have a very partial view of the food-chain (and poor skin). When we read fictions, for instance, we are not concerned primarily or even at all with whether what they say is true or not. Indeed, in some respects, it is a mark of understanding that what you're reading is a fiction that you don't ask 'is this true?' Someone who responded to the first sentence of *Middlemarch*—'Miss Brooke had that kind of beauty which seems to be thrown into relief by poor dress'—by wondering whether she did *really* or hoped to find a photo of her so he could see for himself, would show, just in that desire to check, a basic misunderstanding of what a novel is: you can't check the facts in fiction against the evidence, because what makes it fiction is that there is no evidence for what it says.[1] Literaturists are less used to kinds of writing which derive from checking and depend on accurate

---

[1] George Eliot, *Middlemarch*, ed. David Caroll, 2nd edn. (Oxford: Oxford University Press, 2008), 7.

description. As a result, they tend perhaps to underestimate the virtues of observational patience and careful statement and to worry less than they should about verbal posturing which has only its own lexical flounces to support it.

A related problem arises when people treat works of literature as themselves having direct evidential value, whereas literature's testimony to the world beyond literature is at best oblique and stylized. Professor John Carey took Shakespeare's plays as a good sample of how vivacious the English language was in the playwright's day, as if, down the *Queen Bess* in Jacobean Walford, the air was buzzing with extravagant conceits and searching wordplay:[2] 'Nay, Dot, pout not thy scrawny lips at me, thou crestfallen death's-head, thou Lincolnshire bagpipe.' / 'Have a care ere thou gird at me, Peggy Mitchell, for what is known in Walford is known. And many there be have had their fill of thy Phil, and of thee.' Similar naivety is popular among those who imagine that there was little premarital sex in Victorian England because there is little pre-marital sex in Victorian novels. How they square this belief with the soaring illegitimacy rates of the nineteenth century is a mystery. Literature consists to a great extent of telling people what they want to hear, and that is something quite different from telling them the truth about their lives. Or again, the accomplished historical linguist and phonetician David Crystal tells us much that we ought to know about the pronunciation of Shakespeare's English, in books such as the ear-opening *Pronouncing Shakespeare* or on the website of the same name (where you can hear extracts, including one from *Troilus and Cressida*, Act I, scene 1, done in original pronunciation), but he too has an unexamined notion about literature as evidence—he thinks Shakespeare was trying to transcribe the linguistic realities of sixteenth-century London in his scripts.[3] We know that in sixteenth-century London there were vowel-sounds which were regarded by some as old-fashioned and others which were more up-and-coming. Crystal wonders whether in performing *Romeo and Juliet*, the older Capulets and Montagues should be given the recessive forms and the younger generation, the emergent.[4] He is not bothered that the play is set not

---

[2] John Carey, *What Good Are the Arts?* (London: Faber & Faber, 2005), 215–16.

[3] David Crystal, *Pronouncing Shakespeare: The Globe Experiment* (Cambridge: Cambridge University Press, 2005). The website referred to above has now been incorporated into <*http://shakespeareswords.com/*>.

[4] *Pronouncing Shakespeare*, 72–4.

in London but Verona, and that you can't date its events to the sixteenth century. The linguistic realities around Shakespeare as he wrote are no doubt where the playwright started from but they are not what he was aiming to capture, any more than a rocket, launched from Cape Canaveral, is aiming at Florida—it is headed for the moon, though to describe its flight you need to know about its launch-pad as well as its destination. Comparing different kinds of text should help promote alertness to the differences between them, and keep literaturists aware that the kinds of writing they mostly read (imaginative fictions) are only a fragment of a much larger landmass of language-use, a landmass with which the literary parish remains continuous, and without attention to which even the literary works can't be understood, as an oasis is unintelligible without thought of the dunes which surround it.

Students of imaginative literature are prone to be unimaginative about any writing which isn't imaginative literature. For example, you often find that the word 'list' attracts 'merely', 'only', 'no more than', and the like into its vicinity. Once something has been identified as a list, it seems there can be nothing more to say about it, because lists are inherently dull, prosaic things, part of the fittings in language's utility room, whereas literaturists are keen on more glamorous apartments— sun-lounges, libraries, and bed-chambers. But, as with beauty, list-lessness is in the eye of the beholder, and if you know how to treat a list right, it will repay the time and attention you devote to it.

One reason why lists should matter to literaturists is that lists came before literature; they are, then, part of where literature itself came from. Among the most ancient surviving documents which we can still understand, the clay tablets from Mesopotamia about 3,000 years BC, there are some bits of literature, but the predominant kind of document is a list, an administrative list. The poets like to tell us it was they, the poets, who gave mankind speech and purified the dialect of the tribe and shed light on the gods and other such boasts, but, as far as concerns writing, the evidence suggests we are in debt not so much to the poets as to the warehousemen and civil servants who kept the tallies of grain and oil, recorded the tribute owed from several provinces, or cata-logued the parts of an ox and their respective values. The anthropolo-gist Jack Goody has a fine essay about lists in his *The Domestication of the Savage Mind*, from which I lift this information about ancient lists. He makes the following thought-provoking observations about some of

the things which happen to the human being's mindset when writing
has enabled the keeping of lists:

[Listing] encourages the ordering of the items, by number, by initial sound,
by category, etc. And the existence of boundaries, external and internal,
brings greater visibility to categories, at the same time as making them more
abstract...We can see here [in Egyptian lists of *c.*1100 BCE] the dialectical
effect of writing upon classification. On the one hand it sharpens the outlines
of the categories: one has to make a decision as to whether rain or dew is of
the heavens or of the earth; furthermore it encourages the hierarchisation
of the classificatory system. At the same time, it leads to questions about the
nature of the classes through the very fact of placing them together.[5]

When you recognize the role that lists have played in the flexing and
development of our mental muscles, of our taxonomies and our ability
to retrieve information by searching for it under the headings where
we have filed it, the list which to the parochial literaturist is 'just' a
list—'cornflakes, broccoli, Polo mints, lip-gloss, 2 copies Eric Griffiths:
The Printed Voice of Victorian Poetry, oysters, vodka'—that mundane
document turns out to be a pivotal invention in the development of
cultures, not perhaps quite as dramatic as the invention of the wheel
but up there with the pulley and the world religions. A list, intelligently
considered, can be a real eye-opener and give rise to extremely dramatic
mental events, as in the case of Michel Foucault, who prefaces his
super-famous and reputedly groundbreaking book, *Les mots et les choses*
(*The Order of Things*) as follows:

This book first arose out of a passage in Borges, out of the laughter that
shattered, as I read the passage, all the familiar landmarks of my thought—*our*
thought, the thought that bears the stamp of our age and our geography—
breaking up all the ordered surfaces and all the places with which we are
accustomed to tame the wild profusion of existing things, and continuing long
afterwards to disturb and threaten with collapse our age-old distinction between
the Same and the Other. This passage quotes 'a certain Chinese encyclopaedia'
in which it is written that 'animals are divided into: (a) belonging to the
Emperor, (b) embalmed, (c) tame, (d) sucking pigs, (e) sirens, (f) fabulous,
(g) stray dogs, (h) included in the present classification, (i) frenzied, (j) innumerable, (k) drawn with a very fine camelhair brush, (l) *et cetera*, (m) having
just broken the water pitcher, (n) that from a long way off look like flies.'
In the wonderment of this taxonomy, the thing we apprehend in one great

---

[5] Jack Goody, 'What's in a list?', in *The Domestication of the Savage Mind* (Cambridge:
Cambridge University Press, 1977), 74–111 (pp. 81, 102).

leap, the thing that, by means of the fable, is demonstrated as the exotic charm of another system of thought, is the limitation of our own, the stark impossibility of thinking *that*.[6]

Foucault was an excitable reader and an even more excitable writer—note, for instance, the insistent 'all's of this passage—'all the familiar landmarks...all the ordered surfaces...all the places...' (the translation is faithful in this respect to the French original)—and there are reasons to moderate his squeals of astonishment at the Chinese list. Still, he's admirably responsive to the intriguing and bizarre potential of this list, and of lists generally, and, at least to that extent, is a better reader than the dismissive, 'oh it's just a list' literaturist. Foucault took Borges's fiction as evidence of the possibility of a 'system of thought' implied by the list, and inferred from that possibility the limits of 'our own' mindset—for us, there is a 'stark impossibility' in thinking like that, the list wildly estranges us from all we know and how we think we know it, from '*our* thought'. And this confrontation of one system of thought with another provided him with an analogy for what he believed to be the relations between different historical paradigms or mindsets or *problematiques* or conjunctures within the Western tradition: stretches of our own past are, according to Foucault, another country, and that country is China, in the sense that, for example, the sixteenth century had a way of organizing thoughts, of drawing up lists, sorting stuff into separate boxes, which is now as alien and unthinkable to us as this list of fourteen Chinese categories. From this confrontation, Foucault elaborated his grand project of an 'archaeology of knowing', an inquiry into the conditions of possibility of our thinking some things (and by the same token of the impossibility of our thinking other things). And who are 'we'? Westerners presumably—astounded at the fiendish inscrutability of the oriental mind. But this, on closer inspection, is a very unconvincing Chinese encyclopedia because its classifications are listed according to a Western alphabet. Chinese has no alphabet and so the curious charm of this list, which, on the one hand, careers about wildly between diverse kinds of classification without any immediately evident rationale but also, on the other hand, walks in an orderly, alphabetical manner from 'a' to 'n'—this curious blend of the haphazard and the strict is something produced by Borges's report on the

[6] Michel Foucault, 'Preface', *Les mots et les choses* (1966), trans. as *The Order of Things* (London: Tavistock Publications, 1970), xv.

imagined encyclopedia and cannot have occurred in the Chinese pages where there was no alphabet to follow. (Foucault does mention the presence in the fable of 'alphabetical series' and of 'our alphabetical order', but he sets so little store by this that its presence doesn't hold him back from claiming the list shatters all the familiar landmarks of our thought, though the list is organized by a landmark so familiar— the alphabet—that we barely realize how lost we would be without it.) He is in his own way as naive about what Borges's fiction could be evidence of as Professor Carey is about Shakespeare's plays as a sociolinguistic sample; he ought to have asked whether there could possibly be such an encyclopedia, and the answer is that there could not, and not only because of the incongruous alphabetization.

The character of Borges's passage comes from a discrepancy between what can be guessed to be the Argentinian writer's priorities and what counts most for his imagined Chinese encyclopedist, a discrepancy which is hinted at by the incongruity of alphabetical principles with the character of the Chinese language, or, you might say, with the language of Chinese characters. It is always a question about any list whether it is arranged in a sequence of ascending or descending priority or along more complicated loops or whether it is just disarrayed (and if so, why it is disarrayed—has the writer carefully tousled it, like a photographer artistically mussing a model's hair to look more casual and alluring, or did it just tumble out any old how?). The order of items of information is itself an item of information: this is true of any sequence, whether it is a list or not, so, for instance, it is true of sentences and, more obviously, of longer stretches, such as the stretch of a play: why what comes first, comes first and why what comes second, comes second is something we need to understand to understand the whole communicative act. It matters that we, Horatio, Barnardo, and Marcellus see the ghost before Hamlet does, that we hear about Cassio, Othello, and Desdemona from Iago before we see them, that Macbeth has been described as 'brave', 'valiant', 'worthy', and 'noble' before he comes on stage (a few less unambiguously glowing things are said about him too).

In Borges's case, closer inspection of his list than Foucault devotes to it reveals it as less alien and mindset-shattering than he makes out; makes it, I would say, mildly satirical in an old-fashioned way. Before the Communist revolution in China, the West stereotypically regarded China as an immensely bureaucratic society, converging on the Emperor, a community which took its intense traditionalism and social immobility to the pitch of ancestor worship. The first two items in Borges's list confirm this picture—the prime concerns of the encyclopedist are in relation to the emperor and funerary customs: 'It is the Chinese tombs.../ Usurp the soil' as Empson wrote in 'Missing Dates'.[7] Once these major parameters along which the world is organized—the State, the dead—are laid out, the list proceeds to items of household interest—domestication, the Chinese enthusiasm for crispy pork—before veering off to (e) and (f), sirens and fabulous (this really is odd, do the compilers of this list not include sirens under the more general heading of mythical beings?). That veering is, though, less disorienting than Foucault's response would suggest, because it is so easily explained as proceeding by opposites: it leaps from the very near at hand (crunchy little pigs) to what is never encountered (sirens). That we can bring the list into intelligible line here by subsuming (c) and (d) under the more general head 'familiar', then moving by neat reversal of terms to (e) and (f) as 'unfamiliar', is suggested by the fact that we can then bring (g) 'stray dogs' into line by just reversing the reversal, which gets us back from the remote to the close at hand. I don't deny that Borges's list is strange, with its logical paradoxes at (h), its collapse of taxonomy at (l), and its inclusions of categories which are unusual for an encyclopedia entry because they are deictically organized—that is, they depend for their reference and scope on when and where they are employed as does (m), where when 'having just broken' depends on when the classification is made and so which animals are to be classified under this head must change according to when the 'just' is, but encyclopedia entries, whether Chinese or Western, don't have 'when's like this. Deictic dependence would be weird in a published encyclopedia whose taxonomy is expected not to derive from such variable points of reference in time and space. The questions remain: how strange is this fictional list (in the sense of: is it as strange and mindset-shattering as Foucault makes out?) and how is it strange (in the sense of: what exactly is strange about it?)? My sense is that it is strange in the way jokes are often strange—they have logical inconsistencies or ethical 'naughtinesses' in them without making us feel our intellectual world has come to an

---

[7] William Empson, 'Missing Dates', in *Collected Poems*, 3rd edn. (London: Hogarth, 1984), 60.

end—and Foucault's laughter recognizes this jokiness, though he's not inclined to allow for the way that the humour protects us from the terror of classification run amok which he then delights to conjure up. The sequence in which the items are presented to us also suggests to me that the whole business is less profoundly disturbing than Foucault allows: that is, the list is easily understood as poking gentle fun at the Chinese, kowtowing to the emperor and their dead, experts in pork cuisine, and so on. It doesn't get tricky until its eighth item, and the logical wrinkles with (h) are soon over and we are returned to a world of exotic but stereotypified Chinese-ness, of recognizable human rationales, with (i) 'frenzied' (this repeats the natural concern also apparent in (c)—the most important thing about animals is whether they are going to bite us or we are going to bite them) and with (k) 'drawn with a very fine camelhair brush' (those Chinese, such aesthetes, obsessed with calligraphy). And so on. I can easily reorder the items in the list so that it is much more disorienting than at present, introduces perplexity more abruptly than it currently does, and so I incline to think that epistemic perplexity and disorientation in the Foucault mould are not what Borges's list is primarily up to, but rather a wry *chinoiserie*.

It doesn't matter much whether you agree that Foucault, issuing a position-statement near the start of his international celebrity, misdescribes the implications of the passage he is quoting. What matters is that you take from the example some hints that: (1) the order of items of information is itself an item of information; (2) that the interconnections between items in a sequence can imply more than one rationale, a rationale which may change and have, so to speak, a story of its own to tell; and (3) most importantly of all, that a good way to see how a piece of writing is working is to rewrite it, and consider what difference the rewriting makes, as when I suggest altering the order of the list to make it more disorienting, less cosily humorous, so it goes: *et cetera*; sirens; innumerable; belonging to the Emperor; that from a long way off look like flies. Of course, a reader with sufficient ingenuity will be able to extrapolate a rationale for that sequence too, but it would take more effort than Borges requires of us. Lists are particularly good exercise-machines for developing recognitional skills as a reader, because they are easy to rewrite, and because the rewrites often and sharply bring into focus how they were constituted in the first place.

Jack Goody notes in his essay on lists:

Lists are seen to be characteristic of the early uses of writing, being promoted partly by the demands of complex economic and state organisation, partly by the nature of scribal training, and partly by a 'play' element, which attempts to explore the potentialities of this new medium.[8]

Another way of describing the Chinese encyclopedia more richly than Foucault did would be—taking the hint from the anomaly of a Western alphabetical ordering of a Chinese taxonomy—to consider the passage as the offspring of two different systems of ordering material, coming from two different individuals: the Chinese scribe or clerk, heavily submitted to the 'demands of complex economic and state organisa- tion' and deeply moulded by 'the nature of scribal training', and, alongside the Chinese writer, 'ghosting' him or shadow-boxing with him, Borges, himself a state functionary (Director of the National Public Library in Buenos Aires) and also highly trained, but displaying in his fiction a freedom from checking and accountability, highlighting an aspect of that 'play' which Goody identifies and which a dutiful Chinese bureaucrat, writing a work of supposedly reliable information, would have to rein in more carefully. The humour and the inquisitiveness of the passage lie in a dialectic between work and play, official duty and individual whim, a double-act between the Chinese and the Argentinian but also within each of them, rather than in the melodrama about the culturally Other which Foucault whisks up. Lists should be particularly interesting to the literaturist because their combination of the admin- istrative and the playful helps us to focus on the fact that imaginative writing forms part of a larger landmass of writing which is not only imaginative but may have actual purposes and responsibilities, requires us to place the oasis of fiction amid real dunes.

Consider how Rebecca Gowers quotes from a nineteenth-century railway-manager's list in her study of an unsolved murder-mystery from the busy days of the British Empire:

In a letter to a close friend Stevenson once tried to give a sense of how over- whelming this job [manager of the rail freight that ran through Camden in the mid-nineteenth century] actually was.... The different products mentioned are striking in variety: anchors, beer, blankets from Witney, bobbins, ... cables, cannon balls, Scottish canvas and Worcestershire carpets; American clocks and

---

[8] *The Domestication of the Savage Mind*, 108.

British clogs, clothing for soldiers and corn 'tons on tons'; 'thousands of tons' of cotton goods from the 'clicking, snorting factories of Lancashire'; . . . fish, flax, flour, furniture, glue, grease, grates and grindstones; . . . oil, perfume, pianos and pitch; pumice-stone and reaping hooks, and Coventry ribbons and Coventry watches; salt provisions, biscuits, wines and spirits for voyages in 'astounding' quantities; . . . toys for the wives of manufacturers, beeswax, twine, and woollen bales from Yorkshire plus the terrors of the occasional live tiger or bear and the bother of the occasional unclaimed corpse.[9]

The passage runs on alphabetical lines from anchors to Yorkshire but it remains unclear who has organized it this way, Gowers or Stevenson. Though she explicitly indicates quotation from her source at some points, she nowhere specifies whether she is following his template or reconfiguring his words along her preferred lines. The drama of who is managing whom is full of humane thought about the possible synergies between the clerical Stevenson struggling to keep an orderly grip on the flood of commodities which surges through his station and the writerly Gowers redeploying his efforts to her ends. And then the list sways and threatens to come off the rails of the ABC when 'Witney' comes before 'bobbins', 'Scottish' before 'canvas', and 'Worcestershire' before 'carpets', though a moment's reflection enables us to introduce a second rule which preserves alphabetical tidiness (place-names used adjectivally will not count), steering us from blankets through bobbins to canvas and clogs, and discounting 'American' and 'British' which don't, by virtue of the new rule we have learned to apply, break ranks in the run from 'carpets' through 'clocks' to 'clogs'. Only at 'watches; salt provisions, biscuits, wines and spirits . . . toys . . . beeswax, twine' do the alphabetical wheels come irrecoverably off, and by that time (we are nearing the end of the sentence) this comes as much as a relief from the din of routine as a collapse into disarray. Notice that we have to learn new procedures as we make our way through the sentence (the rule about not counting adjectives); the presence of such learning-processes within writing is one thing which keeps it lively and agile, though lazier readers may resent having to go to the trouble of learning as they go along. Note too that, though what is being listed is the contents of innumerable freight-wagons, all running on the same gauge and looking more or less alike, cogs in a giant, industrialized

⁹ Rebecca Gowers, *The Swamp of Death: A True Tale of Victorian Lies and Murder* (London: Hamish Hamilton, 2004), 109–10.

wheel, the phrase-lengths and organization of the units of writing do not replicate each other, as if mass-produced, but keep changing character and internal composition, so that, for example, the alliteration is sometimes grindingly obvious (fish, flax, flour) and sometimes more subtly variegated (cables, cannon balls, Scottish canvas). The logistical organization of Gowers' prose does not replicate the logistical difficulties of freight throughput in nineteenth-century Camden Town, of course not, but the vivacity with which she cuts and splices Stevenson's account into her own list pays witty respect to what he struggled with, as if recognizing in him, maybe not a kindred spirit, but at least someone with problems not a million miles away from her own. Variety is the spice of prose as well as of life: when describing a passage of writing, we should try to find points in it at which a previously established pattern mutates, a new rule is introduced or the units into which it subdivides change shape or internal organization. The chances that this will happen somewhere and do so significantly are extremely high, especially if the writing is worth reading.

Within a list that is not 'just' a list but a piece of alert writing, the component elements will probably not all be the same shape, so good description will find something to say about where and why they vary. And this is true of poems, because poems are, looked at one way, 'just' a list of their constituent lines. Nor will the rationale of the interconnections always be the same from one entry to the next. This was true of ancient lists, true of Egyptian records, as Goody points out, quoting an Egyptologist:

In Gardiner's words... 'Enough has been said to show that the relations between consecutive entries are by no means always on a dead level of equality, and that consequently we must always be on the look-out for some significant nexus of thought between neighbouring items.'[10]

An ancient historian or anthropologist seeking to unearth a past method of organizing knowledge will need to be particularly alert at spotting where there is 'some significant nexus of thought between neighbouring items'—where a rationale of cataloguing changes, or where a transition is made from one category to another. As, for instance, in one of these old Egyptian lists, the sign for 'dew' is picked out in red ('rubricated' in the jargon) and on inspection turns out to

---

[10]   *The Domestication of the Savage Mind*, 102.

have a pivotal, semantic role, for it is the last in a series of celestial phenomena and the first in a series of terrestrial ones, dew being, as Goody, from whom I take the example says, 'an obvious "mediator" between these two classes'. Consider, then, Robert Burton's list of the 'ordinary recreations which we have in winter', the recreations of the sixteenth and seventeenth century before *The X Factor* had been discovered, and they had to make do instead with: '...jests, riddles, catches, purposes, questions and commands, merry tales and errant knights, queenes, lovers, lords, ladies, giants, dwarfes, theeves, cheaters, witches, fayries, goblins, friers, &c.'[11] A quick glance at this list might mislead you into thinking that its constituents are 'on a dead level of equality'; that impression might arise from the largely asyndetic articulation of the list's items. There are only two 'and's in Burton's list of twenty items; the conjunctions come next to each other at 'questions and commands, merry tales and errant knights', otherwise the sequence trundles along with nothing to oil its wheels but comma after comma. Contrast the list in Borges, which is also asyndetic but which spotlights each element with its own little alphabetical intro, and contrast the list in Gowers, which is polysyndetic. There are ten 'and's in my abbreviated version, with the conjunctions notably not always coming in the same place within the subsections, not, for instance, always introducing the last item in a mini-series.

Why is the asyndetic quality of Burton's list worth noticing? His first 'and' is probably meant to mark the end of a subset, because 'jests' through to 'questions and commands' is a list of games they used to play, interactive verbal games (jests, riddles, purposes, questions, and commands) or musical games like the turn-taking singing of 'catches'. The list then subdivides at 'merry tales', which here plays a role like the 'dew' which Goody mentioned, because it belongs partly to what goes before (storytelling is a kind of group game) but also ushers in what follows, a list of the figures who appear in 'merry tales'. Although these last thirteen components are enumerated with dead level asyndesis, there are several changes of direction or method of sorting in the series, moments when an 'odd one out' crops up, and the asyndetic organization of the list matters because it preserves, so to speak, a poker-face through all these variations, creating innuendoes without

[11] Robert Burton, *The Anatomy of Melancholy* [1621], ed. Nicolas K. Kiessling et al., 3 vols. (Oxford: Clarendon Press, 1989–94), ii. 79.

elbowing the reader in the ribs, relying on the reader to be alive to its delicate suggestions. As at 'errant knights, queenes, lovers, lords, ladies': four of these five terms are words for social status, but 'lovers' doesn't fit that bill—its presence can then have the effect either of suggesting that the series 'knights, queenes' inherently tends to 'lovers' (put a few knights and a few queenes in a castle and leave them alone for twenty minutes and anyone who has heard of Lancelot and Guinevere knows what will happen next) or of implying a wry attitude to chivalric romance in which 'lovers' is tantamount to the name of a profession like 'chartered accountants' (there's a couple of them on every High Street). There are several more of these little swerves or hinting wrinkles in the smoothness of the catalogue; I can't comment on them all, but draw your attention to 'ladies, giants' as a possible 'significant nexus of thought between neighbouring items' and again to 'dwarfes, theeves'. There is something to be worked out about what is happening semantically at both those points of transition. But there is one very large nudge delivered with great asyndetic aplomb at 'fayries, goblins, friers, &c'. The 'friers' meant here are now *friars*, principally the Dominican and Franciscan orders of Catholic religious. To move, without batting an eyelid, from 'goblins' to 'friers' is to pass from mythical beings to kinds of people who really exist. An implication of Burton's move, though, could be that, after the dissolution of Catholic religious orders nearly a hundred years before his book was published, mendicant friars have become for your average English fireside audience the creatures of fairy-tale along with, on a level with, goblins. People romance about them because they have become things of the glamorous past, like knights-errant; maybe parents use them to intimidate children—'be good, or the Franciscans will come and take you away', 'Oh nooo, anything but that'—as I recall my mother used to threaten me with abduction by nuns if I failed to obey her every whim. Whether Burton shares such a folksy, anti-Catholic mythologizing slant or looks at it in some way askance, you can't tell from the passage I quote, and that is because the list doesn't make clear whether its ordering is one that Burton endorses or one he reports without comment but with possible, asyndetic insinuations. Large issues of social, political, ethical, or credal commitment can turn on the question whether a writer aligns him- or herself with the organizational principles of a list, and a good place to look for evidence of this is in the articulations of the list in question, where and when it is asyndetic or polysyndetic.

From the fact that consecutive entries in a list are 'by no means always on a dead level', it does not follow that we can always tell which way the list is sloping. Written lists may tend towards what Goody called a 'hierarchization of the classificatory system', but an operative word here is 'tend', and tendencies can always change direction.[12] So Gary Taylor deserves a gold star for having written an essay about varieties of sixteenth- and seventeenth-century lists, administrative or fictional and, in the case of the lists of *dramatis personae* prefixed to play-scripts, both, because concerned with the administration of a fiction, a play. On the other hand, the gold star has to be taken away again, as Taylor, like, alas, too many literaturists, briskly schematizes the messy realities he should take more time and patience to describe:

Lists inevitably hierarchize their items, because they must give one item literal priority over another. Hierarchies, indeed, are almost invariably conceptualized as lists, in which the diversity of experience is reduced to an ordered sequence from highest to lowest.[13]

But it is absurdly tokenist to infer from the fact that in a list one item comes before another (has 'literal priority' over another), the item which comes first counts for more than what follows. A list of 'cast in order of appearance', for instance, is not 'inevitably' a list of cast in order of importance. Whether or not hierarchies are 'almost invariably' organized as lists (note the wriggle in the phrasing—the overpitch of 'invariably' combined with the hedging of 'almost'; why did Taylor not write 'very often' which is all 'almost invariably' can amount to?) shows nothing about whether lists are 'almost invariably' organized as hierarchies. From 'most A are B', it does not follow that 'most B are A'. It might be true that most literary academics are cheats, but it would not follow from that, alas, that most cheats are literary academics. (The world would be a safer place than it is if that were true.) Though it is a favourite pastime of literaturists to read off the shape of the world from the shape of a sentence or a fiction—Dickens's novels have happy endings, so he and his audience thought that things really turn out for the best in the end most of the time, even 'almost invariably'; sonnets are neatly

---

[12] *The Domestication of the Savage Mind*, 102.
[13] Gary Taylor assisted by Celia R. Daileader and Alexandra G. Bennett, 'The Order of Persons', in *Thomas Middleton and Early Modern Textual Culture: A Companion to the Collected Works*, ed. Gary Taylor and John Lavagnino (Oxford: Oxford University Press, 2007), 31–79 (p. 66).

and ingeniously organized, so sonneteers believed the cosmos fitted together as snugly as their sonnets—this is a bad habit to indulge unreflectively, and if you succumb to it, eventually it will make you go blind (and deaf).

Blind and deaf, for instance, to such tricks of the satirist's trade as the apparently methodical but actually deranged list. Swift is the dab hand here—from towards the end of his *A Modest Proposal*:

> But, as to my self; having been wearied out for many Years with offering vain, idle, visionary Thoughts; and at length utterly despairing of Success, I fortunately fell upon this Proposal; which, as it is wholly new, so it hath something *solid* and *real*, of no Expence, and little Trouble, full in our own Power; and whereby we can incur no Danger in *disobliging* ENGLAND... After all, I am not so violently bent upon my own Opinion, as to reject any Offer proposed by wise Men, which shall be found equally innocent, cheap, easy, and effectual.[14]

Swift originally published this proposal anonymously, so there was no giveaway 'Jonathan Swift' on the title-page to tip the wink: 'what follows is likely to contain ironies, though quite where they crop up will be hard to predict.' It was equally unclear whether this helpful proposal was being made to the Irish by an Irish person or by one of their English masters. That eventually becomes clear six paragraphs in, when the proposer starts referring to the Irish as 'we', as he does in my extract ('we can incur no Danger in *disobliging* ENGLAND'). The nationality of the writer is revealed in the paragraph before he begins to make his, he believes, helpful suggestion, which is that the Irish should eat the one-year-old babies of their poor, and use the profits from the trade in baby-meat to fund desirable public works. The order of information is, as I said before, itself a piece of information; that we find out the writer is himself Irish just before he starts campaigning for mass-infanticide on good, utilitarian grounds alters the angle from which we come at the charred calm with which he introduces his scheme, and gives the satire a sharper edge than if he had turned out to be English. But he doesn't declare himself at the outset as an Irish person, friend to Irish people, an Irish patriot even; there is something more sidelong, offhand even, about the way the information leaks out,

---

[14] [Jonathan Swift], *A Modest Proposal for Preventing the Children of poor People in Ireland, from being a Burden to their Parents or Country; and for making them beneficial to the Publick* (1729), in *The Prose Works of Jonathan Swift*, ed. Herbert Davis et al., 14 vols. (Oxford: Basil Blackwell, 1939–68), vol. 12: *Irish Tracts 1728–1733*, ed. Herbert Davis, 3rd edn (1971), 117.

and that, I repeat, is in its turn another piece of information, a piece of information about the store he sets on being Irish. It is through attention to the implications of his pronoun-system that we discover he is Irish; the 'we' in *A Modest Proposal*, then, is part of the indexicality of the passage, that dimension of writing which tells us about the writer and envisaged audience and the imagined circumstances of writing.

Style is a major source of indexicality, because a writer's style is a way of behaving in language. If you want to get to know a person, you have to attend to what she does as well as what she says (and especially attend to the relation between what she does and what she says). Much comment on literature is, so to speak, disembodied, because it fastens only on a writer's ideas or beliefs or themes, and passes in silence over his or her conduct. It's obvious enough that figuring out the reference of a writer's 'we' will probably tell you something about him, which group he supposes himself to belong to. But indexicality can be more indirect than this, and perhaps more revealing just because it is more indirect, as body language can give away more than a person wants to say. So, in this case, note that both the sentences I quote run to strings of adjectives or adjectival phrases, either pre- or post-modifying their associated nouns: 'vain, idle, visionary Thoughts'; 'this Proposal, which ... is wholly new, ... hath something *solid* and *real*, of no Expence and little Trouble, full in our own Power; and whereby we can incur no Danger in *disobliging* ENGLAND'; 'any Offer proposed by wise Men, which shall be found equally innocent, cheap, easy, and effectual.' These adjectival (or sometimes adverbial) lists are characteristic of the Modest Proposer right from the start: 'whoever could find out a fair, cheap and easy Method ... a young healthy Child, well nursed, is, at a Year old, a most delicious, nourishing, and wholesome Food, whether *Stewed*, *Roasted*, *Baked*, or *Boiled*.'[15] It is part of his sales-pitch for the proposal to chatter on like this, enumerating ever more unique selling points, often superfluously. An archaeologist, whether of the Foucauldian or of a more careful school, studying a list looks for notable transitions between items in the hope they will show up a rationale different from what we now take for granted, a little wrinkle in the arrangement which opens up vistas onto conceptual worlds at variance with our own. He or she needs to be ever ready to ask 'isn't this a bit odd?', as I, for instance, once asked 'isn't this a bit odd?' when I read the proposer's

---

[15] Swift, *Prose Works*, vol. 12, pp. 109, 111.

sequence 'vain, idle, visionary Thoughts'. 'Vain' and 'idle' are both pejoratives but we often speak highly of the visionary—'Mr Blair was much celebrated for his vision of a fairer society', and so forth. The little list struck me as veering off in a new direction at its third adjective, as if the lie of the conceptual land was different at that point from what I would have expected. The OED soon clarified that 'visionary' in Swift's English, and in the English of many writers before him, is usually pejorative, as when Swift speaks of something happening 'faster than the most visionary Projector can adjust his Schemes' and means what we might now phrase as 'faster than the most hare-brained inventor can cook up new plans'. So the adjectival series 'vain, idle, visionary Thoughts' is not equivalent to a modem run such as 'futile, time-wasting, and extraordinarily perceptive'. 'Visionary' comes to be more usually commendatory than pejorative around the time of Wordsworth, whom the great dictionary quotes as remembering in The Excursion, 'What visionary powers of eye and soul / In youth were mine', where he does not mean 'what a prat I was in those days'.[16] The OED is essential for anyone who doesn't want to be trapped in a historically parochial, or 'synchronic', sense of what English is and has been. It helps us dig at those points where the semantic ground has shifted over time—not shifted so terrifically that Foucault's song-and-dance about 'the stark impossibility of thinking that' is in order, but shifted sufficiently that we will stumble if we don't watch our interpretative step.

If you look closely at the modest proposer's runs of adjectival patter, you find they frequently seem a bit odd. What kind of priorities, for instance, are listed at 'innocent, cheap, easy, and effectual'; what, as Taylor might say, is the hierarchy latent in the sequence? It might seem it has to be an ascending order of priorities, because that his scheme would be 'effectual', that is, would work, must be the most important thing about it, as it is the important thing about any political scheme. But if the list goes from least important to most important, then the proposer thinks it is less important his scheme is 'innocent' than that it is 'cheap'. Here we might return to the OED again to check that we are not applying to Swift norms from our English which don't fit.

---

[16] The Excursion (1814), in William Wordsworth, ed. Stephen Gill (Oxford: Oxford University Press, 2012), ll. 110–11 (p. 588).

The dictionary brings into focus how weird the proposer is, for it shows that 'innocent's earliest meaning (derived from the Latin *nocere*, 'to harm') was 'doing no evil, not harming any one', and that it has senses of 'not morally harmful' from 1514, 'not physically or materially harmful' from 1662, and 'not against the law, not legally culpable' from 1811. A good deal more argument than we get in the pamphlet would be needed to show that mass infanticide and cannibalism are 'innocent' in any of these senses. Whatever quite the proposer means, his list lacks a clear direction, a rational hierarchy of priorities (such as we could supply by rewriting it to, say, 'cheap, easy, innocent, and effectual'). Because it lacks a rationale, while yet preserving the outward appearance of methodical enumeration, it drives a wedge between reader and writer, begins to niggle away at our sense of the trustworthiness of this communication. So too with 'wholly new, ... *solid* and *real*, of no Expence and little Trouble, full in our own Power; and whereby we can incur no Danger in *disobliging* ENGLAND'. If this is a series descending from 'wholly new' as the prime consideration to lesser advantages, it suggests a bizarre, self-admiring preference for novelty over whether the plan is solid or can be implemented. If it is a series ascending from 'wholly new', it reaches its climax with 'no Danger of *disobliging* ENGLAND', once again an odd top priority. Odd, that is, until you come back to the question of whether the writer is Irish or not. I answered this question before by noting his habit of referring to the Irish as 'we', but perhaps that was not the whole story. A fuller answer might be that the proposer is Anglo-Irish, a member of a political establishment which straddles the sea between the two islands, and that he has divided loyalties and a divided mind which show up in the way his lists change tack even though it's not clear he himself realizes that is what they do: he wants to help the Irish but he doesn't want to upset the English. A list per se does not entail a hierarchy, it's much too simple to map priority of value directly on to the series of items; and because a list is not of itself a hierarchy, lists can be subtle devices for querying the priorities of those who have compiled them.

One last point about the humble list and why, though humble, it is not 'mere', a mere list. In the old days of Dame Grammar, the written language was taken as the standard by which to measure spoken usage, sometimes even as the stick to beat the spoken language with. Modern linguistics has largely reversed that hierarchy, considers speech a better guide to usage than writing, and certainly does not think the spoken language has to be submitted to the protocols adopted in writing. The encounter of written and spoken forms of the language is a crucial focus for consideration of language behaviour, and perhaps especially so for literaturists who get so used to highly elaborated documents that they forget those documents are not representative of all kinds of language use, like Professors Carey and Crystal each mistaking, though in different directions, Shakespeare's plays for reliable sociolinguistic samples. Jack Goody observes that in the earliest phases of cultures which have developed writing, there often appears a form of discourse 'which is very different from that of ordinary speech, indeed of almost any speech. And the most characteristic form is something that rarely occurs in oral discourse at all (though it sometimes appears in ritual), namely, the list.'[17] What, then, happens when a list crops up in a play, when a written form, even a ritual form, takes over oral discourse, as when Macbeth goads hired assassins to the murder of Banquo and his young son?

> [Macbeth.] . . . Are you so Gospell'd, to pray for this good man,
> And for his Issue, whose heavie hand
> Hath bow'd you to the Grave, and begger'd
> Yours for ever?
> 1. Murth[erer]. We are men, my Liege.
> Macb. I, in the Catalogue ye goe for men,
> As Hounds, and Greyhounds, Mungrels, Spaniels, Curres,
> Showghes, Water-Rugs, and Demy-Wolves are clipt
> All by the Name of Dogges: the valued file
> Distinguishes the swift, the slow, the subtle,
> The House-keeper, the Hunter, every one
> According to the gift, which bounteous Nature
> Hath in him clos'd: whereby he does receive
> Particular addition, from the Bill,
> That writes them all alike: and so of men.[18]

I once heard Simon Russell Beale deliver these lines with a weird fluency as he skated at a great rate over the items in the catalogue. It is that actor's rare distinction that he understands the words of Shakespeare he is uttering, where 'understands' involves much more than just knowing the dictionary definition of each one of them,

---

[17] *The Domestication of the Savage Mind*, 80.
[18] William Shakespeare, *The Tragedie of Macbeth* (Folio I, 1623), III.i.1087–1101.

involves understanding the role they play in the communicative exchange between the people talking and listening to each other on stage. So here, Russell Beale rattled through the items at such a lick, it seemed Macbeth was intent on bamboozling his accomplices, talking not to them but over their heads (he is, after all, the king). The patter was so smooth, it made the speech sound like one he had prepared earlier, as *Blue Peter* presenters used to say, and rehearsed to a pitch of slickness. You could support a case for delivering the lines this way by pointing to the predominantly asyndetic character of Macbeth's two lists—only the first two and the last two items in the catalogue are joined by 'and', the middle six varieties run without interval one into the other; the five-item list beginning 'the swift, the slow' is without any articulating conjunction. This small, linguistic observation might back up the decision to reel it off quickly but wouldn't show that the quickness of Macbeth's tongue was intended to deceive the ear of his hearers. That notion gets support from a different feature of the list. The only member of the list which names a known breed of dog is 'Greyhounds'—a dog of high pedigree, bred for aristocratic sport (recorded as such in the language since 1000). All the other items are either synonyms for 'dog' in general (hound, cur) and / or broad, generic terms for a dog which also had been traditionally applied as insults to men (hound, mongrel, spaniel, cur). All the other items except the last three, that is: for showghes, water-rugs, and demy-wolves are extremely specific names for dogs, so specific that the *OED* records them as occurring only here, and, in the case of 'water-rugs', is so baffled by the term that, if you look up 'rug', you find as sense 4 'a shaggy breed of dog (see WATER-RUG)' but when you turn to 'water-rug', you find only 'A shaggy breed of water-dog (see RUG)'. Looked at closely, the list turns out to move, without signalling, from very common nouns to rare or nonce-words, culminating in the educated, courtly Franglais of 'demy-wolves'. Here it is not the category of thing listed which changes, as in Burton's change from 'goblins' to 'friers', but the kind of classificatory term which is deployed. And this linguistic observation supports a delivery of the lines in which Macbeth is trying to dazzle his slow-witted stooges, teasing them as to whether they can follow him through lexical inventions which take in foreign languages. It is as if he were saying, under his breath, between his lines: 'well, people might sort me into the same box as you—we're all called "men"—but the very way I make this point to you shows you I'm a different kind of creature altogether. I'm an educated man, you're clods.' And his education shows through the polish of the speech, the presence in his talk of the powerful ritual element which is a list. Acting like Simon Russell Beale's is, as he himself has said, just reading closely with your body, though I don't know why I say 'just'.

2

Timing

Let me tell you a joke; it comes from Auden's 'Notes on the Comic':

MOTHER (to her blind daughter): Now darling, close your eyes and count to ten, and when you open them you'll be able to see.
DAUGHTER: One two three four five six seven eight nine ten. But, Mummy, I'm still blind.
MOTHER: April Fool![1]

Auden says that this joke bears 'the same relation to the comic as blasphemy has to belief in God, that is to say, it implies a knowledge of what is truly comic', a knowledge which it then, in some way, perverts. The implied knowledge of true comedy consists in the fact that it is the mother who plays the joke on her child; if it were played by a second cousin, say, or a passer-by, it would scarcely be funny at all. And this is because it is the more shocking that a mother should play with her child in this malign way, that a mother's heart should be thus numbed to her child's feelings, and so the more comically exhilarating that we are provided by the joke with a momentary anaesthesia of the heart about her heartlessness. The joke Auden tells is not malign because it provides only a *momentary* callousness; the joke the mother plays is malign insofar as it suggests a more permanent hardness of heart. The object of the mother's joke is the daughter, but the mother is the object of the joke I have told, an object of shock, bafflement, and gaping laughter at her unnatural behaviour, like the mother in Samuel Johnson's *An Account of the Life of Mr Richard Savage, Son of the Earl*

[1] W. H. Auden, 'Notes on the Comic', in *The Dyers Hand* (London: Faber & Faber, 2012), 265–75 (p. 265).

Rivers. It is important to remember that laughter can express other emotions apart from amusement. (We need not be sure whether a habit of telling such jokes will lead to our adopting really a habit of burned-out unconcern such as that we entertain in imagination when hearing the joke.) I take this joke from Auden, but I have altered it in the telling, for in Auden's version the daughter is told to count to twenty before opening her eyes, and I think the longer waiting-time increases the cruelty of the mother's action so that it is more difficult to laugh at it; normally in children's games, we say 'Close your eyes and count to ten', so that asking the child to count to twenty has a deliberated malevolence to it beyond what even a lecturer in search of the comic could be prepared to find amusing. It seems to me that my version of the joke is better than Auden's, and better because it is more precisely and appropriately timed. The content of this joke concerns mother-love and the way it lets this daughter down, but the technique of the joke centres on how you perform the daughter's counting—the better you judge it, the bigger the laugh. Technically, then, it is an instance of the importance of timing to comedy, a familiar enough fact. But the way in which written literature achieves timing is less familiar and less straightforward. When I perform the joke, my control of the timing is literal; I decide the pace, and my voice measures the duration of words and of the gaps between them. Such literal control is not available to the writer of comic texts, though he must have ways of suggesting a timing for his words so that they can be realized in the precision of their humour by the reader. The basic means of doing this is syntax, or 'word-order' as it used to be called.

It is so important to do things in the right order. I brush my hair with taste and care, satisfy myself with the result in the mirror, and then remember that I have still to put my jumper on over my head, so it will all have to be done again. Human experience is in time; our experiences therefore form a series. Various frustrations, surprises, incoherencies, may arise from the elements of the series not coming in the right order. Our experiences also may form a sequence as well as a series. What I mean by a 'sequence' is a pattern of significance which unfolds in time but in which arches of interrelation are sprung across spans of time to join together in meaning occurrences which are separate in time. A good example of this distinction between 'series' and 'sequence' is a poem. In any decent poem, it will matter that line two comes after line one and before line three; this is the series of the poem. There will also be points of contact between lines two, five, and sixteen, and between lines seven, twenty-three, and thirty (perhaps because they each contain a 'flower-image', or a similar cadence at line-end, or whatever); this is the sequence of the poem. Much the same is true of novels—think of the organization of a mature Dickens work like *Great Expectations*—and there is a very highly developed artistic skill at work in reconciling the demands of series with the requirements of sequence. Some advice, then: when reading a passage, whether poetry or prose, do not succumb to the tyranny of series, don't let it monopolize your attention. Certainly, look at the chronology of the poem, its existence as a series, lines 1, 2, 3, 4, 5, 6, 7, etc., but also give heed to its history, to the sequential meanings which arise in time but arch across temporal instants, for history, as Eliot wrote, is a pattern of timeless moments—not timeless in the sense of 'entirely outside time' but 'timeless' in the sense of 'having a meaning not entirely tied to the point at which they appear in a chronological series'.[2] I'll be talking more about series than about sequence in what follows, but I don't want to do anything to encourage the inclination of some readers to think only of series.

It is important to do things in the right order. Writing and saying are types of doing, forms of conduct. Therefore, it is also important to put words in the right order. The editors of a recent edition of Wordsworth's letters do not remember this wise caution; volume 1 of *The Middle Years*, p. 19 has the following footnote:

Christopher and Priscilla Wordsworth had three sons (1) John, born 1st July 1805, died 30th December 1839, afterwards a classical lecturer at Trinity, Cambridge...[3]

Afterwards? I admit that the fellows of my college are not all as lively as one might desire, and indeed, the classicists amongst them do sometimes seem particularly retiring, but not even Trinity College can have been in the habit of appointing people to its fellowship after their deaths: 'died 30th December 1839, afterwards a classical lecturer at Trinity....' This little snag in the footnote shows how the order of words

---

[2] *The Poems of T. S. Eliot*, ed. Christopher Ricks and Jim McCue, 2 vols. (London: Faber & Faber, 2015), vol. 1: *Collected and Uncollected Poems*, 'Little Gidding', *Four Quartets*, ll. 21–2.

[3] *The Letters of William and Dorothy Wordsworth*, ed. Ernest de Sélincourt et al., 8 vols., 2nd edn. (Oxford: Clarendon Press, 1969–93), vol. 2: *The Middle Years. Part I, 1806–1811* (1969), p. 19 n.

may go unintentionally askew from the order of events—something specially necessary to avoid in English where we have scarcely any means other than the order of words to indicate the articulations of the world our words are supposed to convey.

Comedy can arise from a choice among the possible dictions available to a writer. So too with word order; you can put things in more than one way (diction) and you can put them in more than one order (syntax). The handling of dictions produces a comedy of literary manners, the jokey weighing of proprieties and their infringement; what a writer does with tense and syntax provides that comedy which hinges on pause, teasing delay, sudden surprise, and so on. In *Peter Bell the Third*, Shelley describes Hell—'Hell is a city much like London', as he accurately puts it—and makes a joke on the basis of a skewing of the order of words from the order of events, makes a joke where the editors of Wordsworth become one:

> There is great talk of revolution—
> And a great chance of despotism—
> German soldiers—camps—confusion—
> Tumults—lotteries—rage—delusion
> Gin—suicide—and Methodism;[4]

At some points in this stanza, it is possible to read the order of words as following exactly the order of time, and indeed, not only giving us a regular succession of events but hinting that a series of events is also a causal chain. There are German soldiers who come and build camps and their presence results in confusion; perhaps it is because people talk so much about revolution, and talk so grandly about it ('great talk' is not quite the same as 'much talk'), that there is such a chance of despotism. Someone who drinks too much gin—the crude gin of those days, not the refined and life-enhancing liquor of our times—might be brought thereby to suicide and then—ah but here the temporal series goes wrong, and the joke arises. 'Gin—suicide—and Methodism'; it sounds as if nonconformity were a posthumous state of a soul already dead, and dead at suggestion, but this is not the point I want to press. What the joke alerts us to is how completely this stanza depends for its effects on the way that the series of words, because we know that it is a deliberately calculated series, alerts us at every point to the possibility

---

[4] *Percy Bysshe Shelley: The Major Works*, ed. Zachary Leader and Michael O'Neill, 2nd edn. (Oxford: Oxford University Press, 2009), *Peter Bell the Third* (1819), ll. 147, 172–6.

of sequence, to the possibility that words don't just happen to follow each other in this order, and that, by implication, the things they refer to don't just happen to follow each other either, but also follow from each other. The infernal chaos which Shelley wishes to depict comes over partly in the absence of all but the most rudimentary syntax in the passage; there are two 'ands', and that is all, apart from the punctuation, to articulate everything which hangs on that bare 'There is'. A result of that absence of syntax contributes even more to the hellish textures in the verse: because we are told so little how things relate to each other, we are the more incited to work out bearings for ourselves. Consequently we search at every point in the process for a significance to the process, and our interpretations are baffled by the disorderliness Shelley has carefully planned. We may read 'German soldiers—camps—confusion— / Tumults' with a conviction growing on us that this series is also a sequence, a causal and explanatory chain; the sequence disappoints us when we come to 'lotteries' because it is less easy to see how lotteries arise from tumults than it is to see how tumults arise from confusion and confusion from soldiers' camps. When the kink in the sequence comes at 'lotteries', we are thrown sceptically back on the sequence we had just established, perhaps it was only a mere series after all, as the relation between 'Tumults' and 'lotteries' appears to be mere series. This is what Hell will *be* like: time will appear to be logic and then it will just turn back into endless, invalid time; we will seek the significance of sequence and be crammed instead with infinite, empty series. This tormenting vacillation between series and sequence also appears in the dashes with which the stanza is punctuated. On the one hand, they indicate a sardonic relaxation on the part of the writer ('While I'm on the subject, I may as well also mention x and y too'); on the other, they begin to look like hyphens, a sort of conjunction which comes closer to a logical connective, as if 'lotteries-rage' or 'Gin-suicide' were double-barrelled words, binding their parts together in a nightmare of causal intimacy.

In conversation with William Archer, Thomas Hardy asked, with modest rhetoric: 'What are my books but one plea against "man's inhumanity to man"—to woman—and to the lower animals?'[5] Now, Hardy did not speak the dashes William Archer gives him in transcription, though

---

[5] Thomas Hardy, quoted in William Archer, *Real Conversations* (London: W. Heinemann, 1904), 46–7.

I suppose that Archer was trying to convey in writing the nature of the pauses between the elements of the sentence he remembered Hardy saying. The timing of this sentence, to which the clue is the dashes, is decisive for its meaning. If Hardy spoke just casual dashes such as, in one aspect, we find in Shelley's stanza, then the series 'to man—to woman—and to the lower animals' is not only innocuous but reveals also how extensive Hardy's tenderness was. If, however, we read these dashes as coming closer to the condition of the hyphen, to logical rather than temporal connectives, and so construct an inflection for the sentence such as 'man's inhumanity to man' (first priority of any protests), 'to woman' (second priority), 'and to the lower animals' (third and least important factor), then we shall have spotted Thomas Hardy in the toils of sexism. Thomas Hardy thought women came halfway between men and the lower animals, the bastard. Detecting sexism in the writers of the past forms a major part of the literary-critical endeavour these days, so we might well be pleased with such a result, but let us attempt to preserve fairmindedness and fair hearings at whatever cost of renunciation of the impulse to triumph over Hardy for not being as enlightened as we are. There is, after all, a series / sequence ambiguity in what Archer has written here, just as there is in Shelley's stanza, though Archer probably did not contrive his ambiguity as cunningly as Shelley. The ordering of the words can be interpreted as psychological or logical, and there is not only one possible interpretation of the logic or the psychology. Hardy was a methodical man, but not even the most methodical man always speaks in an absolutely orderly manner. It is possible, for example to imagine a little psychological drama in this order of the words. Hardy starts off with a slightly clichéd defence of his own work; he quotes the old tag about 'man's inhumanity to man', but then realizes, as he realized often elsewhere, that his style of thinking doesn't quite fit with the familiar models of the past. He recalls his dedication to the cause of women's rights and his interest in wronged women and feels the need to revise the tag by adding 'to woman'. Having once broken out of the apparently impregnable familiarity of 'man's inhumanity to man' by the first addition, he recalls further his concern for animal welfare, and adds this last qualification. The process of revising and amplifying you can imagine in the series seems to me to Hardy's credit, setting aside all question of the merit of the causes he espoused.

A writer like Swift can make series imply less respectable psychological processes. The mock-writer of *A Modest Proposal for Preventing the Children of poor People in Ireland, from Being a Burden to their Parents or Country* argues that things have got to such a pass amidst the paupers of Ireland that the only practical way of alleviating their condition is that pauper children of up to one year old should be sold as delicacies for the tables of the rich. He dismisses alternative remedies and concludes:

> But as to my self, having been wearied out for many Years with offering vain, idle, visionary Thoughts, and at length utterly despairing of Success, I fortunately fell upon this Proposal; which as it is wholly new, so it hath something *solid* and *real*, of no Expence, and little Trouble, full in our own Power; and whereby we can incur no Danger in *disobliging* ENGLAND: For, this kind of Commodity will not bear Exportation, the Flesh being of too tender a Consistence, to admit a long Continuance in Salt...
>
> After all, I am not so violently bent upon my own Opinion, as to reject any Offer proposed by wise Men, which shall be found equally innocent, cheap, easy, and effectual.[6]

Is that last series—'innocent, cheap, easy, and effectual'—an ascending or descending scale of priorities, or are all these conditions on a par for this mock-writer? He may think that the most important thing about the scheme is that it is innocent (in the old sense of 'not harming anybody'); it would then be the next most important point that it was 'cheap' and so on down to 'effectual'. But he can't believe—can he?—that the least of his plan's charms is that it would work. Perhaps we should reverse the direction of the scale of priorities: what matters most about this scheme as contrasted with the many other proposals for assisting Ireland is that it will work, the next thing is that it will work easily, then that it would not cost much to implement, and, finally, that it is 'innocent'. This puts innocence low down on the list, too low for ethical comfort. The moral bankruptcy of the mock-writer shows nowhere more clearly in the text of *A Modest Proposal* than in the reversibility of his series of considered priorities. He has the trick of series, this genocidal buffoon who believes himself to be so comprehensively methodical and who shows his madness in his method: 'vain, idle, visionary Thoughts', '*solid* and *real*, of no Expence, and little Trouble, full in our own Power; and whereby we can incur no Danger

---

[6] *The Prose Works of Jonathan Swift*, vol. 12, p. 117.

in *disobliging* ENGLAND'. It's always worth looking in a passage for categories of words which are grammatically or functionally equivalent, and considering how the whole set of such words works together, and here is an instance of what such looks produce. The mock-writer of this piece is characterized in the text by a fondness for enthusiastic series of adjectival phrases, a kind of incontinence of qualification which he thinks is judicious but which judges him because of the senselessness of the order in which the phrases come, or because the order in which they come betrays his warped sense of what counts. Swift creates significant sequences out of what the mock-writer writes as harried, excitable, would-be persuasive series, and the imaginative drama of Swift's relation to his stooge in the piece plays itself out before us once we begin to attend to the fact that the writer runs on (in a series) but that his chatter has been composed into a significance beyond his guessing (in a sequence).

It is essential for literature that human experience is always in time; our language bears the marks of that timing, but literature can bend the language, and therefore the timing of a piece of writing may come at various angles into alignment or disarray with this prime fact of human experience. Human beings in time have imagined a stop to time, and an eternity beyond time; the literary weight of these imaginings has almost no proportion to philosophical questions about whether or not such remarks as 'time that takes survey of all the world must have a stop' have any clear sense or not. Still with Swift, from his *A True and Faithful Narrative of What Passed in London* which details what is supposed to have occurred when a Mr Whiston prophesied on 'Tuesday the 13th of October' that the world would come to an end on the following Friday. One great businessman tried to set his accounts in legitimate order but couldn't, even with the Day of Judgement looming over him, bring himself to admit all the shady details of his dealings:

Another seem'd to be very melancholy, which his flatterers imputed to his dread of losing his power in a day or two; but I rather take it, that his chief concern was, the Terror of being try'd in a Court that could not be influenc'd, and where a majority of Voices could avail him nothing. It was observ'd too, that he had few Visiters that day; this added so much to his mortification, that he read thro' the first Chapter of the Book of *Job*, and wept over it bitterly; in short, he seem'd a true Penitent in everything but Charity to his Neighbour...

Three of the *Maids of Honour* sent to countermand their Birth-day Cloaths; two of them burnt all their Collections of Novels and Romances, and sent to a Book-seller's in *Pall-mall* to buy each of them a Bible, and Taylor's *Holy Living and Dying*... A grave elderly Lady of great erudition and modesty who visits these young Ladies, seem'd to be extreamly shock'd, by the apprehensions that she was to appear naked before the whole world; and no less so, that all mankind was to appear naked before her; which might so much divert her thoughts, as to incapacitate her to give ready and apt answers to the Interrogatories that might be made her. The Maids of Honour who had both modesty and curiosity, could not imagine the sight so disagreeable as was represented; nay, one of them went so far as to say, she perfectly long'd to see it; for it could not be so indecent, when every body was to be alike: and they had a day or two to prepare themselves to be seen in that condition. Upon this reflection, each of them order'd a Bathing-tub to be got ready that Evening, and a Looking-glass to be set by it. So much are these young Ladies both by nature and custom addicted to cleanly appearance.[7]

Imagine this passage a little different. Reverse the order of the two coordinated sentences which begin the second paragraph: 'Two [Maids of Honour] burnt all their Collections of Novels and Romances...; Three of the *Maids of Honour* sent to countermand their Birth-day Cloaths'. The joke is ruined. The order Swift put the sentences in implies that all three could give up their new dresses, but one of them could not give up novels even on the verge of apocalypse; and it is this one implied maid of honour who provides the comedy of human tenacity in the passage, human adherence to foible even as the skies fall. She is not named, or even mentioned in the text, she is implied by the order of Swift's sentences. Or consider the 'grave elderly Lady'. He mentions her 'erudition' first and then her 'modesty', probably because of an eighteenth-century prejudice that well-read women had loose morals, so that the 'and modesty' should be given a protesting weight by the voice—'erudition, and—don't get me or her wrong—modesty'. Reverse the order of the nouns and the nuance is flattened out. This lady seems pure of heart and punctilious when he tells us that she was shocked by the thought of appearing naked before the whole world; not many of us have such beautiful physiques and such unstained souls

[7] Jonathan Swift, *A True and Faithful Narrative of what Passed in London, During the General Consternation of All Ranks and Degrees of Mankind, on Tuesday, Wednesday, Thursday, and Friday Last* (1736), in *Miscellanies in Four Volumes. By Dr. Swift, Dr. Arbuthnot, Mr. Pope, and Mr. Gay* (London: Charle[s] Bathurst, 1747), vol. 3, pp. 245–6. *A True and Faithful Narrative* has also been attributed to Alexander Pope and John Gay.

that we wouldn't sympathize with that shyness. But then Swift adds:
'and no less so, that all mankind was to appear naked before her; which
might so divert her thoughts, as to incapacitate her to give ready and
apt answers to the Interrogatories that might be made her.' It seems she
is not so much a shrinking violet, as a Venus fly-trap who worries that
she may be distracted from God's probing of her character by all those
assembled flunky men before her. The joke depends on the order of
the sentences, as also on the dexterous change of circumlocutions; she
is to appear naked before the whole world, but all mankind is to appear
naked before her; if you change it to 'She was to appear naked before
all mankind' and 'the whole world was to appear naked before her', the
point is blunted. Remove the series, and you destroy the sequence, the
meaning which lies here not in the words but in the word order.
A comparable infiltration of psychological sequence into the series of
the text occurs when one of the maids of honour 'could not imagine
the sight so disagreeable as was represented'. At first, she sounds full of
a properly religious egalitarianism—'it could not be so indecent, when
everybody was to be alike'—but then we discover that she has her eye
on the main erotic chance because she observes that they have a 'day
or two to prepare themselves', not by reading Taylor's *Holy Living and
Holy Dying* but by bathing and primping; so that when she says she 'perfectly long'd to see it' we know she is not talking about a saintly longing for perfection. These facets of human duplicity are revealed in the
ordering of the considerations, though they also affect dictional jokes
such as the way 'Upon this reflection' is set against their commanding
a 'Looking-glass'; the sort of reflection these maids of honour are capable of is neither maidenly nor honourable. The little phrase 'a day or
two' in 'a day or two to prepare themselves' has come in earlier when
the great businessman has a 'dread of losing his power in a day or two',
and it witnesses in miniature to the deeply comic superfluity of the
human soul; these people believe the world is coming to an end on
Friday next, and yet they still count the hours left them for worldly
ends. The exceptional comic genius of the passage comes from this
clash of the human being—soaked to the bone in life in time—and the
divine judgement—ever there, immobile, on the lookout, impending.
Swift's comic precisions about these weak adherences to the measurement of time even when time has had a halt called to it come themselves from an artistic handling of the timed quality of human
experience; he is proficient with literary timing where his butts are

helpless in real time, but this skill doesn't stop him recognizing the general comic condition of the human being who knows what he or she should do, who sees the ideal, and who yet *postpones* living up to or for it, a comic condition which the art of Swift's writing submits to even as he diagnoses it.

There are less intelligent ways of handling the reciprocal demands of human existence in time and the divine judgement: an extract from the *Evening Standard*:

PREACHER CREATES AN UNHOLY ROW

An elderly preacher is causing an unholy row with his sermons.

Neighbours say he shouts his messages from his windows, often at night. The council taped him for 10 days from a nearby house—and issued a noise abatement order.

But people living in Radford Road, Lewisham, say Mr Simeon Walters, who is in his 60s, is still preaching.

They have organised a 34-name petition and threatened a rate strike and court action unless Lewisham Council puts a stop to it.

One resident said: 'It's like the Sermon on the Mount every night—but someone ought to tell him this isn't Mount Sinai. We have all tried to reason with him, but it's no good.'

Mr Walters said: 'I've had my windows smashed while spreading the word of God. I don't trouble anyone—they trouble me.'

His house is painted red, white and blue. The window-sills and walls are daubed with the word 'Peace' and covered in felt-tip written biblical texts.

After taping Mr Walters's sermons, council environmental officers decided the noise amounted to a nuisance. The noise abatement order was issued by the general purposes committee.

It states: 'You must abate the nuisance arising from loud speech, shouting, chanting or similar noise amounting to a nuisance.'

Here again, human senses of what is timely are at odds with the demands of eternity. The comic quality of the passage arises from the reciprocal glowering of the two imperatives, a decent timeliness and an uncompromising absolute. 'It's like the Sermon on the Mount' / 'every night'; the suggestion is that the Sermon on the Mount wouldn't be so objectionable if it came only every other night, which in this case may be true enough but brings the Sermon on the Mount into the category of those good things which it is possible to have too much of, a category that doesn't quite fit the incarnate deity's words of revelation, though Jesus had at least more tact than Mr Walters; he delivered his sermon only once. Or take: 'Mr Walters said: "I've had my windows

smashed while spreading the word of God. I don't trouble anyone—
they trouble me."' If you take out the 'while', rewriting the sentence
as, for instance, 'I've had my windows smashed because I spread the
word of God', you alter the balance of competing demands and destroy the comedy. 'I've had my windows smashed because I spread the
word of God' tells us only that Mr Walters has suffered for his calling,
which may or may not be funny, but the temporal simultaneity of
'while' keeps the balance between the demands of time and the
demands of eternity on which the comedy of the passage hinges; it
conjures a sound-picture, Mr Walters in full, exhorting spate and his
neighbours lobbing stones at him: 'And I say unto you, brethren...
CRASH! tinkle, tinkle...died for you all, for your sins...CRASH!
tinkle, tinkle....' This simultaneity compacts orders, levels of living a
human life in time under the pressure of a possible eternity; these pres-
sures also make themselves felt in the amusing thought that someone
living in Lewisham needs to be told that he isn't on Mount Sinai
(which is not, by the way, where the Sermon on the Mount was
delivered, so perhaps Mr Walters's neighbours have something to learn
from him if only in the way of history) and in Mr Walters's fondness
for writing the word 'Peace' in 'felt-tip pen'. Of course, Mr Walters
doesn't have letters of fire at his disposal as God does, and so can't be
looked down on for using whatever is to hand, but nonetheless there
is a disproportion between his aspirations and his techniques for realizing them which is comic. Comic, because it provokes an oscillation
of attention, a clash of scales of judgement—is Simeon Walters a
prophet or a lunatic?—which can become a mechanism of pleasure in
this passage because the balance of allegiances between the timely and
the timeless is so precise.

Freud thought that 'a clergyman entirely overlooks the comic in the
human weaknesses which the writer of comedies can bring to light
so effectively'.[8] Clergymen were yet another thing that Freud didn't
know much about. They are the butts of many jokes partly because
they are the professional interface between the timeless and time,
partly because they embody the failures of human beings to live up to
the ideals they proclaim, a failure which is a constant preoccupation of

    [8] Sigmund Freud, *The Joke and Its Relation to the Unconscious*, trans. Joyce Crick, ed.
Adam Phillips (London: Penguin, 2002), 214–15 (the translation differs slightly in this edition from that given above).

comic writing. But they also make jokes. I think of a friend of mine who is a Benedictine monk saying to me: 'Oh, I'm so holy these days, visions and illuminations the whole time, and why not? The trouble with these other monks is they don't drink nearly enough.' Perhaps I should give an example in which I have no personal interest, Goldsmith's Vicar of Wakefield. This Anglican minister has lost his comfortable fortune, but his wife and daughters are slow to adapt themselves to their new, reduced circumstances, and wish to continue going to church in a carriage, despite his objections:

The next morning I perceived them not a little busy in collecting such materials as might be necessary for the expedition; but, as I found it would be a business of time, I walked on to the church before, and they promised speedily to follow. I waited near an hour in the reading desk for their arrival; but not finding them come as expected, I was obliged to begin and went through the service, not without some uneasiness at finding them absent. This was increased, when all was finished, and no appearance of the family. I therefore walked back the horse-way, which was five miles round, though the footway was but two, and, when got about half-way home, perceived the procession marching slowly forward towards the church; my son, my wife, and the two little ones exalted on one horse, and my two daughters upon the other. I demanded the cause of their delay; but I found by their looks that they had met with a thousand misfortunes on the road. The horses had at first refused to move from the door, till Mr Burchell was kind enough to beat them forward for about two hundred yards with his cudgel. Next, the straps of my wife's pillion broke down, and they were obliged to stop to repair them before they could proceed. After that, one of the horses took it into his head to stand still, and neither blows nor entreaties could prevail with him to proceed. It was just recovering from this dismal situation that I found them; but perceiving everything safe, I own their present mortification did not much displease me, as it would give me many opportunities of future triumph, and teach my daughters more humility.[9]

And that is the end of a chapter. As we are considering the relation between the order of words and the order of events narrated through words, we easily observe how heavily this passage marks the fact that its order follows the order of events—'The next morning'; 'I walked on to the church before'; 'I waited near an hour'; 'when all was finished'; 'The horses had at first refused'; 'till Mr Burchell'; 'Next, the straps'; 'To repair them before they could proceed'; 'After that'. And so

[9] Oliver Goldsmith, *The Vicar of Wakefield* (1766), ed. Arthur Friedman and Robert L. Mack (Oxford: Oxford University Press, 2008), 48.

on. Particularly towards the end of the passage, the comicality of the occurrences is enriched by the determined fidelity of the writing to the order of events, by pointing up of the 'and then... and then' quality of the events which gives the piece its 'it never rains but it pours' quality, its lugubrious resilience. If you remove these explicit time-markers from Goldsmith's prose, you hollow out the character of the fictional narrator: try 'The horses had refused to move from the door, but Mr Burchell was kind enough to beat them forward... The straps of my wife's pillion broke down...'. Taking out 'At first' and 'till' and 'Next', you turn the piece into a mere narration and wash out the colour with which it is narrated. Hegel catches that colour excellently in a passage from his *Aesthetics*:

The comical therefore plays its part more often in people with lower views, tied to the real world and the present, i.e. among men who are what they are once and for all, who cannot be or will anything different, and, though incapable of any genuine 'pathos', have not the least doubt about what they are and what they are doing. But at the same time they reveal themselves as having something higher in them because they are not seriously tied to the finite world with which they are engaged but are raised above it, and remain firm in themselves and secure in the face of failure and loss. It is to this absolute freedom of spirit which is utterly consoled in advance of every human undertaking, to this world of private serenity, that Aristophanes conducts us. If you have not read him, you scarcely realise how men can take things so easily.[10]

We don't have to believe everything Hegel says, but we can be grateful for his phrase, as the translator gives it to us, 'utterly consoled in advance of every human undertaking', because it describes so well the effect of these time-markers which precede each recounted incident in Goldsmith's prose, and the 'Wouldn't you just know it?' comic prediction which those markers create and convey. The Vicar of Wakefield manages to show that he is not seriously tied to the finite world with which he is still engaged by the care with which he marks out that world; the energy of the narration frees him, in Hegel's sense, from what he narrates. Just the very precision with which he feels the fetter of time enables him to slip the chain; he accepts the weight of these tiresome incidents, he shows his acceptance in the detail of his care to recount them clearly, and the thoroughness of his acceptance gives him

---

[10] Georg Wilhelm Friedrich Hegel, *Aesthetics: Lectures on Fine Art*, trans. Thomas Malcolm Knox, 2 vols. (Oxford: Oxford University Press, 1975), vol. 2, pp. 1220–1.

something like what Hegel calls, with a thrilling exaggeration, 'absolute freedom of spirit'. Distracted during the church service by worries about his family, he half-admits his own lack of concentration: 'went through the service', he writes, risking a proximity to such phrases as 'went through the motions' but not worried by the neighbourhood of the phrases. It would not do to be moralistic about this vicar's failings of spiritual attention; he tells us about them with such a placid sense of how natural they are, his responsibilities as a clergyman are entirely accommodated within his domestic frame of reference, and, as an Anglican, he thinks this is how it should be. The temporal and the eternal are hand in glove. Consider how open-hearted and unruffled the admission is at the end of this passage: 'but perceiving everything safe, I own their present mortification did not much displease me, as it would give me many opportunities of future triumph, and teach my daughters more humility.' This isn't so heartless as the April-fooling mother about the distresses of the daughter (it's important that he only contents himself with the state of affairs after telling us that he had found everything 'safe', no serious harm has been done), but, in its own way, it rejoices in the offspring's comedown. The balance of phrasing— 'give me many opportunities of future triumph' against 'give my daughters more humility'—covers the fact that the attitude expressed is a little unbalanced, because a person who approves of humility should not be too keen on triumphing. That balance also tones down what we might otherwise feel as vengeful and self-satisfied on the Vicar's part because it produces a literary pleasure in near phrasing which matches his pleasure in the convenient way things have turned out for him; events happen fortunately, and words occur felicitously. The order of words *gelatinizes* the possible nastiness of the order of events; his sentiments about what has happened come to us in the palatable aspic of style. 'Pretty!', as Pope, with his lip a-curl, observed about the way pigmy critics preserve themselves by writing annota-tions on works of permanent genius, 'Pretty! in Amber to observe the forms / Of hair, or straws, or dirt, or grubs, or worms' (that last line itself a very notable use of series to imply a sequence).[11] Pope meant to be sarcastic about such preservations of the ephemeral in the perman-ent, but the fact remains, despite his sarcasm, that it is pretty to observe

[11] Alexander Pope, *Epistle to Dr Arbuthnot* [1735], in *Alexander Pope: Selected Poetry*, ed. Pat Rogers, 3rd edn. (Oxford: Oxford University Press, 2008), ll. 169–170.

hair in amber, the ephemeral in a still medium. Here, then, is a further operation of literature on the time of human experience. Fixing the contours of an emotional complex such as that the Vicar feels in face of his family's humiliation, the writing offers us an algebra of the transient, a general formula, a governing shape which contains and maintains what, without it, would pass.

Lineation in verse is a special technique for the construction of such an algebra of the transient. John Berryman, part of the fourth of his *Dream Songs*:

> Filling her compact & delicious body
> with chicken paprika, she glanced at me
> twice
> Fainting with interest, I hungered back
> and only the fact of her husband & four other people
> kept me from springing on her
>
> or falling at her feet and crying
> 'You are the hottest one for years of night
> Henry's dazed eyes
> have enjoyed, Brilliance.' I advanced upon
> (despairing) my spumoni.[12]

Spumoni is a frothy pudding, something so evanescent and unresisting that it is excess of zeal to 'advance upon' it in this military way, just as it might seem excess of zeal to advance on so small and so issueless an incident as this with all the machineries of poetry. The vigour with which Henry attacks his pudding is, of course, deflected from the vigour with which he would like to throw himself at her feet; you feel the strength of the curb which demands that deflection of what he would have like to have done the more strongly because his imaginary declaration to her is ended in mid-line, and the sad spooning of froth into his mouth begins in the same line as the account of what he would have, frothily, said to her. If you imagine a different lineation, so that 'Brilliance' comes at a line-end, you alter the tenor, and the drama of the joke. So too, the placing of '(despairing)', because of its grammatical oddness, gives the line an exact contour, and in that exactness of shape lifts the passing moment recorded into the dimension of a sustainable configuration, something you can keep thinking about even as

---

[12] John Berryman, 'Dream Song 4', in *The Dream Songs* [1964–9] (New York: Farrar, Straus & Giroux, 2014), ll. 1–11.

it passes and has passed. You feel his despair, the inner sinking, as he lifts the spoon—like Simeon Walters's '*while* spreading the word of God'— the grind of his feelings against his circumstances, which you would not get unless you had a jar of diction in '(despairing)' against 'spumoni', unless you had the syntactical hiccough of that inserted parenthesis between the verb phrase 'advanced upon' and its required object 'my spumoni'. The very intensity of the experience, 'Fainting with interest', produces its own transition into the laughable, especially as Berryman goes on to write 'I hungered back', and so tips the wink that 'Fainting with interest' was formed out of the cliché 'fainting with hunger'; that makes us wonder if there aren't comparisons to be made between his longing for this stranger and his waiting for the next course of his meal, to calibrate different kinds of appetite against each other. There is a skill in the narration of this disaster, like that of the Vicar of Wakefield, a meticulousness with regard to catastrophes undergone which frees the storyteller from being completely bound to his own predicament. Consider the lineation 'she glanced at me / twice'. Everything hinges on the vivid sidelong quality Berryman gets into the verse by veering the reader's eyes round the line, the corner of the line, we might say, rather than its end, in order to try to put over how the reader's eyes repeat the flick of her eyes at him. But our eyes alight only on the meagre word 'twice' when we round that corner. Imagine how different it would have been if we read 'she glanced at me / passionately' or 'she glanced at me / unbuttoning her blouse'. The small word 'twice' all by itself as a line looks so little to put weight on, but all the better matches then how much weight people put on little looks— the tiniest gesture can be the occasion for a hopeful inflammation in such a context. The possible tones which the lineation produces open up new reaches of the laughable; should we say 'she glanced at me / TWICE' (twice, eh? nudge, nudge, you're on to a good thing there, mate) or 'she glanced at me / twice' (oh dear, only twice? Well yes, I admit, only twice, but still, that's more than once, isn't it, I think there must have been something in it, don't you? No? Oh well, perhaps you're right, the spumoni was excellent anyway); the doubt of interpretation as regards the lines meets the doubt of interpretation as regards the glances. The shape of the lines conveys, captures, the shape of the recounted experience, but in doing so it also replaces the experience with the lines, gives us an established contour of words which we cannot understand without bringing them into line with the experience

which they point to but which, once we understand them, offer us a
pleasure different from the pleasure of the experience, a shape of words
in which there is a pleasure beyond the present moment they record, an
algebraic equation, with many solutions, for dismay. This is Aristophanic
comedy in Hegel's sense, a 'world of private serenity' in the words. If you
had not read it, you could scarcely have realized how men can take things
so easily.

3

Timeliness

When is it chic to be antique? In 1922, *The Waste Land* seemed to be in at least two minds about this as about so much else. Its second section, which begins with a pastiche of Enobarbus's description of Cleopatra on the river Cydnus, contains the following note on interior design:

> Above the antique mantel was displayed
> As though a window gave upon the sylvan scene
> The change of Philomel, by the barbarous king
> So rudely forced.[1]

Here it seems that, if you like that sort of thing, an 'antique mantel' is a good thing to have on display (especially if it's topped with a picture of a 'sylvan scene', that phrase coming from the description of Eden in *Paradise Lost*).[2] However, later in the same section of the poem, two women have a conversation in a pub, part of which went, according to one of them:

> If you don't like it you can get on with it, I said.
> Others can pick and choose if you can't.
> But if Albert makes off, it won't be for lack of telling.
> You ought to be ashamed, I said, to look so antique.
> (And her only thirty-one.)[3]

—where looking 'antique' is supposed to be a source of shame, at least for a woman who wants to keep her man. Not only does the poem

---

[1] *The Poems of T. S. Eliot*, vol. 1, *The Waste Land* (1922), 'II. A Game of Chess', ll. 97–100.
[2] John Milton, *Paradise Lost* (1667), ed. Stephen Orgel and Jonathan Goldberg (Oxford: Oxford University Press, 2008), Book 4, l. 140.
[3] Eliot, *The Waste Land*, 'II. A Game of Chess', ll. 153–7.

have two attitudes to the fact of being 'antique', it may even have two
ways of pronouncing the word, for on its first appearance, someone
determined to hear T. S. Eliot as writing iambic pentameters would
have to pronounce the line: AbOVE the ANTique MANtel WAS
disPLAYED—whereas the second time around, there's no such metrical
reason not to stress the word on its second syllable as has been normal
since the eighteenth century. But if Eliot had read Shakespeare, as he
evidently had because he is pastiching his style, he would have known
that in those old days the word took stress on its first syllable. *The Waste
Land* is a mock-heroic poem, as Joyce's *Ulysses* is a mock-heroic novel,
and so it has, as good mock-heroic usually does, two attitudes to the
past, two attitudes which are expressed in these two diverging usages
of the word 'antique'—on the one hand, the past is prestigious, an
object of cultural reverence; on the other hand, it is a load of old junk,
clapped-out. Hence the poem's title, *The Waste Land*, not *The Wasteland*,
as you sometimes see it called.

   Troilus and Cressida is Shakespeare's most 'antique' play. It is set
furthest back in historical time of his dramatic works whose events can
be dated—about 1100 BC, if we suppose that Shakespeare would more
or less have agreed with Sir Walter Ralegh's date for the Trojan War in
his *History of the World* (modern chronology thinks Priam's city fell
about 200 years earlier than Ralegh believes).[4] It is also a very 'antic'
play in the sense of 'grotesque', 'uncouthly ludicrous', 'grinning'. The
two words 'antique' and 'antic' have distinct careers in English, though
they enter the language at about the same time, in the 1530s–40s and,
for a while, they became capable of being mistaken for each other, not
only in writing, because either of them could be spelled 'antick(e)' or
'antik(e)', but also in speech, for they were both stressed on the first
syllable. Shakespeare quite liked the word 'antique'; we may guess he
thought it classy because all fourteen uses of it in his works are from
passages in verse and because he used it most often of all in the *Sonnets*
(five times), which were first published in 1609, the year of the Quarto
publication of *Troilus and Cressida*. But Shakespeare was not the only
writer in the sixteenth century to have been drawn to 'antique' or its
cognates, and to have had something like the double attitude to
antique-ness we find in *The Waste Land* and which also expresses itself

---

   [4] *The Works of Sir Walter Ralegh*, 8 vols. (Oxford: Oxford University Press, 1829), vol. 4:
The History of the World, pp. 440, 527.

in the fact that what is 'anticke' (ancient) may also for that very reason be 'anticke' (grotesque). A quick scan of the relevant pages of the *Oxford English Dictionary* gives us:

antiquary, A. *adj.* Of antiquity; ancient; antique. *rare.*
1606 SHAKS. *Tr&Cr.* II.iii.262 Here's Nestor Instructed by the Antiquary times.
B. *sb.* **1.** A man of great age, an ancient. *Obs. rare.*
1581 CAMPION. *Hist. Irel.* vii Had it beene my chaunce...to meet and conferre with this noble Antiquarie [a man aged two thousand and forty one years]
2. An official custodian or recorder of antiquities. (Bestowed as a title by Henry VIII on Leland.) *Obs.*
1563 GRAFTON *Chronicles* The booke of the excellent antiquary John Leland.
3. A student...or collector of antiquities.
1586 THYNNE in *Animadv.* Introd. 80 It hath beene some question among the best antiquaries of our age, that, etc.

antiquate, *ppl.a. arch.* Rendered or grown old; obsolete through age; ANTIQUATED.
1537? TYNDALE *Exp. I John* It was antiquate, and clean out of knowledge.

antiquate, *v.* **1.** To make old, or out of date; to make obsolete; to abolish as out of date.
1596 SPENSER *State of Irel.* 22 Now through change of time [they] are cleane antiquated.

antiquated, *ppl.a.* **2.** Out of use by reason of age, obsolete.
1623 B.JONSON in *Shaks Centurie of Praise* Neat Terence, witty Plautus, now not please; But antiquated and deserted lye

antique, *a.* and *sb.* **A.** *adj.* **1** Belonging to former times, ancient, olden. (Now generally rhetorical = of the 'good old times'.)
1541 R COPLAND *Galyen's Terap.* And that this reason and maner were antyke. **1595** SPENSER *Sonn.* lxxix, The famous warriors of the anticke world
2. Having existed since olden times; of a good old age, aged, venerable. *arch.*
1536 *Thynne's Animadv.* The old and antyk bulding.
1596 SPENSER *State of Irel.* 28 A nation so antique, as that no monument remaines of her beginning.
B. *sb.* **1.** A man of ancient times; *pl.* the Ancients. *Obs.*
1563 J. SHUTE *Archit.* Vitruvius one of the most parfaictest of all the Antiques.
2. A relic of ancient art, or of bygone days.
1530 PALSGR. If this antique were closed in golde, it were a goodly thing.

antiquity, I. As abstract sb.

I. The quality of being old (in the world's history) or ancient; long standing, oldness, ancientness.

*c.*1450 *Court of Love* This statue was of old antiquite.

2. Old age (of human life); seniority. *Obs.*

1596. SHAKS. *2 Hen. IV.*, I.ii.208 Is not your voice broken?... and every part about you blasted with Antiquity.

II. Elliptical senses.

4. The time of antiquity, olden time. **a.** generally.

*c.*1380 *Sir Ferumb.* 1316 An old for-sake yeate of the olde antiquytee.

b. *spec.* The period before the middle ages, the time of the ancient Greeks and Romans.

*c.*1450 *Songs & Poems* Famous poetis of antyquyté, In Grece and Troye.

c. The early ages of the Christian era; the early centuries of the Church...

1564 HARDING *Answ. Jewel* 173 To see antiquitie for proufe herof... Let him reade...

5. The people (or writers, etc.) of ancient times collectively; 'the Ancients'.

1538 STARKEY *England* Aftur the opynyon of the wyse and auncyent antyquyte.

6. Matters, customs, precedents, or events of earlier times; ancient records

1557 NORTH *Diall of Princes* Paulus Diaconus... sheweth an antiquitie right worthy to remember.

7. Remains or monuments of antiquity; ancient relics.

1513 MORE *Hist. Edw. V* The great care... that hath alwaies been observed... for the preservation of antiquities.

We need to be careful with information such as the *OED* can supply, for several reasons. In the first and simplest place, the great dictionary is not wholly reliable; even a comparative ignoramus can find usages which pre-date the dictionary's first date for a sense of a word—I've done so myself. The dictionary evidently can record only written usages for periods before we were blessed with means for recording speech, and so the history of English it records is overwhelmingly that of written English. And we should not forget that well into the nineteenth century less than half of the population of these islands could read and write. A historical linguist will also rightly warn us that the early editors of the *OED* had a particularly high esteem for evidence from literary sources as contrasted with, say, court records, popular 'broadside' pamphlets, and the like; this means that its evidence is slanted in ways which are troublesome for a historian of the English language but not troublesome in the same way for people who are particularly interested in the history of the literary language. These considerations can all be found, along with a wealth of detail, in Jürgen Schäfer's *Documentation in the O.E.D: Shakespeare and Nashe as Test Cases* (1980).

Professor Schäfer estimates, for example, that the *OED* is likely to be no more than 93.1 per cent reliable in assigning first uses to Shakespeare; this is a deplorably low figure for serious, scientific purposes, but for literary critics it could be regarded as a barely attainable ideal.[5] I would be very happy if I were sure that what I say about Shakespeare is 93.1 per cent accurate. More generally, there is a philosophical consideration which needs to be remembered: a word is not the same thing as a concept. People can show by their behaviour, for instance, that they possess a concept for which they don't in fact have a word—some children demonstrably have a notion of 'fairness' or 'distributive justice' (we can tell from the way they share out their sweets) before they start using these terms. And conversely, the fact that Mr Blair says 'fairness' very often indeed is not in itself a proof that he has any secure or subtle grasp on the concept of social justice. It can be very misleading to write intellectual history on the unchecked basis of when people started using words in certain senses; the example of Raymond Williams's *Keywords* might be mentioned here.[6]

Nonetheless, the rash of new senses for 'antique', 'antic', and their cognates in sixteenth-century English *is* evidence that the period had an intense and many-faceted concern for old things, and perhaps even more for 'olde' things. The past was found appealing, and people appealed to it; it could be treated as a source of 'period charm', an ethical standard, a reservoir of correct practice, legal precedent, and permanently applicable principle, or it could be looked down on as thoroughly disjoint from present needs—as the dictionary shows 'antique' could refer to the 'good old times' but 'antiquated' could mean dead and done with, obsolete through age. One source of the enthusiasm for old things was Renaissance humanism, so largely fuelled by rediscovery of the classical past, or by a certain idealization of that past which sometimes came up hard against the facts of antiquity, as when archaeological excavations in Rome uncovered ancient bathhouses decorated with less than tasteful frescos: these baths, which had over time sunk below ground-level, were regarded as caves—Italian *grotte*—from which the word 'grotesque'

---

[5] Jürgen Schäfer, *Documentation in the O.E.D.: Shakespeare and Nashe as Test Cases* (Oxford: Oxford University Press, 1980), 38.

[6] Raymond Williams, *Keywords: A Vocabulary of Culture and Society* (London: Fontana; Croom Helm, 1976).

was formed to register the shocking nature of their decoration, hence the sense of 'grotesque' which attaches to the 'antic' side of the 'antique'. The Renaissance tends to appear in those cartoons which serve most of us most of the time as our sense of history as a period of peaceable enlightenment and forward-looking tolerance—people started painting nudes and observing the world around them, whereas previously they had all been glumly worshipping the Pope when not dying of plague. But the Renaissance was also fiercely pedantic and quite ruthless in ignoring realities when they did not fit its enthusiastic schemes to revive Greece and Rome. The Senate of Venice, for example, in 1526 was keen to build some ships to combat the pirates who were interfering with Venetian traders; they had before them some eminently practicable designs from a master-craftsman, but opted instead for a completely useless replica of a quinquereme on the best ancient lines which was sold to them by a feverish humanist called Faustus. The attempts in France or England to write French or English poetry according to the rules of Graeco-Roman prosody are another case where scholarly faddism overwhelmed a sense of reality, because neither language was remotely adapted to such schemes. As J. G. A. Pocock has written:

> the humanists aimed at resurrecting the ancient world in order to copy and imitate it, but the more thoroughly and accurately the process of resurrection was carried out, the more evident it became that copying and imitation were impossible—or could never be anything more than copying and imitation.[7]

There are two senses of 'imitation' at work here: 'imitation' in the sense of 'following an example' and 'imitation' in the sense of an 'artificial likeness', a 'counterfeit', and both these senses are alive and at odds with each other in the England of *Troilus and Cressida*:

> 1502 ATKINSON A full devoute & gosteley treatyse of ye Imitacion & folowynge ye blessyd lyfe of our most mercifull saviour cryst.
> 1601 SHAKS. *Jul. C.* IV.i.37 One that feeds On Objects, Arts, and Imitations.

One of the sad truths the humanists discovered in their impassioned researches into the past was that there was less of it than they had supposed, or at least that some of the past was not nearly so reverendly old as had been claimed. The Papacy had long rested its claims to temporal, political power on a document called the 'Donation of Constantine', in

---

[7] J. G. A. Pocock, *The Ancient Constitution and the Feudal Law: A Reissue with a Retrospect*, 2nd edn. (Cambridge: Cambridge University Press, 1987), 4.

which it was claimed that the fourth-century Emperor Constantine had conferred rights of political dominion on the Bishop of Rome; the great scholar Lorenzo Valla in 1440 showed on philological grounds that it had been craftily backdated by an eighth-century forger. Nor was it only the Pope who sought to draw advantage from antique documents of doubtful authenticity; many political radicals had rested part of their case on the supposedly ancient *Manner of Holding Parliaments*, but the constitutional historian Selden showed in 1614 that it was a forgery and advised people 'not to trust to its pretended antiquity'.[8] 'Pretended antiquity' can be taken in either the sense of 'a claim to antiquity' (an older, Frenchified sense of 'pretend' current in the language until at least the eighteenth century, when the Stuart claimant to the throne was known as 'the Pretender') or in the sense of 'faked antiquity', but in either sense 'pretended antiquity' was of great practical and theoretical moment in sixteenth-century England: the ancient claims of the Bishop of Rome and the Catholic Church could be resisted by appeal to the supposed, primitive purity of the early Church ('antiquity' as sense 4c in the list I've given). Certainly, Henry VIII's break with Rome in the 1530s and the decades of ferocious argument about theology, church-government, and liturgy which followed brought questions of the new, the old, and the 'neo-' into prominence, as Cranmer noted about his countrymen in his 1549 note 'Of Ceremonies' to the Book of Common Prayer (the State prayer-book):

in this our time, The Minds of men are so diverse that some think it a great matter of conscience to depart from a piece of the least of their Ceremonies, they be so addicted to their old customs; and again on the other side, some be so new-fangled, that they would innovate all things, and so despise the old, that nothing can like them, but that is new.[9]

The right to the throne too was often debated via a curious mishmash of archaic legend and tenuous birth-lines along with the still-familiar argument from *force majeure* or winner-takes-all. When Henry Tudor came to the throne in 1485, the old story that 'Britain' derived its name from 'Brut[us]', a son of Aeneas and hence a Trojan, came back into vogue—this is the 'matter of Britain' or the 'British history' which wove in King Arthur too, and which plays a large role in *The Faerie*

[8] John Selden, *Titles of Honour* (London: John Helme, 1614), 274.
[9] Thomas Cranmer, 'Of Ceremonies', *The Book of Common Prayer: The Texts of 1549, 1559 and 1662*, ed. Brian Cummings (Oxford: Oxford University Press, 2011), 215.

Queene, I am told. Probably nobody except Tudor spin-doctors and demented Welshmen ever really credited it, though Henry Tudor evidently thought it had its uses, for he named his first-born Arthur. Sir John Price was still arguing desperately in the 1570s that the Trojan ancestry of the ancient Britons was demonstrated by the prevalence of names like Hector, Achilles, Ulysses, and Helena in these islands; he also thought that Welsh, 'Cymraeg', derived from 'cam-Graec', twisted or lame Greek.[10] But once again, antiquarian researches resulted in there being less antiquity on hand than some people hoped, and the notion that the Britons were originally Trojans was largely derided by the 1590s; I think the vogue for claiming that Britons were originally Trojans—as, for instance, in the Lytescary family, whose motto was *Fuimus Troies* ('Once we were Trojans')—and its fall from popularity made some contribution to the mock-heroic zest with which Shakespeare treats the old Trojan story in *Troilus and Cressida*.

'Pretended antiquity' was a serious business in those days; it could, therefore, also be turned into a game. Thomas Nashe wrote of 'Antient antiquitie' with a full, witty confidence that the alert reader would recognize his implied joke about the distinction between 'antient' and *nouvelle* 'antiquitie';[11] Daniel thought the attempts of writers like Campion to model English verse on Graeco-Roman metrical models were absurd and disdained 'his new-old arte' (long before the 1662 the *OED* gives for this lovely compound).[12] Perhaps in order to distinguish really up-to-date writing from such 'new-old arte', Gabriel Harvey coined 'new-new' in 1592—and there are many other compounds with 'new-' from the last decade of the sixteenth century: new-coined (1598), new-comer (1592), new-minted (1593), news-man (1596, astonishingly from that arch-archaizer, Spenser), and, according to the *OED* all from the pen of Shakespeare: new-create; new-fallen; new-devised; new-risen; newsmonger; and new-sprung. The buzz of not always coherent excitability about what was old and what was new, what genuinely English and what a horrid import, can be heard in that curious production E.K.'s 'Epistle' to *The Shepheardes Calender*, where he offers several, mutually inconsistent defences for Spenser's newfangled antiquations of the language:

---

[10] John Price, *Historiae Brytannicae defensio* (London: Humphrey Toy, 1573), 60.

[11] Thomas Nashe, *The Anatomie of Absurditie* (London: Thomas Hacket, 1589), 9.

[12] Samuel Daniel, *A Defence of Ryme: Against a Pamphlet entituled: Observations in the Art of English Poesie* (London: Edward Blount, 1603), 4.

[his] framing his words: the which of many thinges which in him be straunge, I know will seeme the straungest, the words them selves being so auncient, the knitting of them so short and intricate, and the whole Periode and compasse of speache so delightsome for the roundnesse, and so grave for the straungenesse.... for oftimes we fynde ourselves, I knowe not how, singularly delighted with the shews of such naturall rudenesse, and take great pleasure in that disorderly order.... in my opinion it is one special prayse, of many which are dew to this Poete, that he hath laboured to restore, as to theyr right-full heritage such good and naturall English words, as have ben long time out of use and almost cleane disherited. Which is the onely cause, that our Mother tonge, which truely of it self is both ful enough for prose and stately enough for verse, hath long time ben counted most bare and barrein of both. Which default when as some endevoured to salve and recure, they patched up the holes with peces and rags of other languages, borrowing here of the french, there of the Italian, every where of the Latine, not weighing how il, those tongues accorde with themselves, but much worse with ours: So now they have made our English tongue, a gallimaufray or hodgpodge of al other speches.[13]

So shocking a 'gallimaufray' or 'hodgpodge' had English become as a result of these borrowings that E.K. had to use the borrowed French words 'gallimaufray' and 'hodge-podge' to describe it ('hodge-podge' from '*hocher*' to shake about and '*pot*', a pot). Like many nationalists even today, E.K. has a shaky sense of what is 'genuine' English (other borrowings in this passage include: 'straunge', 'auncient', 'intricate', 'singularly', 'naturall', 'Poete', 'heritage', 'default', 'salve', 'recure'—to name a few). Other writers of the period have a wide variety of attitudes to borrowing, attitudes which range from the linguistically protectionist to the lexically free-trading. Diverse though their attitudes are, many of them end up in E.K.'s position of having to use foreign words to characterize what is and what is not 'proper' English ('proper', by the way, is a borrowing from the French). Thus, Puttenham:

language ... when it is peculiar unto a countrey ... is called the mother speach of that people: the Greekes terme it *Idioma*.... this word *Idiome*, taken from the Greekes, yet serving aptly, when a man wanteth to expresse so much unles it be in two words, which surplussage to avoide, we are allowed to draw in other words single, and asmuch significative: this word *significative* is borrowed of the Latine and French.[14]

---

[13] E.K., 'Epistle' to Edmund Spenser, *The Shepheardes Calender* (London: Hugh Singleton, 1579), [n.p.].
[14] George Puttenham, *The Arte of English Poesie* (London: Richard Field, 1589), 120–2.

He could have said the same of 'surplussage' which is from medieval Latin. E.K. and Puttenham strike me as more or less hapless in their attempts to find a pure-bred English, but such haplessness could also be played for comedy, as a comic ice-skater pretends not to be able to skate but displays his virtuosity by the skill with which he teeters on the edge of calamity. Thomas Nashe is the specialist in this trick, as when he berates his enemy and stooge, Gabriel Harvey, for the pedantic excesses, the 'inkehornisme[s]' to be found in his writing; Nashe gives a catalogue of Harvey's lexical crimes (which I abbreviate) and then comments:

Conscious mind: canicular tales:...putative opinions: putative artists:...materiallitie:...
Fantasticallitie; divine Entelechy:...addicted to Theory:...addoulce his melodie:...
amicable end: extensively emploid:...negotiation: mechanician.

Nor are these all, for everie third line hath some of this over-rackt absonisme.[15]

But Nashe knew perfectly well that 'absonisme' is also a coinage, as is 'over-rackt', for he coined them both. I am 93.1 per cent certain of this. One thing Nashe's list of absurd linguistic novelties indicates—a cheering thing—is that in some respects writing of the 1590s is easier to understand now than it was then, because many of the period's lexical innovations have since entered the language and grown familiar to us—conscious mind, addicted to theory, negotiation—whereas they were more troublesome then. This is worth bearing in mind when scholars tell you that 'Shakespeare's audience would instantly have recognized...' some allusion to Ovid or some complex word-play; this has a depressing effect on us now, I think, but we should not trust the scholars 100 per cent, only about 93.1 per cent, for, setting aside the fact that Shakespeare's audience was made up of people with diverse levels of education, and that some of them were probably trying to pick their neighbour's pocket, or ogling the peachy boy who was playing Cressida, many of the things they heard on the Shakespearean stage were unfamiliar to them though they are familiar to us now.

Shakespeare's *Sonnets*, *A Lover's Complaint*, and *Troilus and Cressida* are liberally sprinkled with words which have been resurrected from fifteenth-century English or earlier; it seems likely, given the previous uses of these words which the *OED* records that he had been reading

---

[15] Thomas Nashe, *Strange Newes, of the intercepting certaine Letters and a Conuoy of Verses* (London: John Danter, 1592), 'The Arrainment and Execution of the Third Letter', [n.p.].

up in earlier versions of the Troy story by Chaucer or Lydgate or in *The Recuyell of the Historyes of Troye*. Shakespeare shared to some extent Spenser's fondness for a linguistic 'wonder of antiquitie' and, like Spenser, was not above faking new words along old lines to produce an illusion of datedness in his language; I think myself that the reasons why Shakespeare engaged in this fabrication of the antique, this production of 'distressed pine' or 'stone-washed jeans', as it were, are much more searching and interesting than any motive Spenser may have had, but this may be only because I mostly find Spenser unreadably dull. So in *A Lover's Complaint* and *Troilus and Cressida* we find new words produced by affixation, particularly with prefixes such as 'en-' or 'em-' (enpatron, empleached, enswathed) or with suffixes such as '-ure' or '-ion' (extincture, annexions). These affixes all have in common a strongly latinate, and an especially frenchified, timbre, and they produce when they appear *en masse* an air of faded courtliness, a sense of outdated refinement; they have an 'indexicality' rather like that which attaches to certain linguistic usages in old families, or families which like to pretend to antiquity, in the Southern United States. In *A Lover's Complaint*, as John Kerrigan notes in his excellent edition of the poem, this fondness for lavendering the language extends even to spelling, for the poem often deliberately opts for spellings which were overtly quaint at that time, so that even words which are not fake-antique may be perfumed with a whiff of olden times: 'plattid' (for 'plaited'), 'carkas' (for 'carcase'), 'trew' (for 'true').[16]

In *Troilus and Cressida*, words formed by similar affixation include: 'abruption' (III.ii.64), 'rejoindure' (IV.iv.35), 'soilure' (IV.i.57), 'immures' (Prologue), 'insisture' (I.iii.67) or, in the *Sonnets*, 'rondure'. An exhaustive list of all the play's lexical novelties would be very long and would have to include also: 'allayment'; 'appertainments'; 'assubjugate'; 'conflux'; 'constring'd'; 'convive'; 'corresponsive'; 'embrasure'; 'exposure'; 'imminence'; 'oppugnancy'; 'persistive'; 'plantage'; 'tortive'; 'transportance'; and so on. The *OED* credits Shakespeare with the first recorded use of all these words, if credit is the word for what he deserved, but we need not commit ourselves as far as the dictionary does; the evidence may show only that he was extremely alert to the massive influx of coinages in sixteenth-century English, and that he was extremely intelligent about

---

[16] William Shakespeare, *The Sonnets and A Lover's Complaint*, ed. John Kerrigan (London: Penguin, 1999).

how such rarities could be deployed in a play to give it a time-warped verbal atmosphere, entirely appropriate to its mock-heroic treatment of the ancient story.

It might be said that all these observations about the play's vocabulary may be of interest for a historian of the language, that it may even show something about Shakespeare's terrific on-the-ball-ness about the state of the words he heard all round him, but that it draws us away from an imaginative response to the dramatic qualities of the play. But this is not so. Consider Troilus in Act V, scene ii. Cressida has been exchanged for Antenor shortly after she and Troilus have come together; he now stands with the wiliest of Greeks, Ulysses, watching from a hiding-place his beloved flirting with Diomedes. Ulysses tries to persuade him to leave, because they have seen enough, more than enough, and there is nothing to be done—'Why stay we then?', to which Troilus replies:

> To make a recordation to my soule
> Of every syllable that here was spoke:
> But if I tell how these two did coact;
> Shall I not lye, in publishing a truth?
> Sith yet there is a credence in my heart:
> An esperance so obstinately strong,
> That doth invert th'attest of eyes and eares;
> As if those organs had deceptious functions,
> Created onely to calumniate.[17]

'Recordation', 'coact', 'credence', 'esperance', 'attest', 'deceptious' are all either neologisms, rare senses, or uses of a word in a new grammatical category. Someone might wonder whether this is genuinely the language of heartbreak, might object that Troilus cannot be much moved by what he sees if he has the mental energy to come out with such a string of far-fetched linguistic novelties. But this objection forgets that Troilus is not alone on stage to witness Cressida's flirtation; Troilus knows that Ulysses is watching him. So he does not pour his heart out, he decants it in this finicky, stilted manner. Ulysses's brief comments in the scene show how embarrassed he is by and for Troilus—'Come, come', 'My lord', 'All's done, my lord'—and in these circumstances Troilus stands on the dignity of his vocabulary; he is putting a brave

---

[17] *Troilus and Cressida*, V.ii.3110–18 (Folio text, but preferring Quarto 'th'attest' to F 'that test').

face on the situation by talking about it in a big voice with big words. Considering the vocabulary of the play can then yield us an intimate sense of how the scene needs to be acted. It might even make us the more sympathetic to Troilus, if we reflect that the very far-fetchedness of his words could show the effort he has to make on himself, the strain of grasping this horrible new truth drives him to these linguistic exotica.

It is not only Troilus we need to think about when considering the effect of such rapid density of new vocabulary in this scene (there are many other similar passages in the play) but also the audience. An obvious consequence of such a density of 'hard words' is that the audience too, as well as Troilus, is confronted with the unfamiliar at a rate which is hard to take in. How was it thinkable for Shakespeare to write for the theatre lines such as:

> ... by the conflux of meeting sap,
> Infects the sound pine and diverts his grain
> Tortive and errant from his course of growth[18]

which have five lexical curiosities in twenty-eight syllables? He may have taken for granted that his audience could recognize and quickly understand new words, especially if the new words were formed along old familiar lines; but we should also realize that lexical far-fetchedness was itself something of a production-value in Shakespeare's theatre, something equivalent to the dry ice and hydraulic sets of Sir Andrew Lloyd Webber or the fact that Nicole Kidman gets her kit off in Act 2.

Troilus and Cressida offered its audience an experience at once thrilling and disorienting of linguistic up-to-date-ness, an experience something like going to a very fashionable night-club indeed, where the people look weird and behave in scary ways but where you are nonetheless pleased with yourself for having got in. There are fashions in speech as in clothes or music, and Shakespeare was extremely fashion-conscious. Indeed, it could be said with little exaggeration that he invented the modern sense of the word 'fashion', for, before him, it meant mostly 'a manner of doing something' or 'the construction of an object', and so on. But Shakespeare gave us 'the glasse of Fashion, and the mould of Forme' in *Hamlet*, the phrase 'in fashion' in *Julius Caesar*, 'out of fashion' in *All's Well That Ends Well*, and 'fashionable' in its still-current sense in

---

[18] *Troilus and Cressida*, I.iii.464.

Troilus and Cressida.[19] If you look at the scene between Hamlet and Osric, for example, and check its words out in the dictionary, you'll see that Hamlet is genuinely innovative whereas Osric, who thinks he's so *chic*, is in fact merely following verbal fashions which had already been set by others. Barbara Everett has brilliantly described what Shakespeare does in *Troilus and Cressida*, and does particularly through the play's super-sharp sense of lexical fashion and fashioning:

> the verse most characteristic of the play makes us see and feel things both as History and as Now, as very great and very small, as far removed and detached and also as the stuff of the most immediate sensation.... *Troilus and Cressida* often seems Swiftian, not merely in its scabrousness, but because it plays games like this with scale. Its embodying of existence lived between History and 'Now' makes us look at things, at one moment with the extreme detachment of History, at another from the sensational immersion of 'Now'.[20]

To which I would add that it is not only 'things' which the play makes us look at through both ends of a telescope but also words, for it is by the density of such fake antiques in the play's vocabulary that Shakespeare principally creates the veering sense of scale which Everett so well describes. We often hear of the 'theme of Time' with a capital T in Shakespeare's works, in the *Sonnets*, for example, or in *Troilus and Cressida*, which has a long speech on the subject of Time, but we hear much less often about Shakespeare's timing of his plays. A dramatist can 'time' his or her plays in many ways: think of how much faster and shorter Harold Pinter's plays would be if he did not so often write in the stage direction '(*Pause*)'; by the inclusion of very long speeches only indirectly related to the narrative action of the play—as, for instance, Ulysses' 'degree' speech in this play, which Dryden cut by half in his rewrite of the piece, leading one modern editor to praise him because 'so long a speech about general principles makes action stand still in the theatre' (a comment which ignores the very special effect that can be obtained by making time seem to stand still, as also the appropriateness to a play about a ten-year siege of such experiences of futile protraction as Cressida has during Pandarus's stupid shaggy-dog story about the hair on Troilus' chin, after which she comments, 'it has

[19] *Hamlet*, III.i.1819; *Julius Caesar*, V.v.2645; *All's Well That Ends Well*, I.i.161; *Troilus and Cressida*, III.iii.2018.

[20] Barbara Everett, 'The Inaction of *Troilus and Cressida*', *Essays in Criticism* 32 (1982), 119–39 (pp. 132–3).

beene a great while going by'); or by the arrangement of scenes and events—in Dryden's version of the play, for example, Troilus and Cressida get it together in Act II, scene ii (not till Act III, scene 2 in Shakespeare) and have, in effect, two love-scenes separated by 433 lines: this makes their love seem 'outside' the march of military events, something Shakespeare never permits, for the delay and the rush Shakespeare's Troilus and Cressida experience are wholly submitted to the rhythms of war.[21] But a dramatist can also 'time' the events in a play by varying the datedness and the up-to-dateness of the play's language, so the audience experiences it as now remote and stilted, now racy and urgent. It is through such lexical composition that Shakespeare produces the diffuse mock-heroic atmosphere of his play and thereby expresses his historical self-consciousness, his sense of the fact which Fontenelle expressed in his *Dialogues of the Dead*: 'Antiquity is a remarkable sort of object; the further you are away from it, the bigger it looks.'[22]

The play has a reversible, telescopic style; the writing can switch between belittling and aggrandizing its material and can, even more remarkably, do both at once. This process begins in the Prologue:

> To *Tenedos* they come,
> And the deepe-drawing Barke do there disgorge
> Their warlike fraughtage.[23]

If you ask why he wrote one six-syllable line, 'To Tenedos they come', in the run of the blank verse, the answer is probably that he is pastiching Virgil, who sometimes has these half-lines (hemistichs) in the run of his hexameters. So here there is a small 'up-market' moment in the versification (which would sound out in the theatre as an impressively long pause). But then immediately a lexical play moves our attitudes in a different direction, because 'disgorge' can mean, as Shakespeare could have found in Caxton, 'to vomit' or 'to throw up'. The ships are deep-drawing because they are very large and very laden and so sit low in the water, but they are also metaphorically

---

[21] John Dryden, *Troilus and Cressida, or, Truth Found Too Late* (1679), in *The Works of John Dryden*, 20 vols. (Berkeley: University of California Press, 1956–89), vol. 13: *Plays; All for Love; Oedipus; Troilus and Cressida*, ed. Maximillian E. Novak and George Robert Guffey (1984); Shakespeare, *Troilus and Cressida*, I.i.323.

[22] *Fontenelle's Dialogues of the Dead*, trans. John Hughes (London: Jacob Tonson, 1708), 75. Hughes's translation differs slightly from that given above.

[23] *Troilus and Cressida*, Prologue, ll. 12–14.

deep-drawing, they have taken deep draughts, sunk many pints, and so are the more likely to throw up—the Greek troops are then vomited on the plains around Troy. There is a variety of linguistic bulimia at work from the very start of the play; its language is gorgeous, engorged, but then permanently queasy and about to disgorge. Jürgen Schäfer has stressed in great detail 'the fluid state of the English lexicon in the sixteenth century', and calls it 'a period afloat in uncharted seas of new words'; in *Troilus and Cressida*, the period is not only afloat on words but seasick of them.[24]

It has often been observed that the play has a lot of 'food imagery'; this is a regrettable way of expressing a fact, regrettable because it is tainted by the unexamined assumption that 'imagery', figurative language, is more important than non-figurative usages. There's no good reason, either literary-historical or linguistic, to assume this, so I'll just say: the play has an extensive semantic field related to cooking and eating. Shakespeare deploys a set of words which have a (usually ancient) culinary sense and also (usually more recent) senses which more or less forget their humble, homely origins. If we remember the earlier sense while hearing the newer sense, we perform an act of mock-heroic realization of the word itself, and hence about the speaker of the word. For example, the words 'chaf'd' and 'broyles':

> IN Troy there lyes the Scene: From Iles of Greece
> The Princes Orgillous, their high blood chaf'd
> Have to the Port of Athens sent their shippes...
>   ...our Play
> Leapes ore the vaunt and firstlings of those broyles,
> Beginning in the middle.[25]

The Prologue starts out very finely: 'orgillous' is a swanky spelling of a swanky Old French word for 'proud'; the intercalated phrase 'their high blood chaf'd' is an anglicized ablative absolute and so carries the high-cultural prestige of Latin. 'Chaf'd' too has linguistic connections in high places (you can find it, among the *OED* citations, in a version of the *Aeneid* and in *The Faerie Queene*), but the root sense of the word is from a less-than-courtly French, *chauffer*, and that sense had long been alive in the kitchens of England in such words as 'chafing-dish'.

[24] Jürgen Schäfer, *Early Modern English Lexicography*, 2 vols. (Oxford: Clarendon Press, 1989), vol. 2: *Additions and Corrections to the O.E.D.*, p. 5.
[25] *Troilus and Cressida*, Prologue, ll. 2–4; 27–9.

We are to think of the 'Princes Orgillous' as both nobly enraged and in a mock-sweat. Similarly 'broyles' means 'disagreement', 'warlike encounter', but 'to broil' is also a way of cooking things, as it is when Ulysses speaks of Achilles as one who 'broyles in loud applause' (I.iii.846). The most startling of these culinary sub-meanings occurs when Thersites, watching Diomedes chuck Cressida under the chin, exclaims: 'How the divell Luxury with his fat rumpe and potato finger, tickles these together: frye lechery, frye' (V.vii.3039). The translation of which into modern cookery is 'steak and chips', because 'fat','rumpe','potato finger', and 'frye' all have their culinary senses, though the potatoes involved here (by virtue of a wild, mock-heroic anachronism, because the delectable tuber was not known in Europe until 2,600 years or so after the events here staged) are probably sweet potatoes, which were thought to have aphrodisiac properties. It is a horrifying moment of sexual disgust of a kind which Shakespeare was expert at creating as if, for a moment of hyperbolic lucidity, for a 'naked lunch', Thersites saw the whole business of love and procreation as a steak-house chain, endlessly serving up the same, mass-produced, finally tasteless dishes. Thersites' bitter insight is a self-conscious, mock-heroic version of a truth the British Foreign Secretary, Lord Halifax, expressed with weird bathos in 1938 when contemplating the rights and wrongs of appeasing Hitler: 'the world is a strangely mixed grill of good and evil.'[26]

The language of *Troilus and Cressida* is, in the play's own word, 'crammed'. Its copious verbiage eventually conveys a sense of surfeit, which then impels the dramaturgy to moments of silence, passages of inaction. Amid all its clamour, the play longs for silences, speaks of 'tongue-tied maidens', 'dumb cradles', 'dumb-discoursive devil[s]', of Ajax turned into 'a very land-fish languageless', where 'languageless' was invented by Shakespeare for the occasion, according to the *OED*. *Troilus and Cressida*, contrary to the *OED*'s findings, also has the first recorded use of 'infancy' in its radical, etymological sense of 'unable to speak'. 'Infancy' is particularly Troilus's word of self-description: 'skilless as unpractis'd infancy' or 'I am as true as truth's simplicity / And simpler than the infancy of truth'—though study of Troilus's vocabulary shows that this a self-delusion on his part, because he is in fact a noticeably high-flown speaker. It is Cassandra who has the word

---

[26] Halifax to Roger Lumley, 31 Mar. 1938, cited in Andrew Roberts, *The Holy Fox: The Life of Lord Halifax* (1991) (London: Head of Zeus, 2014), 410.

clearly as meaning 'incapable of speech': 'Soft infancy, that nothing canst but cry, / Add to my clamours'—a grave irony: the woman who was doomed never to be listened to, calling for aid to those who cannot speak. This longing for silence may also be why something happens in *Troilus and Cressida* which happens nowhere else in Shakespeare's plays. The phrase 'to stop someone's mouth' as meaning 'to kiss' occurs several times in his works—Beatrice to Don Pedro: 'stop his mouth with a kisse'; Richard II to his queen: 'One Kisse shall stop our mouthes, and dumbely part'[27]—but there is only one occasion when somebody asks for his or her mouth to be stopped, Cressida:

> Sweet, bid me hold my tongue,
> For in this rapture I shall surely speake
> The thing I shall repent: see, see, your silence
> Comming in dumbnesse, from my weaknesse drawes
> My soule of counsell from me. Stop my mouth.[28]

It is a relief, for her, for all in the theatre, when he obeys her command: 'Pretty, yfaith', as Pandarus comments. It is *Troilus and Cressida*'s unique and fugitive moment of happiness, when these two mouths close on a kiss. For mouths, that take survey of all the world, must have a stop. And that's the moral.

---

[27] *Much Ado About Nothing*, II.i.709–10; *Richard II*, V.i.2357.
[28] *Troilus and Cressida*, III.ii.1760–64.

4

Beasts

I have an old friend, with whom I once went to see *Poltergeist*. The film consists of a satisfying crescendo of supernatural horrors unleashed, as such horrors should be, on a normal and likeable American white middle-class family. There is a particular scene in which a piece of steak falls from a plate to the kitchen-floor, and then begins rapidly and inexplicably to decompose and churn with maggots. We were in the front row, as usual, because I do not find the cinema satisfying unless I am as close to the screen as possible. At the moment when the squirming beasties began streaming out of the steak, the rest of the audience and I fell silent, appalled, wondering what atrocity could be coming next. My friend burst out laughing. He has an extremely loud laugh, something between a carthorse and the 'Hallelujah' chorus. I could have killed him. I felt moral disapproval drilling into the back of my neck and sank lower in my seat, hoping we wouldn't be turfed out or publicly vilified for a deviant sense of humour and lack of decent human feelings. We were, in fact, left unpunished and my friend now has a good job on the *Independent*'s arts page.

Looking back, I have to admit that he was right. Not only right, but insightful, because it is nothing new for monsters and monstrosities in artistic representations to be comic: this is what we call the 'grotesque'. Comedy is often monstrous and laughter is part of the basic reaction to monsters. I stress the phrase 'in artistic representations'; I am not vindicating, or even considering, those who might snigger at a famine, or torture, or betrayal by a friend, or the murder of the innocent. The relevance of this to Rabelais is that it seems likely he was prompted to write the first of his chronicles, *Pantagruel Roi des Dipsodes*, by a fierce drought which France had undergone in the 1520s and 1530s. He gives a comically false etymology for the name Pantagruel, pretending that it comes from the Greek and means 'all thirst'. Hence, too, the genuinely Greek 'Dipsodes' of whom he is King: 'the Thirsty Ones'. As Professor Screech writes: 'this prolonged heatwave was a national disaster...Rabelais uses it as a source of humour, not as an excuse for breast-beating...[in] the comic tradition by which we are often made to laugh, not weep, at what we are really afraid of'.[1] If somebody were indignantly to ask, 'How can you laugh at such things?', one reply would be: 'What else can I do?' That is, one criterion by which we could differentiate the comic from the callous would be whether the laugher has any alternative, more practical charitable course of action open to him. One person dying of thirst at my feet when I have a bottle of water in my hands is not a laughing matter; thousands suffering in a drought when I have no supplies may be grotesquely—that is, painfully—comic. Laughter has, looked at from this angle, connections with a sense of human impotence, and this is one reason why comedy may be deeply religious. And facing the world of artistic representation, we are always helpless; a fictional person dying of thirst has no mouth into which we can pour anything. (Or rather: only the creator of an artistic representation can get at the mouth of his creature.) And this is one source of the pleasure we take in works of art, whether comic or tragic: they offer us worlds we cannot change, before which we are without recourse, as we are at times helpless in our own world, but now our incapacities have become a spectacle for us rather than a dilemma or a source of the despair.

A large question is opened up by this modest but necessary caveat: just what is an artistic representation? I shall not answer that question, but I shall include jokes and other varieties of the comic such as caricature under this heading. One reason why monsters are often funny is that our technology for representing the unimaginably awful, in films and suchlike, itself develops quickly, so that monsters soon become dated. Perhaps in 1954 the Creature from the Black Lagoon was genuinely awesome, though it is difficult to see why anybody should have been scared of a man in a rubber suit with an odd mask on (in the context of watching the film, I mean; if I found one in my bed, I might well feel a certain trepidation). To find this creature risible in his menaces and, indeed, rather cute because so unfrightening is to experience an illusion of historical progress which is in itself both pleasing and

---

[1] M. A. Screech, *Rabelais* (London: Duckworth, 1979), 37–8.

funny; I laugh quite as much at the 1954 audience who shuddered at the Creature from the Black Lagoon as at the Creature himself—how paltry their fears were, how I have now outgrown them as I have outgrown the fear of many things which, when I was a child, frightened me. Yet such a laughter at passé objects of terror would do well to include itself in the joke, for I have to recognize that much which fools or shocks me in current films will itself some day look hilariously unconvincing, and that I too will be outgrown. The recognition of a monster as amusingly grotesque rather than truly threatening is part of the comedy of humanity's notion of itself as progressively enlightened. But if there is such a thing as progressive enlightenment, we can be sure that such progress will eventually put us too in the shade. And this too is relevant to Rabelais, for he is a writer with one foot in each of what seem to us now two worlds—the passing world of medieval schools and monasteries, the coming world of the new learning. His writing makes a constant comparison between 'le savoir de vos rêveurs matéologiens du temps jadis et les jeunes gens de maintenant', between 'the learning of your nothingological dreamers of yesteryear and the young people of today'.[2] And, though his formulated sympathies are with the up-and-coming he has, at least, as is only decent, a comedian's gratitude to the targets of his ridicule, the stuck-in-the-mud, the old-timers. Hence the mixture in his work of, on the one hand, fairy-tales, deliberate linguistic archaisms, compendious superstitions, and, on the other, upper hand, up-to-the-minute scriptural erudition and reform-ist views. He is a master of that arena where the utopian encounters the inveterate, and one of the depths of his humour lies in his recog-nizing something like what I suggested we recognize when we laugh at the Creature from the Black Lagoon: that if we have superseded the past, we too will be overtaken in our turn. So, for instance, the many catalogues in his work are at the same time both epic and mock-epic, parodies of the compendious and futile learning of the old clerks and also of the garrulous anecdotalism of peasants, but also straight dem-onstrations of the solidity of the new imaginative world he is creating. His is the permanent comedy inherent in proverbs such as 'you can't teach an old dog new tricks', the sense of each individual as, so to speak, unevenly developed, with some old habits dying hard and some

---

[2] François Rabelais, *Gargantua* (1534), ed. Emmanuel Naya (Paris: Gallimard, 2004), ch. 15, p. 84 (text modernized).

bright new ideas, good resolutions for the future, and a constant tendency to backsliding.

One of the puzzles of reading Rabelais is an inverse of the effect produced by my friend's laughter during *Poltergeist*. He found something funny that appalled others, and so seemed a bit of a beast; people evidently used to find Rabelais extremely funny but a great deal of it now strikes us only as obscene. Take this passage, describing a merry prank Pantagruel's companion Panurge played on the theologians of the Sorbonne:

il feist une tartre Borbonnoise, composée de force de hailz, de *galbanum*, de *assa fetida*, de *castoreum*, d'estroncs tous chaulx, et la destrampit en sanie de bosses chancreuses, et de fort bon matin engressa et oignit tout le pave, en sorte que le diable n'y eust pas duré. Et tous ces bonnes gens rendoyent là leurs gorges devant tout le monde comme s'ilz eussent escorché le renard: et en mourut dix ou douze de peste, quatorze en feurent ladres, dix et huyct, en furent pouacres, et plus de vingt et sept en eurent la verolle; mais il ne s'en soucioit mie.

he made a sort of quiche with a great deal of garlic, gum resin, *assa foetida*, beaver's musk, piping-hot dog turds, all steeped in the issue of running sores, and bright and early in the morning he greased and anointed the whole pavement, so that not even the devil could have stood the smell. And so all these nice folk spewed up with a technicolour yawn in full view of everybody: with the result that ten or twelve of them died of plague, fourteen caught leprosy, eighteen were infested with lice, and more than twenty-seven got the pox; but he didn't give a fig.[3]

'Technicolour yawn' is, I'm afraid, a tad anachronistic and much too mild for 'comme s'ilz eussent escorché le renard', which means, literally, 'as if they flayed the fox', but it is in Rabelais's French a vulgar idiom for vomiting, based obviously on the idea that the intestines all become visible in such a spasm (I have merely tried to find a modern equivalent in tastelessness). And quiche is a joke of mine, though a 'tarte Borbonnoise' is indeed a tart made with cheese and eggs.

Much is lost in the translation. Rabelais is at times a great master of a sublime primness and insouciant precision in his narrative—it is one of the tricks Swift learned from him. He recounts this yucky incident with a spritely calm, a Pollyanna-ism in his locutions which both goads the reader and preserves a fixed smile of faux-naiveté: as if to suggest

---

[3] François Rabelais, *Pantagruel Roi des Dipsodes* (Paris: Gallimard, 2006), ch. 16, p. 231.

that Rabelais would be astounded to hear that what he has written is disgusting: take, for instance, 'estroncs tous chaulx', which is reasonably translated as 'piping-hot dog turds', it is the 'piping-hot' which carries the narrator's tone, as again at 'et de fort bon matin engressa at oignit', 'bright and early in the morning he greased and anointed', where the '*fort* bon matin', 'bright and early in the morning', does the trick. The absolute pretence of unruffled innocence was even stronger in the first edition, where Rabelais had 'oignit theologalement tout le treilliz de Sorbonne'—'devoutly anointed'. Such phrases can be easily turned round and made sarcastic; and part of the joke is evidently in a gibe at the stuffed shirts of the theologians and the pleasure in the public spectacle of stiff-necked people contorted with retching ('tous ces bonnes gens . . . devant tout le monde'). The equableness of all this, and its concern for expository clarity, stop, as it were, at least the narrator's nose against the offensiveness of what he recounts; he hasn't the faintest intention—he implicitly protests—of uncleanly imagination, nor of taking swipes at theologians; they really *are* 'bonnes gens'. The narrator, like Panurge, 'ne s'en soucioit mie'—there is a joke I haven't managed to get over there, the phrase meaning literally 'he didn't give a crumb' so that 'foie' evidently picks up from the immense 'tarts Borbonnoise' which Panurge has baked. The effect of this narrative trick is a complex questioning of what might be meant by innocence. To the pure all things are pure, the tone seems to say, even such sights, and stories about them. Were we to protest about the passage, he would throw up his hands in horror, how could we think such a thing of him, it never occurred to him that . . . etc., etc. The mock-horror implicit in the narrator's relation to a deliberately provoked response of the reader, which he then feigns to be entirely unconscious of, cannot engage us, though, unless in some sense we credit the possibility of somebody's really being impervious, in an oddly saintly way, to the implications of what they themselves have said. (An equivalent might be Dame Edna Everage's frequent claim to be 'caring' and to have won an award for 'niceness', the pleasure with which we hear her say, 'Oh dear, this is a terrible thing to say', but we must, in some sense, grant these claims to 'niceness' for the joke to work.) The grotesque is comprehensible only in relation to an imagination, sometimes hyperbolic, sometimes calculatedly implausible, but ever present, of the celestial, a sphere of righteousness against which the kinks show up. One evidence of this truth is that all the best gargoyles are in churches.

On this matter of the monstrously comic, the comically monstrous, compare Swift. Take part of the 'Digression concerning...Madness' from *A Tale of a Tub*; we are on a tour of a madhouse:

Accost the hole of another kennel (first stopping your nose), you will behold a surly, gloomy, nasty, slovenly mortal, raking in his own dung, and dabbling in his urine. The best part of his diet is the reversion of his own ordure, which, expiring into steams, whirls perpetually about, and at last reinfunds. His complexion is of a dirty yellow, with a thin scattered beard, exactly agreeable to that of his diet upon its first declination; like other insects, who, having their birth and education in an excrement, from thence borrow their colour and their smell...

...even I myself, the author of these momentous truths, am a person whose imaginations are hard-mouthed and exceedingly disposed to run away with his reason, which I have observed, from long experience, to be a very light rider, and easily shaken off; upon which account my friends will never trust me alone, without a solemn promise to vent my speculations in this or the like manner, for the universal benefit of human kind; which perhaps the gentle, courteous, and candid reader, brimful of that modern charity and tenderness usually annexed to his office, will be very hardly persuaded to believe.[4]

The narrator's imperturbability here comes less from a mock-innocence as in Rabelais and more from the clinical numbness of his diction. He is a professional, insulated in the terms of his competence against encounter with the miseries he catalogues—'reversion', 'ordure', 'expiring', 'reinfunds', 'declination': Swift has concocted for him a fantastical medico-legal-Miltonic terminology which cloaks the horrors he describes but then becomes itself the focus of a further horror, his appalling unconcern. When he writes 'The best part of his diet', he means just 'What he mostly eats', but 'best part' lacks contact with its other possible senses (such as 'the most pleasant thing he gets to eat') in a way which indicates the prose's lack of contact with what it itself represents. Similarly, 'His complexion is of a dirty yellow, with a thin scattered beard, exactly agreeable to that of his diet'—'agreeable to' is meant to mean only 'in conformity with', 'matching', but by being meant to mean only this has semantically blinkered itself against the disagreeableness it purveys. Having got this far in remoteness from his subject, the narrator finds it easy to write 'like other insects'; rather than 'like insects';

[4] Jonathan Swift, *A Tale of a Tub* (1704; text modernized), in *The Prose Works of Jonathan Swift*, vol. 1: *A Tale of a Tub with other Early Works 1696–1707*, ed. Herbert Davis, 3rd edn. (1965), pp. 112–14.

for he writes from a lexical point of vantage to which the sequence 'surly, gloomy, nasty, slovenly mortal' is an ascending sequence of horrors which the word 'mortal' caps, as if for the narrator mortality was an offence which, like surliness, nastiness, and the rest, was something of which he could not conceivably be accused. Being a mortal, this wretched lunatic is not of the same species as the person who tells this story—is, in fact, an 'insect', something apart, as if he were not an animal himself and could not die. The calm of this prose is calloused rather than celestial, and it is self-righteousness rather than righteousness which casts the grotesque into relief, yet here too a sense of exactitude, correctness, is essential to the production of the comic effect.

It is comforting to be indignant about moments like these, and Swift is indeed partly indignant himself and expects his alerted reader to be so too. But we are not to rest complacently on our quarrels with this expertise. As he comes to the end of his digression on madness, the hack-narrator turns to his own case in a wonderfully tortuous passage. Part of the joke here is that phrases such as 'even I myself, the author of these momentous truths' strike us as obviously symptomatic of the lack of self-knowledge, the preening, of the narrator which we have long been used to, though it continues at each new instance to amaze us. That is, there is at one level a simple and sarcastic reversal of what he means to say into what we take him to give away about himself by meaning that—'there he goes again', we readily think at a moment such like this, as we watch him in his implicit arrogation to himself of a sanity not shared by his subjects ('even I', he writes, as if it were surprising that he of all people should be touched with the wing of battiness, whereas readers would replace his 'even I' with 'especially you'), or again, 'vent my speculations, in this or the like manner, for the universal benefit of human kind', the mad self-importance of 'universal benefit of human kind' is a give-away, which shows him up as merely furiously venting when he believes himself to be reasonably speculating. If he weren't so laughable, he'd be dangerous. But thinking that about the Swiftian hack, we have placed ourselves as spectators at a Bedlam, unconcerned, irresponsive spectators of the very sort we have previously diagnosed him to be. And so, the final turn is doubly inculpatory: 'which perhaps the gentle, courteous, and candid reader, brimful of that modern charity and tenderness usually annexed to his office, will be very hardly persuaded to believe.' If we think in reply to this: 'what a sycophant he is, buttering up his readers by telling them what nice feelings they've got', we are admitting of ourselves what the joke actually tells—that we are not brimful of modern charity and tenderness. Not being so, who were we then to take such high-toned umbrage with the writer's earlier failings in sensitivity? And that last phrase 'which perhaps the gentle . . .' scathingly sounds in two voices at once—that of the writer we had taken him to be, fawning on the herd instinct for self-approbation, but also the voice of Swift, icily catching us out as actually practitioners of what we affect to disdain. Nor is the double-tongue of the humourist an entrapment that Swift invented for his readers; Rabelais has his versions of the same trick, as when, in the Preface to *Gargantua*, he addresses us as 'Beuveurs tres illustres, et vous, Verolez tres precieux', 'Distinguished drunkards, and you, esteemed and poxy readers', and says that it is particularly for drunkards and the poxed that he writes.[5] If we laugh this address off ('Of course, he doesn't really think we are such dreck'), we put ourselves in a self-righteous and haughty position which is risible; if we are flattered to be 'illustres' and 'tres precieux', we pay for that flattery by admitting that we are drunk and/or poxed. In the case of Rabelais and Swift, such comic turns on the reader are in fact jokes made out of the fact that Christ came to save sinners, and that his grace is received on condition of admitting our need for it, our fault, much as we are Rabelais' preferred audience on condition of admitting our risibility. But the joke need not always be Christian; it is part of a long-standing comic tease by which all kinds of comedian get us to admit that we are beasts, and laughable at that.

Rabelais is perhaps read less often than he is invoked by students of comedy nowadays; the percentage of those who use the word 'Rabelaisian' who have read him is probably small. For this we have to thank or blame Mikhail Bakhtin, whose book on *Rabelais and His World* has been monstrously influential. I would like to suggest a few reasons for thinking Bakhtin's influence regrettable. I take it, for starters, that the 'Rabelaisian' in comedy would be regarded by many as in some sense the antithesis of the 'Swiftian'. Rabelais is the great celebrant of the earthly, festive, sprawling, amoral, etc., etc., Swift the eternal party-pooper. Yet, as I have mentioned, Swift learned a great deal from Rabelais, and we know he was fond of Rabelais's work, so it was not an

⁵ Rabelais, Preface to *Gargantua*, 13.

unacknowledged or involuntary debt. It may be that Swift is no more 'Swiftian' than Rabelais is actually 'Rabelaisian', and that the opposition is, like other talismanic antitheses, not precisely dependent on fact. Rabelaisian comedy, according to Bakhtin, is essentially this-worldly, it accepts bodily functions with a hearty frankness, it subverts official ideologies, it is 'carnivalesque'. He puts his case eloquently in the following description of laughter:

Laughter purifies from dogmatism, from the intolerant and the petrified; it liberates from fanaticism and pedantry, from fear and intimidation, from didacticism, naiveté and illusion, from the single meaning, the single level, from sentimentality. Laughter does not permit seriousness to atrophy and to be torn away from the one being, forever incomplete. It restores this ambivalent wholeness. Such is the function of laughter in the historical development of culture and literature.

Or, more succinctly, 'Laughter...overcomes fear, for it knows no inhibitions, no limitations'[6]. Bakhtin's account of Rabelais has been widely accepted as true of all comedy worthy of the name, comedy has become for many critics the 'nice guy' of the literary world—affable, acquiescent, endlessly forgiving, joyous, etc., made in the image of Pantagruel himself as he eventually becomes in the *Tiers Livre*, 'le meilleur petit & grand bon hommet, que oncques ceignit espée',[7] 'the best little, big little chap who ever carried a sword'. This kind of comedy clearly differs from the 'Swiftian' as that is usually conceived—a form of comedy scarred with horror at the physical world, in the service of embittered political factionalism, in some respects an 'Establishment' humour, arising from many tortuous inhibitions and concerned to stress, as an ethical imperative, the need for human beings to recognize their own limitations. The mere existence of a Swiftian comedy is enough to prove that Bakhtin's account of 'laughter' is one-sided, but set this to one side for the moment. What Bakhtin says of Rabelais both is not true of Rabelais and could not be true of any form of practised comedy, not even the Rabelaisian as Bakhtin liked to imagine it.

If laughter overcomes fear, when we laugh at something monstrous, we do not fear it, we do not regard it as truly monstrous, but only as a

---

[6] Mikhail Bakhtin, *Rabelais and His World* (1965), trans. Hélène Iswolsky (Bloomington, Ind.: Indiana University Press, 1984), 123, 90.

[7] François Rabelais, *Le Tiers livre des faits et dits Héroïques du noble Pantagruel* (1546).

Creature from the Black Lagoon. But this is not so. We have the phrase 'screamingly funny', and it means something, as does the phrase 'I almost died laughing' (equivalents of which exist in other European languages). It is not an accident that people wet themselves in terror as well as in laughter: Rabelais knew this quite well, and one of the major elements in his writing is a co-occurrence of laughter and fear, in which we laugh at the frightening and fear our laughter, such as could not be comprehended within Bakhtin's sentimentalized scheme. The title-pages of the first two books of Rabelais' work both make this clear: *Pantagruel Roy des Dipsodes . . . avec ses faictz et prouesses espouventables* (1532) (*Pantagruel, King of the Dipsodes . . . with an account of his terrifying deeds and abilities*) and *La vie très horrifique du grand Gargantua, père de Pantagruel* (1534–5) (*The very horrific life of the Giant Gargantua, father of Pantagruel*). His writing, in a strict sense, is outrageous not only in that it concerns the deeds of giants, their hyperbolical eating and excreting, but in such plain facts as that Rabelais' narration reverses the order of nature, for he wrote the story of the birth of Pantagruel's father after the story of the birth of the son (though Gargantua features in the first book too). These and suchlike games make little sense unless they constantly reawaken and so preserve the very dogmas and fears which they at the same time flout; an infringement requires and reinstates a rule, and has to do so if it is to be felt as an infringement; breaches call up customs as do observances of the same custom. (This is part of the logical reason why Bakhtin could not possibly be right.)

Consider an instance of comic beastliness. Rabelais tells with pride how his hero was more amazing a baby than Hercules. In doing so, he at once summons to mind the epic conventions of remarkable infancies, thereby nods to them, and then takes a swipe at them. Hercules strangled two snakes; small deal, according to Rabelais—Pantagruel, while in his cradle, was being suckled by a cow:

Il se deffit des liens qui le tenoyent au berceau un des bras, et vous prent ladicte vache par dessoubz le jarret, et luy mangea les deux tetins et la moytie du ventre, avecques le foye et les rognons, et l'eust toute devoree, n'eust este qu'elle cryoit horriblement comme si les loups la tenoient aux jambs, au quell cry le monde arriva, et osterent ladicte vache a Pantagruel[.]

he freed one of his arms from the cords which held him down to his cradle, and took hold of the said cow underneath its hams and ate two of its teats and half its stomach, along with its liver and kidneys, and would have eaten it all, had it not been that the cow screamed horribly as if wolves had it by its legs; at which scream everybody rushed in and they took the said cow away from Pantagruel[.][8]

Just as the joke does not begin to work without the allusion to Hercules, so too its recounting calls upon fastidious officialise without which it would not begin to amuse ('ladicte vache', 'the said / aforementioned cow', and the finical subjunctive of 'n'eust este qy'elle cryoit horriblement', 'had it not been that the cow screamed horribly'). What is Rabelaisian here is exactly what would have been Swiftian in the same passage, and what Swift so well learned from Rabelais: the decorous impassivity amidst horrors, for the poor cow's screams (what happened to her after she had been rescued?), in this prose made more acute by being thus muted, are not far from the silenced cries of the Irish poor as they sound through Swift's *Modest Proposal*.

Writing such as this is characteristic of even the most 'carnivalesque' moments in Rabelais and contradicts the Bakhtinian notion of the Rabelaisian. Some more facts may be useful at this point in considering what Bakhtin has made out of *Gargantua* and *Pantagruel*. Bakhtin emphasizes the 'popular' character of Rabelais' work; he explains his fall from esteem in the seventeenth and later centuries as a result of the ideological freezing of culture under the grip of the absolutist French state. But the opposition between popular and official culture on which *Rabelais and His World* is built lacks historical substance; it does not seem to be the case that carnivals or fairs or feasts of fools and suchlike were 'popular' in the sense that officials and nobles did not attend them or know about them. On the contrary, they were mainly run by petty officialdom and not by the 'people'; European culture in the sixteenth century does not divide between 'official' and 'popular' culture in the sense that each sphere excluded the other. Rather, the 'popular' culture was shared by all, including those of highest rank; there was indeed a second, 'high' or learned culture which was closed, in some respects, to the uneducated. The spheres are not opposed to each other, but rather concentric. Then, it is not easy to see how Rabelais can be regarded as a popular author. Bakhtin may have meant that only the poorer people talked about farting or fucking, but this seems both unlikely and patronizing. Even *Pantagruel*, which is demonstrably raunchier than the later works in the sequence, is by no stretch

[8] Rabelais, *Pantagruel*, ch. 4, p. 75.

of terms popular. In the first place, it is a printed book, and so available to the illiterate majority of the population only through the mediation of the educated. Secondly, you have to be quite well educated to read, for instance, chapter 9 of that volume, in which Panurge speaks German, a corrupt Arabic, Italian, Biscayan, Low Breton and a jumble of other dialects, Low Dutch, Spanish, Danish, Hebrew, Greek, Gascon, and Latin. Rabelais' endless stylistic jokes, erudite puns, theological parodies, and so on do not square with Bakhtin's account of the popular character of the work.

Bakhtin himself describes the relation between popular and official culture very inconsistently (I am relying on the translation of his work here, which might be at fault, but then most of those who adopt Bakhtin's terms with enthusiasm rely on the same translation). On the one hand, he asserts that the Middle Ages had 'forbidden laughter in every official sphere of life and ideology', that 'Laughter was eliminated from religious cult, from feudal and state ceremonials, etiquette and from all the genres of speculation'.[9] Yet he also tells us that feasts of fools were 'held in the churches and bore a fully legitimate character'; he quotes a fine defence of fooling:

foolishness, which is our second nature and seems to be inherent in man might freely spend itself at least once a year. Wine barrels burst if from time to time we do not open them and let in some air. All of us men are barrels poorly put together, which would burst from the wine of wisdom, if this wine remained in a state of constant fermentation of piousness and fear of God. We must give it air in order not to let it spoil. This is why we permit folly on certain days so that we may later return with greater zeal to the service of God.[10]

This was drawn up not by popular wisdom but by the Paris School of Theology in 1444, drawn up, that is, by the predecessors of those theologians for whom Panurge prepared his monstrous quiche. He also mentions the existence of the *Risus paschalis* (Easter laughter), a tradition by which, in celebration of Our Lord's resurrection, sermons and services were lightened by clerical jokes, and he acknowledges that the many parodies of liturgy produced in the Middle Ages were the work of clerics. (He might more fairly have admitted that virtually all writings in the period have clerical authors, and so that virtually all the records he can have had to go on in constructing his notion of

---

[9] Bakhtin, *Rabelais and His World*, 71, 73.   [10] Bakhtin, *Rabelais and His World*, 74–5.

popular culture are, in fact, on the 'official' side of his dividing-line.)
Take the wonderful fifth chapter of *Gargantua*, which consists entirely
of unassigned clichés which people say when they are drinking;
amongst the bits of chatter is: 'J'ai la parole de Dieu en bouche: *Sitio.*'
'I've got the Gospel on the tip of my tongue: *I thirst.*'[11] *Sitio* is the
Vulgate's rendering of one of the last words of Christ on the cross:
'I thirst.' Should we describe this tippler's witticism as 'popular' or
'established/high-cultural/learned'? It seems reasonable to think that
only the quite well educated would know the quotation, and so be
able to turn it to this jocular purpose. And there is not one joke here,
for there is both the joke the tippler makes by quoting Our Lord's
agonized word in new and more relaxing circumstances, but also the
joke Rabelais makes by listing the tippler's joke along with a couple of
hundred other such sallies, in a list which both develops into a wild
good time being had by all, as it goes on and on in its merry-making,
but also winds down into a sense of forced humour, exhausted attempts
to 'keep the party going', flags, grows boring, as binges do.

Yet despite such considerations, Bakhtin insists on referring to the
'monolith of the Christian cult and ideology'.[12] The price he pays
for this perverse insistence is that he offers an equally monolithic and
unconvincing account of popular culture. We hear nothing of such
folk traditions as mourning rituals, keenings, the blessing of crops and
livestock, or the veneration of local saints, all of which involve a far
from oppositional relation between religious and folk culture. This
popular laughter which 'purifies from dogmatism', from the intolerant
and petrified and 'liberates from fascism ... fear and intimidation ... naiveté
and illusion' does not seem to have been remarkably efficacious on a
peasantry which we can quite as plausibly conceive of as such in what
Brecht called a 'mittelalterlicher Dunst von Aberglaube und Pest'
('a medieval fog of superstition and plague') as we can conceive them
rollicking, open-minded, sceptical, and permissive.[13] Indeed, the fundamental point of objection to Bakhtin, which goes deeper than his
misconception of the empirical evidence for his case, is that we must
conceive popular culture as integrally involving both these sides—the
laughing and what Bakhtin imagines to be the gloomy, religious

---

[11] Rabelais, *Gargantua*, ch. 5, p. 41.   [12] Bakhtin, *Rabelais and His World*, 75.
[13] Bertolt Brecht, *Leben des Galilei* [*Life of Galileo*] [1938], ed. Günther Busch (Berlin:
Suhrkamp, 1972), 124–5.

aspect—if we are to understand even only its laughter. And this follows not from the nature of the Middle Ages but from the nature of the comic.

Consider Bakhtin's claim that: 'For the medieval parodist everything without exception was comic.'[14] This cannot be true, for an essential element in parody is the guying of an original which is serious—not just an original which mistakenly takes itself seriously but an original which is in some sense seriously mistaken about itself. The original of a parody must be making a claim which the parody then counters; it may be that the parody in fact pretends to believe things about the original which are not true, but then that pretence itself has to be serious. The various angles at which original claim and parodic counter-claim meet and diverge cannot be specified in advance—the tone of parody can range from the openly indulgent to the nakedly hostile—but the element of genuine disagreement remains essential across the spectrum of parodic possibility. Not, of course, that it is impossible to parody comic originals, though it is less usual. My point here is that comedy and tragedy, or the comic and the serious, stand in relation to each other as do two natural languages; it is always possible to translate between them, though, as with other translations, something may well be lost (or something gained) in the translation. Bakhtin's account of the comic in relation to the serious, the popular to the official, while managing to be incoherently various, is also sadly one-sided. That is, he writes, for instance: 'forms of pure laugher were created parallel to the official forms'; but he also writes that the comic empha-sizes 'the element of relativity and of becoming . . . in opposition to the immoveable and extratemporal stability of the medieval hierarchy'—but to be 'parallel with' is not the same as to be 'in opposition to'.[15] He is also prepared to say that 'medieval parody played a completely unbridled game with all that is most sacred and important from the point of view of official ideology'.[16] Here perhaps the translation has granted Bakhtin an ambiguity he did not intend, because to play a game with something or somebody can involve cooperation as much as antagonistic derision. We should also note the difficulty of the con-cept of an 'unbridled game'; most games constitutively involve rules,

[14] Bakhtin, *Rabelais and His World*, 84.

[15] Bakhtin, *Rabelais and His World*, 74, 82.

[16] Bakhtin, *Rabelais and His World*, 84.

and so cannot be completely unbridled, though they may have a game-some relation to their own rules. Certainly, the game of parody is unintelligible without rules, rules of correspondence to its imputed original, though again, these rules may themselves be parodically treated and are often not formulable in advance.

'Laughter does not permit seriousness to atrophy and to be torn away from the one being, forever incomplete. It restores this ambivalent wholeness.'[17] This is a fine saying of Bakhtin's, and it is unfortunate that we cannot say the same of his own work, but we cannot do so because *Rabelais and His World* shows us a comedy which is in entire atrophy, wrenched apart from its symbiotic role in an ambivalent wholeness, itself now as monolithic as Bakhtin, quite wrongly, claims seriousness became in the seventeenth century and thereafter. His work expresses a prejudice, provides slogans for a partisanship, which is no doubt why it has become popular. It is merely a prejudice, though one that many share, to assume that people are simply 'freed from the oppression of such gloomy categories as "eternal", "immovable", "absolute", "unchangeable" by laughter' and 'instead...exposed to the gay and free laughing aspect of the world, with its unfinished and open character'.[18] Can it always be good to be 'unfinished' (try telling that to the tourist who arrives to find his hotel unbuilt) or 'open' ('You've been sleeping with six of my colleagues'. 'But, darling, you should be glad. You *see*, I decided ours should be an open marriage')? Does it mean anything to regard 'immovable' or 'unchangeable' as a gloomy category (to feel immovable trust in a friend one knows is unchangeably trustworthy is not a gloomy experience)? Not everyone laughs all the time in the world, nor is laughter impossible in eternity; the end of *Troilus and Criseyde*:

> And whan that he was slayn in this manere,
> His lighte goost ful blisfully is went
> Up to the holughnesse of the eighthe spere,
> In convers letyng everich element;
> And ther he saugh, with ful avysement,
> The erratic sterres, herkenyng armonye
> With sownes ful of hevynyssh melodie.
>
> . . .

---

[17] Bakhtin, *Rabelais and His World*, 123.
[18] Bakhtin, *Rabelais and His World*, 83.

> And in himself he lough right at the wo
> Of hem that wepten for his deth so faste.[19]

It was, we know, Bakhtin's quiet intent in his celebration of the Rabelaisian to speak indirectly against the murderous officialdom of the Stalinist state, but he would have spoken better against such authoritarianism had he recalled that one of the elements of popular culture which that regime brutally repressed was Christian devotion. The attempt to portray the Christianity of Rabelais' time in terms of such totalitarianism, though historically implausible, has evidently had considerable appeal to liberal and literary intellectuals, given the breadth of acceptance which Bakhtin's work has commanded. But its appeal is that of a myth. There is indeed a charm to believing that, for instance, by having a good laugh and a few drinks one is in some way engaging in a dedicated struggle against forces of repression, but in fact freedom-fighters have usually to spend their time less convivially, and the overthrow of tyranny, the freeing of slaves, is not brought about by fun-loving merriment but through the blood of martyrs, whether religious or political. The adulation of the 'carnivalesque' which Bakhtin has promoted among students of comedy blinds its adherents to things more important than the nature of Rabelais' imagination, important though that is, blinds them to such things as what this earthly world is like, and how laughter sounds in it.

Yet Bakhtin has his allies, and in unusual places. Baudelaire, in his essay on the essence of laughter:

Le Sage, c'est-à-dire celui qui est animé de l'esprit du Seigneur, celui qui possède la pratique du formulaire divin, ne rit, ne s'abandonne au rire qu'en tremblant. Le Sage tremble d'avoir ri; le Sage craint le rire, comme it craint les spectacles mondains...le Sage par excellence, le Verbe Incarné, n'a jamais ri. Aux yeux de Celui quit sait tout et qui peut tout, le comique n'est pas. Et pourtant le Verbe Incarné a connu la colère, il a même connu les pleurs.

The wise man, by which I mean the man who is filled with the spirit of Our Lord, the man who holds in practice the key to the divine code, does not laugh, or gives himself up to laughter only with tremblings. The wise man trembles at having laughed; the wise man fears laughter, as he fears all earthly shows... The wisest man of all, the Incarnate Word, never laughed. In the eyes

---

[19] Geoffrey Chaucer, *Troilus and Criseyde*, in *The Riverside Chaucer*, ed. Larry D. Benson, 3rd edn. (Oxford: Oxford University Press, 2008), Book 5, ll. 1807–13, 1821–2.

of the omniscient and omnipotent, the comic does not exist. And yet the Incarnate Word felt anger, he even shed tears.[20]

This is as gloomy as Bakhtin is jocund, and yet (and for the same reason) it is misleading. We have in both cases a monolithic tokenism which takes the varieties of laughter, selects from them a narrow range of instances, and then fabricates from that narrow range the elements of a theory to which the writer can cling, a platform onto which his readers may climb. For Bakhtin, laughter achieves an essential freedom for the earthly from the eternal; for Baudelaire, it is a mark of human fallenness, imperfection, indeed it is essentially connected with evil, is satanic. Both writers from their divergent perspectives fail to *see* (or will not acknowledge) how manifold creation is, and how, therefore, laughter as part of creation joins in that manifoldedness. Had Baudelaire, for instance, looked at the Bible rather than spinning out his passionate and melancholy sentences, he would have found that God, monstrous as he may be in many ways, is not a humourless monster. Job observes how like God is to my friend who laughed at *Poltergeist*—'This is one thing, therefore I said it. He destroyeth the perfect and the wicked. If the scourge slay suddenly, he will laugh at the trial of the innocent'; the Psalmist notes: 'He that sitteth in the heavens shall laugh: the LORD shall have them in derision'; and 'The wicked plotteth against the just, and gnasheth upon him with his teeth. The Lord shall laugh at him for he seeth that his day is coming.'[21] It cannot, then, be the case, as Baudelaire implies, that omniscience and omnipotence exclude the possibility of laughter (indeed, there is a certain oddity in suggesting that an omnipotent being cannot laugh). Yet it may be that we would think better of him if he couldn't, for God in the Book of Job and in much of the other wisdom literature does sound as if he laughed at actual calamities in a way I mentioned could well be deplorable, though I allowed laughter at calamities in artistic representations. But, for God, all the world appears as an artistic representation because he sees it all *sub specie aeternitatis*, and, as Wittgenstein said:

The work of art is the object seen *sub specie aeternitatis*: and the good life is the world seen *sub specie aeternitatis*. This is the connexion between art and ethics.

---

[20] Charles Baudelaire, 'De l'essence du rire' [1855], in *Oeuvres complètes de Charles Baudelaire*, 7 vols. (Paris: Michel Lévy frères, 1868–73), vol. 2: *Curiosités esthétiques* (1868), p. 362.

[21] Job 9:22–3; Psalms 2:4; Psalms 37:12–13.

The usual way of looking at things sees objects as it were from the midst of them, the view *sub specie aeternitatis* from the outside. In such a way that they have the whole world as background.[22]

Such a point of vantage is one that comedy can offer beings lesser than God for moments (it is not the only one, laughter is possible in the midst of things as well as from above them). In its ability to offer such a point of vantage, comedy shows that it need not be a liberation of this-worldliness, but a liberation from this world, as in Troilus's laughter. On the other hand, such a point of vantage is of its essence only temporary for those of us who are not God or gods; were we always and only to laugh at the trial of the innocent, we would not know what 'trial' or 'innocent' meant. This very temporariness of a comic attitude makes it hard to talk about without simplification, just as it is hard to describe the character of a person whose moods often change. But the alternative to such difficulty is to pretend that a person has only one mood—say, Bakhtinian or Baudelairean—and such a person would not be a character but a cartoon.

Baudelaire and Bakhtin are strangely at one not only in their inadequate segmentation of the serious from the comic, their narrowed view of the religiousness of comedy, but also in their constant recourse to laughter as *the* token of the comic. The idea appears to be that if we understand laughter we shall understand the essence of comedy (and this appears also to have been the view of Bergson in *Le rire* and to a certain extent of Freud in his decision to focus on jokes as a key to the comic). But laughter is only one manifestation of the comic, though clearly an important one. If you turn back to the account of laughter which I quoted above from Bakhtin—'Laughter purifies from dogmatism... Laughter does not permit seriousness to atrophy'—it is evident, both that this is a sentimentalized notion of laughter (for there are such things as the laughter of in-groups against outsiders, in-groups which can be extremely dogmatic, or pompous and self-satisfied laughter which dismisses any new notion out of hand as absurd) and also that such an account cannot provide us with a full notion of the comic just because of its concentration on laughter, just because it ignores all those other expressions of a comic sense, which these descriptions do

---

[22] Ludwig Wittgenstein, *Notebooks 1914–1916*, trans. G. E. M. Anscombe, ed. G. H. von Wright and G. E. M. Anscombe, 2nd edn. (Oxford: Blackwell, 1979), '7.10.16', p. 84.

not fit. What of the snigger? the wry smile? the twinkle? the gloating cackle? the insult? the raised eyebrow? the limp wrist? and particularly, that intriguing and central comic abstention from expression, the poker-face? Theorists of the comic are over-impressed by laughter and under-impressed by things that comedians do in order to provoke laughter, and what it is that we have to do in order to be provoked into laughter. J. L. Austin has some fine remarks about philosophical over-concentration on a narrow range of examples, and how such over-concentration warps our thinking. In aesthetics, for instance, he rightly wishes that we would stop talking about the beautiful all the time 'and get down instead to the dainty and the dumpy'. Similarly, in thinking about comedy and the comic, we should take a holiday from laughter, from the carnivalesque, the open, the liberating, the subversive, and turn our attention to the snide, the outrageous, the Jeevesian twitch of the lips. For this too is a matter in which the collection of an appropriately wide range of instances is essential to making progress in conceptualization, for the reasons Austin gives:

It seems to be too readily assumed that if we can only discover the true meanings of each of a cluster of key terms, usually historic terms, that we use in some particular field (as, for example, 'right', 'good' and the rest in morals), then it must without question transpire that each will fit into place some single, interlocking, consistent, conceptual scheme. Not only is there no reason to assume this, but all historical probability is against it, especially in the case of a language derived from such various civilizations as ours is. We may cheerfully use, and with weight, terms which are not so much head-on incompatible as simply disparate, which just do not fit in or even on. Just as we cheerfully subscribe to, or have the grace to be torn between, disparate ideals—Why must there be a conceivable amalgam, the Good Life for Man?[23]

By the same token, it might be asked: 'why *must* there be such a thing as the relation of the comic to the serious?' or even 'the essence of laughter'? Taking Austin's point, it will, then, I hope be clear that it is not just because of the pleasure to be derived from slagging off fellow-critics that I spend time carping at Bakhtin and his followers. Something important needs defending against these theorists of comedy as a fairground or amusement arcade. Or indeed, several important things need defending against them, including fairgrounds and amusement

[23] J. L. Austin, 'A Plea for Excuses', in *Philosophical Papers* (1961), ed. J. O. Urmson and G. J. Warnock (Oxford: Oxford University Press, 1979), 184, 203 n.

arcades. The next time you feel inclined to use the word 'canivalesque' or its associated terms as appropriate to comedy, go and look at the faces of the customers of an amusement arcade—how drawn they are—observe how relentlessly the coins are slotted into machines for the promotion of avarice and deflected aggression, listen to the clatter of the toys and the absence of conversation. Reread Jonson's *Bartholomew Fair*, and recall that carnivals are golden opportunities for pickpockets. There you have a full and ponderable instance of the grotesque. And comedians also need to be defended against such theorists: Aristophanes, for instance, who sent his Dionysus into the underworld to find a poet who would save the city, and who gave to Dikaiopolis in *The Acharnians* the great plea: 'Don't hold it against me, gentlemen, if though a beggar—and a comic poet at that—I make bold to speak to the Athenian people about matters of state. Not even a comedian can be completely unconcerned with matters of truth and justice'; or Erasmus, who praised Christian foolishness in protest against the power-brokers and warmongers of his time; or indeed Rabelais himself, disciple of Erasmus, who equally wrote in favour of law-abiding tolerance, peaceableness, and the amiable decencies.[24]

Remembering Austin's philosophically grounded plea for a keener attention to a greater variety of examples, it will, I hope, be clear that it is not in a spirit of anti-intellectualism or anti-theory that I offer no formulation of the essence of comedy. Thinking about comedy does have to submit to the test and the pleasure of examples, and has to deny itself the relaxations of the Big Idea. So I end not with a conclusion, but three exemplary remarks about laughter which are worth keeping in mind and taking to heart—

Beckett, a conversation between a priest and one of his flock:

I...told him how worried I was about my hens, particularly my grey hen, which would neither brood nor lay and for the past month and more had done nothing but sit with her arse in the dust, from morning to night. Like Job, haha, he said. I too said haha. What a joy it is to laugh from time to time, he said. Is it not? I said. It is peculiar to man, he said. So I have noticed, I said. A brief silence ensued. What do you feed her on? he said. Corn chiefly, I said.

---

[24]   Aristophanes, *Frogs* (405 BC), trans. Judith Affleck and Clive Letchford, ed. John Harrison and Judith Affleck (Cambridge: Cambridge University Press, 2014); Aristophanes, *The Acharnians* (425 BC), in *Aristophanes. Acharnians. Knights*, trans. and ed. Jeffrey Henderson (Cambridge, Mass.: Harvard University Press, 1998), ll. 497–500 (p. 119).

Cooked or raw? he said. Both, I said. I added that she ate nothing more. Nothing! he cried. Next to nothing, I said. Animals never laugh, he said. It takes us to find that funny, I said. What? he said. It takes us to find that funny, I said loudly. He mused. Christ never laughed either, he said, so far as we know. He looked at me. Can you wonder? I said. There it is, he said. He smiled sadly.[25]

Newman, on the devil:

Yes! he is a master who allows himself to be served without trembling. It is his very art to lead men to be at ease with him, to think lightly of him, and to trifle with him. He will submit to their ridicule, take (as it were) their blows, and pretend to be their slave, that he may ensnare them. He has no dignity to maintain, and he waits his time when his malice will be gratified. So it has ever been all over the earth. Among all nations it has been his aim to make men laugh at him; going to and fro upon the earth, and walking up and down in it, hearing and rejoicing in that light perpetual talk about his which is his *worship*.[26]

The Gospel according to Saint Luke:

And he lifted up his eyes on his disciples, and said, Blessed be ye poor: for yours is the kingdom of God. Blessed are ye that hunger now: for ye shall be filled. Blessed are ye that weep now: for ye shall laugh.[27]

---

[25] Samuel Beckett, *Molloy* [1951; 1955], ed. Shane Weller (London: Faber & Faber, 2009), 105.
[26] John Henry Newman, Sermon 23: 'Christian Reverence' [8 May 1831], in *Parochial Sermons*, 6 vols. (London: J. G. & F. Rivington, 1834–42), vol. 1 (1834), 351–2.
[27] Luke 6:20–1.

5

A rehearsal of *Hamlet*

My title is 'a rehearsal of *Hamlet*' for three reasons: people say 'I needn't rehearse all the details' when they are about to offer their own slant on an issue or event; they strip the subject bare of what is not to their purpose and ask us to trust them that their edited version is all we need to know, although, unless we know the details which they tell us don't need rehearsal, we can't know whether we ought to trust them when they leave those details out. I will not be asking you to trust me in this way. The details are not extraneous to my purpose; they *are* my purpose. Not that I pretend to rehearse *all* the details of *Hamlet*; even if I knew them all (which I don't), that would take years. There is no such thing as a 'complete rehearsal' any more than there is such a thing as a 'complete explanation', if by 'complete explanation' is meant 'an explanation which precludes any possible misunderstanding'. Misunderstanding is always possible; like hope, it springs eternal in the human breast.

The second reason for 'a rehearsal of *Hamlet*' is that the kind of attention to detail I am mostly paying is the kind of attention which actors and directors and playwrights and stage-hands are paying when they rehearse a play; in particular, I repeatedly ask what the words on the page suggest about staging—about tone of voice or pace of delivery, about movement, about what those onstage but silent at any moment might be doing, about, that is, the kinds of things which it is easy to forget when reading a play without thought of the fact that a script is only a plan which needs to be put into practice. 'Putting a plan into practice' is the third sense of 'rehearsal' in the title, for the nearest thing I have to a general over-view of the play is that it represents a group of people engaged in rehearsing, in forming plans and then envisaging how they might be put into practice; Prince Hamlet himself is the most prominent of these rehearsers, but not the only one. And I think of the play as a rehearsal by Shakespeare of his skills and aptitudes, of what the theatre could do when he got his hands on it, and as rehearsing also more general competences in the socio-political world he inherited, for Shakespeare too, like an actor rehearsing, is engaged in memorizing and then bringing to a not entirely foreseeable new life what has gone before him.

I'll begin just before the beginning, with the title.

A text of Shakespeare's play, or something roughly like it, was entered in the Stationers' Register for 26 July 1602 as 'A booke called the Revenge of Hamlett Prince Denmarke'. In 1603, the first published version of the play, the bad Quarto 1, calls it 'The Tragicall Historie of Hamlet Prince of Denmarke'; the 1604 Quarto 2, the fullest contemporary text of the play, has shifted ground slightly to ·'The Tragedie of Hamlet *Prince of Denmarke*', which is also the name under which the play appears in the Folio of 1623. A similar shift happened to *Lear*, whose first Quarto (1608) introduces the play as 'M. William Shake-speare: HIS True Chronicle Historie of the life and death of King LEAR and his three Daughters', though the Folio gives us just 'The Tragedie of King Lear'. Publishers were as sloppy about the meaning of words then as they are now, and printers even then were or had demons, so we should not make a meal of these small alterations, but they still offer a few sustaining and tasty snacks. There isn't as much that matters in the varying titles of *Hamlet* as in some other titles which are so often mangled that their mutilated forms are now more or less a part of Western tradition: the *Divina* in *Divina Commedia* is a publicist's hype, not the poet's title—Dante never referred to the poem as anything but the *Commedia*, and *Divina* has no more warrant than any other enthusiastic adjective you feel like applying to his work, such as *Lunga*, *Ilaria*, or *Unputdownabile*; T. S. Eliot did not write a poem about a rubbish-dump, *The Wasteland*, but a poem about a devastated realm, *The Waste Land*; Joyce's last work has no apostrophe in its name, not *Finnegan's Wake* but *Finnegans Wake*, because Joyce meant by his title something plural before he meant something possessive, meant a plural noun followed by a verb in the indicative or imperative, not a singular proper name + apostrophe-s + a noun.

But still, there are a few things to note particularly about the smaller changes in the title of this play.

First, though the first record of Shakespeare's work calls it 'the Revenge of Hamlett', the word 'revenge' disappears from the title of later texts. This matters to me because I shall be arguing that *Hamlet* is not a 'revenge tragedy' but a quizzical pastiche of what we now categorize as revenge tragedies and of the ethic such plays imply, insofar as these plays imply anything so definite as an 'ethic'. *Hamlet* stands to 'revenge tragedy' as *The Royle Family* stands to soap-opera or *Little Britain* to a tourist-board video; it is a derisive instance of a rule, not the rule itself. The *Oxford English Dictionary* records 'revenge tragedy' as a literary-critical term only from Northrop Frye in 1957, though it is clear from such titles as *Antonio's Revenge* (Marston, Quarto, 1602) or *The Revenger's Tragedy* (Middleton, 1607) that the category was more or less known, even if not precisely labelled, much earlier.[1] People may have a concept without having a specific term for that concept, but it's worth recognizing that the labels we now have so convenient to hand for pasting on past works may not quite fit them (as, for instance, the label 'soliloquy' meaning 'a literary representation of someone talking to him- or herself' did not come ready-made to mind until further into the seventeenth century, and is applied only with the backward stretching of a limbo-dancer to Hamlet's so-called soliloquies). It is comforting to have a supply of such labels; they save time and mental labour and give us the pleasant sensation of knowing what's what. But there are occasions when we do well to do without such tags, when, for example, we encounter something new or newish and need, not familiar labels, but the courage to realize that our labels are the wrong shape and the patience to undergo our ignorance, that patience which is a condition of discovery. This point applies particularly to Shakespeare's Danish play, because the relation between known categories and present realities, between what Hamlet calls 'All sawes of Bookes, all formes, all presures past'[2] and what is happening even as he speaks, is a pivotal subject of the play. At many levels, including the level of genre-classification, what has gone before, what 'we all know', is in question in *Hamlet*.

Second, there is a slide in the case of both *Lear* and *Hamlet* from a Quarto classification of the plays as 'history' (whether 'Chronicle

---

[1] Northrop Frye, 'The Mythos of Autumn: Tragedy', in *Anatomy of Criticism: Four Essays* (1957), ed. Harold Bloom (Princeton: Princeton University Press, 2000), 206–23 (p. 209).

[2] *Hamlet*, I.v.785.

Historie' or 'Tragicall Historie') to 'Tragedie' pure and maybe simple. This slide crosses a boundary which Aristotle laid down and which a certain strand of critical opinion in Shakespeare's time observed, the boundary between the realm of history, of contingent facts, and that of poetry, of general rules. History tells us what in fact happened, poetry lays out the pattern according to which we could have seen the event coming. Aristotle makes the distinction as follows in his *Poetics*:

[history] describes the thing that has been, and [poetry] the kind of thing that might be. Hence poetry is something more philosophic and of graver import than history, since its statements are of the nature rather of universals, whereas those of history are singulars. By a universal statement I mean one as to what such or such a kind of man will probably or necessarily say or do—which is the aim of poetry, though it affixes proper names to the characters.[3]

'Statements' which are 'of the nature...of universals' are statements such as 'All vain people begin by deceiving themselves and then try to fool others into thinking of them as well as they think of themselves' or 'Politicians can always manage a passable impersonation of sincerity'; a 'singular' statement instantiating the truth of these two 'universals' might be 'Tony Blair is untrustworthy'. This distinction between history which 'merely' records what happened in all its particularity and poetry which gives, as it were, a template for how in general things happen, the pattern or rule of events, has counted in various ways for a lot in literary history. As far as concerns England: it lies behind Sir Philip Sidney's maxim that poets don't lie because they don't make factual claims; Dr Johnson's Imlac is a good Aristotelian when he says it is not the poet's business to number the streaks of a tulip; Coleridge makes explicit appeal to Aristotle's division of poetry from history when he complains of the 'accidentality' in some of Wordsworth's poems, their 'matter-of-factness', by which he means that they rehearse details such as only a chronicle could be interested in, details which Coleridge thought superfluous to the grander, general aims of poetry.[4]

---

[3] *Aristotle on the Art of Poetry* (1920), trans. Ingram Bywater, 12th edn. (Oxford: Clarendon Press, 1974), *Poetics*, Sect. 9, p. 43.

[4] Philip Sidney, *The Defence of Poesie* (London: William Ponsonby, 1595); *The Yale Edition of the Works of Samuel Johnson*, vol. 16: *Rasselas and Other Tales*, ed. Gwin J. Kolb (New Haven: Yale University Press, 1990), 43; Samuel Taylor Coleridge, *Biographia Literaria* (1817), in *Samuel Taylor Coleridge: The Major Works*, ed. H. J. Jackson, 3rd edn. (Oxford: Oxford University Press, 2008), 391.

Luxuriant and even superfluous detail is, however, near the heart of *Hamlet*, in ways which I shall describe as the occasion arises. In particular, the play inquires into and reorients our sense of dramatic character, the confidence with which we guess or the fervour with which we debate 'what such or such a kind of man will probably or necessarily say or do', because its dramaturgy stands in so constantly searching a relation to an audience's sense of social types, of 'such or such a kind of man'. This is one source of the work's staying-power, for every generation more or less newly shades its sense of the plausible, what kind of thing a certain kind of person is likely to say or do, and, engaged as it is in such a renovation of the plausible, *Hamlet* has the key to eternal relevance (which is not the same thing as eternal youth), and so came in handy for, say, J. Alfred Prufrock as for James Joyce. In *Hamlet*, the figures onstage and the audience in the theatre are both often engaged in asking what kind of person so and so is, changing their mind about previous judgements they have made, and Shakespeare's dramaturgy encourages this because this play shows many figures in the process of development, a development which is partly a matter of individual life-histories but also partly something wider than that, something that could be called, in Norbert Elias's phrase, the 'civilizing process'.[5] By which Elias meant such changes over time in acceptable behaviour as the shift in the West from eating with your hands to eating with a knife and fork, along with the internalization of such social norms so they come to seem a 'second nature' to those who obey them: in *Hamlet*, for instance, there seems to have been a quite recent shift away from the more physically adventurous style of kingship represented by Old Hamlet and his fondness for smiting Polacks to the prudent self-regard of a Claudius who employs mercenaries (Switzers) and of the Prince who thinks himself un-Herculean compared to his father; there are some old heavy-drinking customs which the Prince turns his refined nose up at; and so on.

By 'dramaturgy', I mean: the staging implied by a script and the further implications of that staging; I mean 'what is distinctive about what a playwright does in writing a play as contrasted to what is done by other writers in other forms'. Among the distinctive occupations of

---

[5] Norbert Elias, *The Civilizing Process* [*Über den Prozeß der Zivilisation*, 1939], trans. Edmund Jephcott, ed. Eric Dunning, Johan Goudsblom, and Stephen Mennell (Oxford: Blackwell, 2000).

a playwright is the playwright's design of information: what we are told, when, by whom, in what circumstances, and so on; how scenes are begun and ended; the perpetual situatedness of utterance in a play and the consequent need to bear in mind and ear that, for example, when Hamlet says he has recently lost all his mirth, has a heavy disposition, and regards the earth as a sterile promontory,[6] he is not confessing directly to us, nor is he in the role of a BBC newscaster passing on information, which to the best of his knowledge is true, nor has he suddenly metamorphosed into the narrator of a novel whose insights into the psychology of the book's characters we have little option but to trust. He is talking to Rosencrantz and Guildenstern, whom he suspects of being spies, as indeed they are; his suspicion is clearly established in the twenty lines immediately preceding his sudden declaration that he is suffering from depression, or 'melancholy' as it might have been called in those days. And his announcement of his state of mind begins with the sardonically helpful remark that he'll let them into his secret so they can continue their career of 'secrecy' in service of the king and queen; what's more he stresses that he doesn't know why he is so sad—'I have of late, but wherefore I know not, lost all my mirth'[7]—although we in the audience who have seen him on the battlements with the Ghost know part of the reason for his low spirits, and know that he too knows it. His exquisite words about the 'excellent Canopy the Ayre' and the following, celebrated exclamation, 'What a piece of worke is a man',[8] have provoked scholars to intensive researches on Renaissance conceptions of melancholy and prompted actors of the role into various postures of elegant gloom. These responses to his lines depend on the belief that Hamlet here is a straight-talker, though Shakespeare's dramaturgy, his design of the scene, devotes considerable pains to bringing out how densely refractive the inter-personal acoustic in which the prince hears himself speak is, how little he trusts Rosencrantz and Guildenstern to whom some suppose he is unbosoming himself. Perhaps the lines are, at least in the immediate situation of their utterance, something less grand than a self-expressive aria—a red herring, for instance. Which would not prevent there being some truth in what Hamlet says with his characteristically wry 'mirth', even as he speaks of having lost his sense of humour (like Beckett in a

---

[6] *Hamlet*, II.ii.1342–46.   [7] *Hamlet*, II.ii.1343.   [8] *Hamlet*, II.ii.1346–57.

very late text, *Stirrings Still*, whose best joke is the laconic self-description, 'No trace of humour any more').[9]

Take a second, larger-scale instance of Shakespeare's dramaturgy in the play. Imagine what difference would be made if *Hamlet* began with what is now Act I, scene 2. The first scene of the play tells us nothing of consequence for the plot which we are not told again in its successor; a strict, efficient script-editor, considering the treatment for Hollywood, would have cut it altogether. In Act I, scene 1, we are told of the political problems the Danes are having with Fortinbras, but this information is repeated in Act I, scene 2; in Act I, scene 1, we see and hear about the Ghost, but in Act I, scene 2 Horatio provides an extremely accurate summary of what happened in the earlier scene. An impatient critic might complain: either Act I, scene 1 serves purposes other than those of grounding the main lines of the plot, or it had better be got rid of (*Hamlet* being already grossly too long by Shakespeare's usual standards of length). What might be said in defence of poor, redundant Act I, scene 1? Well, for one thing, it establishes that Horatio is a trustworthy witness, for we saw what he saw in Act I, scene 1, and so are in a position to judge his reliability when he gives his synopsis in Act I, scene 2—and this matters because he is Hamlet's best friend in the play, so his decency rubs off, as it were, on the Prince. It will also matter at the end of the play, when he is charged with the task of telling the story of the entire play as he had, in Act I, scene 2, told most of the story of its first scene. What's more, though it is true that both the Ghost and the war with Fortinbras are gone over again in Act I, scene 2, they are repeated differently because separately: it is Claudius who talks about the Fortinbras problem in Act I, scene 2 and Horatio who talks about the Ghost; but in Act I, scene 1 Horatio discusses both—the Ghost and Fortinbras appear *as connected one to the other* in Act I, scene 1, for the suggestion is made in that scene that the Ghost appears because of the trouble with Fortinbras, a suggestion which may turn out to be misleading but which raises the issue of how large-scale political difficulties are linked to more domestic problems, whereas they appear uncoupled, one after the other in Act I, scene 2. Then again, Act I, scene 1 is an 'outdoor' scene which contrasts with the 'indoors' of the castle of Act I, scene 2, just as the last act of the play

[9] Samuel Beckett, *Stirrings Still* (1989), in *Company; Ill Seen Ill Said; Worstword Ho, Stirrings Still*, ed. Dirk Van Hulle (London: Faber & Faber, 2009), 65.

(however little weight we give to act-division in Shakespeare's texts) opens outdoors and then moves into the castle. I'll have more to say later about the dramaturgical genius of the opening scene, but one way of expressing its brilliance would be to notice that if Shakespeare had not written it, nobody would have guessed it was missing or hankered after its many superfluous details—the recent, frantic increase in shipbuilding (even on a Sunday); the appearance and behaviour of zombies at the time of Julius Caesar's death; the power of Christmas over fairies.

But these details can be discounted as 'superfluous', beside the main point, and thrust of the play, only when we have been clued in to what that is, but after Act I, scene 1, we still don't know what is going to count in what follows. Shakespeare's *Hamlet* is a retelling of an already-told sad story of the death of a king, though its predecessor play, the ur-*Hamlet*, is now lost. Some members of Shakespeare's audience may have known the earlier play or one of its sources, and so would have known—as nobody onstage in Act I, scene 1 does—why the Ghost walks and other such drifts of the plot to come as are hinted at in the opening scene. But they would not have known what sort of treatment the pre-existing story was going to get at Shakespeare's hands—whether, for instance, Christmas was going to bulk large in it, so that Marcellus's lines about the festive season would have more of a part to play than just making clear to us that we are in an officially Christian society, which is all they turn out to do.[10] Aristotle thought that tragedies are about 'what such or such a kind of man will probably or necessarily say or do', but the opening scene of *Hamlet* does not settle which kind of play is to follow, and so we do not know what such or such a kind of play will probably or necessarily do to its inherited story.[11] *Hamlet* is a sequel to a play which has now disappeared, and it is the responsibility of a sequel to be both a continuation of, and a change to, what has gone before; Shakespeare's play sets out to be an updated version of an old theatrical warhorse, with better special effects and an intriguingly novel slant on more or less familiar characters; it is, in effect, an equivalent to recent new series of *Dr Who*. We are therefore not as yet oriented with regard to the importance or relevance of details—that mention of Julius Caesar may turn out to be a clue, that apparently

---

[10] *Hamlet*, I.i.157–63.   [11] Aristotle, *Poetics*, Sect. 9, p. 43.

innocuous puddle of goo at the door of the TARDIS will be overlooked at your peril.

Another result of the profuse detail in *Hamlet* is that its events do not readily shape themselves for our attention according to the law-like pattern of inevitability, which Aristotle considered a prime requirement of the tragic plot, but amount rather to a stark and messy actuality of 'accidentall judgements, casuall slaughters', as Horatio puts it.[12] Coleridge thought such 'accidentality' contravened the 'essence of poetry'; if this is so, then *Hamlet* is not a 'poetic drama', and if that is so, so much the worse for poetic drama.[13] My sympathies are with Dr Johnson, who remarked, 'we must allow to the tragedy of *Hamlet* the praise of variety',[14] a plain remark with wide ramifications, especially for our ability to categorize the play even if we resort to hybrid terms such as the bad Quarto's 'Tragicall Historie'. As is often the case with this acutely self-conscious work, the play itself comments on the problems and the pleasures it raises, for 'Tragicall Historie' is one of the categories in Polonius's silly list of literary kinds in which the players at Elsinore excel:

The best Actors in the world, either for Tragedie, Comedie, Historie, Pastorall; Pastorall-Comicall-Historicall-Pastorall; Tragicall-Historicall; Tragicall-Comicall-Historicall-Pastorall; Scene individible, or Poem unlimited.[15]

Such uncertainty about what *kind* of play this is affects other plays which were written apparently under the influence of *Hamlet*, such as Marston's two-part *Antonio and Mellida* (1602), whose first part is, more or less, a romantic comedy and whose second part is, more or less, a revenge tragedy, or his *The Malcontent* (first published 1604), often referred to as a revenge tragedy and found in collections such as Oxford University Press's *Jacobean Tragedies*, though Marston himself in his dedication calls it 'ASPERAM HANC SUAM THALIAM' ('this his harsh comedy'), and it is called in its 'Induction' a 'bitter play'.[16] *Hamlet*

[12] *Hamlet*, V.ii.3879.

[13] Samuel Taylor Coleridge, *Biographia Literaria*, in *Samuel Taylor Coleridge: The Major Works*, 391.

[14] *The Yale Edition of the Works of Samuel Johnson*, vols. 7–8: *Johnson on Shakespeare*, ed. Arthur Sherbo (New Haven: Yale University Press, 1968), 1011.

[15] *Hamlet*, II.ii.1444–8.

[16] *Jacobean Tragedies*, ed. A. H. Gomme (Oxford: Oxford University Press, 1969); John Marston, *The Malcontent* (London: Valentine Simmes, 1604); John Webster, 'The Induction to *The Malcontent*' (1604), in *The Complete Works of John Webster*, ed. F. L. Lucas, 4 vols. (London: Chatto & Windus, 1927), iii. 292–310.

too is a 'bitter play'—it seems, incidentally, that in the early seventeenth century for a play to be advertised as 'bitter' meant much what it now means when a new play is called 'disturbing'. As soon as the word 'disturbing' goes up in lights over a theatre, queues form round the block of eager people for whom the world we live in is not disturbing enough and who want to pay to be given a good disturbing before their after-theatre supper. It was for some such reason, no doubt, that Lear kept for so long his 'bitter Foole'[17] until on the heath the world became quite bitter enough and he could do without his fool, having learned to play the fool for himself, as Hamlet has—'Oh God, your onely Jigge-maker'.[18] A good term for such 'bitter' plays is one invented by T. S. Eliot for different purposes: 'savage farce.'[19]

One thing remains constant in the changes the name of the play went through: Hamlet himself always keeps his title, 'The Prince of Denmarke'. '*Hamlet* without the Prince' is now a cliché for something which lacks a crucial feature, but speaking of the figure Hamlet without remembering his status as 'Prince' describes well a strong tendency in responses to him from at least the mid-eighteenth century on, responses which conceive him as an isolated individual, a sole, quintessential human, notable because he is quick-witted, sweet though weird, and in a sticky situation, not because he is a prince of the blood. Nearly halfway into the play, Hamlet notices: 'Now I am alone.'[20] He has the stage to himself for fewer than 200 of the play's 3,900 lines. Yet commentators began talking of the play as the Prince's solo long before Romanticism made lonely pallor necessary for those who would be *chic*. The Earl of Shaftesbury in 1710 had eyes and ears only for the play's leading man, finding in it nothing but 'a series of deep Reflections, drawn from one Mouth... It may properly be said of this Play, if I mistake not, that it has only ONE *Character* or *principal Part*'.[21] Mallarmé saw the play as 'a pivotal moment in the history of the theatre, a transition in Shakespeare's own work between the old-style, multiply-plotted drama and the Monologue, the drama of the future'.[22] Gordon Craig

---

[17] *King Lear*, I.iv.666.   [18] *Hamlet*, III.ii.1978.

[19] T. S. Eliot, 'Notes on the Blank Verse of Christopher Marlowe' (1920), in *The Sacred Wood: Essays on Poetry and Criticism* (London: Faber & Faber, 1997), 72–80 (p. 78).

[20] *Hamlet*, II.ii.1589.

[21] The Earl of Shaftesbury, *Soliloquy: or, Advice to an Author* (London: John Morphew, 1710), 117–18.

[22] Stéphane Mallarmé, 'Scribbled at the Theatre: *Hamlet*', in *Divagations* (1897), trans. Barbara Johnson (Cambridge, Mass: Harvard University Press, 2009), 124–8.

was blunt and sure: 'All the tragedy of Hamlet is his isolation.'[23] How this notion managed to grow up around the play Shakespeare wrote, crowded, maybe overcrowded, as it is with individuals in pitilessly nervy relation to each other, entangled in backchat, constantly looking out of the corners of their eyes at those around them, is more than I can explain; I leave that to historians of culture. But not paying attention to detail will have had something to do with it, as it does with most 'major cultural shifts'.

Hamlet is like all of Shakespeare's tragedies, early and late, in that its central protagonist is a community, not an individual, though a 'community of individuals' rather than a mere collectivity or shoal. There are no tragic heroes in Shakespeare, and it is consequently a waste of time to explore what may or may not be the hero's tragic flaw. Rome, Denmark, the realm of Albion, 'poor Scotland', Venice—these are the subjects of Shakespearean tragedy. Which is the 'tragic hero' of *Romeo and Juliet* or *Antony and Cleopatra*? What Isolde in Wagner's *Tristan und Isolde* fastens on as the all-important little word 'and' is vital to Shakespeare's tragedies too. Asking which is the tragic hero of *Antony and Cleopatra* seems to me like asking which is the *really* funny one of Laurel and Hardy, a question which shows only that the person who asks it has not understood the essential dynamics of a double-act.

Shakespeare's dramaturgy as he introduces us to Prince Hamlet shows how mistaken it would be to be preoccupied with the play's principal boy to the exclusion of all around him, because Hamlet himself is not even mentioned until line 169, and is introduced to us more obliquely, more refractively *through* other people's eyes and words, than any other Shakespearean protagonist. We hear Claudius's account of his state of mind before he begins to speak out, in an aside, for himself. Contrast the first appearance of other leading figures in mature Shakespearean tragedies: Othello arrives first as 'him' in line 10, becomes 'his Mooreship' at line 35, 'the *Moore*' at line 43, which is how he is then referred to, repeatedly, until Act I, scene 3 when the character of highest status in the play, the Duke, greets him with his name as 'Valiant *Othello*'; he is a functionary before he is christened.[24] Lear is there as 'the King' from

[23] Edward Gordon Craig, 'Stanislavsky and Gordon Craig Discuss *Hamlet*' (1909), trans. Ursula Cox and Mikhail Lyklardopoulos, 29 Apr. 1909, in Laurence Senelick, *Gordon Craig's Moscow Hamlet: A Reconstruction* (Westport, Conn: Greenwood Press, 1982), 62–71 (p. 64).

[24] *Othello*, I.i.10, 35, 43; I.iii.382.

the first spoken line of his play; the witches name Macbeth in the play's eighth spoken line; Antony and Cleopatra enter at line 15 of their play.[25] Here, then, is another dramaturgical purpose in the design of Act I, scene 1: it establishes Denmark, the Ghost, and so on before it even mentions the Prince; it stresses the world from which he cannot be separated (however much he may wish to leave it) without losing his reality. Once he appears, Hamlet often delays performing his crucial task of revenge, but in that delay of performance, he is only behaving as his creator made him, for his appearance itself is delayed by Shakespeare: we do not know 'which one' Hamlet is when the court processes on (or even that he's onstage) till the play's 244th line, when Claudius turns to him, singles him out: 'But now my Cosin *Hamlet*....'[26] Compare this with Lear, who is identifiable as Lear because he issues all the orders, at line 36 of that play. Whatever the myth of Hamlet suggests, the dramaturgical facts of Shakespeare's play show the prince as a thoroughly socialized individual, indeed one it takes us a while to be able to pick out from the crowd; he cannot be sheerly the loner of legend, because familiarity with the ways of a sociable world is a necessary condition of his being the adept, satirical mimic he is. One way of demonstrating how important it is not to forget 'the Prince' when thinking of Hamlet is by noting how careful Shakespeare is to have him consistently addressed with honorifics—my Lord, sir, sweet Prince—almost every time he is spoken to, and how startling the effect then is when someone drops his title, as Ophelia does at 'I was the more deceived', or as Rosencrantz does when searching for Polonius' body: 'Tell us where 'tis, that we may take it thence, / And bear it to the Chappell.'[27]

Having considered the names of the play, it remains for me to say something about the names *in* the play and then I can get to I.i.1. In the passage I quoted from Aristotle, the philosopher, whether rightly or wrongly, regards the fact that figures in tragedies have 'proper names' as a dispensable machinery of fiction:

poetry is something more philosophic and of graver import than history, since its statements are of the nature ... of universals ... By a universal statement I mean one as to what such or such a kind of man will probably or

---

[25] *King Lear*, I.i.4; *Macbeth* (Folio 1, 1623), I.i.10; *Antony and Cleopatra*, I.i.15.
[26] *Hamlet*, I.ii.244.   [27] *Hamlet*, III.i.1775; IV.ii.2637–8.

necessarily say or do—which is the aim of poetry, *though it affixes proper names to the characters*.[28]

The characters of tragedy, according to Aristotle, are, that is, 'token individuals' who stand as more or less transparent instances of general rules about human dispositions and conduct. All the figures of tragedy, in this account, are like the one child of colour in the schoolroom at *South Park*, the little Afro-American boy who is called, of course, 'Token'. Aristotle's account treats all tragic narratives as if they were allegorical fictions, but *Hamlet* is only very unclearly an allegory, or, we might say, if it is an allegory, it is an allegory *of* individuality. The play is set in Denmark, and Shakespeare seems to have known a good deal about that country and relied on some knowledge in his audience; details about this matter can be found in Cay Dollerup's '*Denmark, Hamlet and Shakespeare*'; there are also some characteristically pert and stimulating thoughts in Barbara Everett's *Young Hamlet*.[29] Denmark had acquired a sharp, topical interest for our islands in the late sixteenth century, because Denmark then looked for a while as if it might become the Argentina in the Falklands conflict of those days. The Danes had asked for Orkney and Shetland back in 1585; it had been suggested that James VI of Scotland should marry a Danish princess to solve this dispute and, four years later, on 22 October 1589, he married Anne of Denmark, so that after his accession to the English throne in 1603, the united kingdoms of Scotland and England had a Danish queen (compare the kingdoms of Denmark and Norway united in the person of Fortinbras at the end of the play). Informed and subtle as Shakespeare's sense of Denmark is, he represents one aspect of that kingdom bizarrely—what its inhabitants are called. It has a king with the name of a Roman emperor, Claudius, the stepfather of Nero; Claudius's stepson, Hamlet, prays 'let not ever / The Soule of *Nero*, enter this firme bosome'.[30] Its queen is named for the patron saint of Germany, Gertrude, though this name is decently Danish too (it appears in the chronicles which first tell the tragic story of Amlotha/Hamlet, unlike 'Claudius', who is known there as 'Feng' or 'Fengon'). The chief

---

[28] Aristotle, *Poetics*, Sect. 9, p. 43.

[29] Cay Dollerup, *Denmark, Hamlet and Shakespeare* (Salzburg: Institut für Englische Sprache und Literatur, Universität Salzburg, 1975); Barbara Everett, *Young Hamlet: Essays on Shakespeare's Tragedies* (Oxford: Oxford University Press, 1989).

[30] *Hamlet*, III.ii.2264–5.

royal counsellor we meet in the play is called 'Polonius', a Latinate name which implies that he is of Polish extraction (and there are Poles in the play at Act I, scene I, line 66—Hamlet's father creditably smites them as Young Hamlet later discreditably smites Polonius); this Latinized Pole seems to have a fondness for all things Greek, because his two children have names deriving from the Greek—'Laertes', who was the father of Odysseus, and 'Ophelia' which means 'help, succour'. The Norwegian prince, Fortinbras, has a French-sounding name which, were it French, would signify, aptly enough for lovers of allegory, 'strong in arm'. Horatio says of himself that he is 'more an Antike Roman then a Dane',[31] and this holds good at least of his evidently Latinate name. Shakespeare may have been drawn to the name because it figures prominently in Kyd's *The Spanish Tragedy*, a principal target for *Hamlet's* parodic brilliances, where the son whose murder is avenged by his father—spot the difference—is called 'Horatio'; the name may also have appealed to the witty Bard because it contains the Latin word for reason, 'ratio', thereby allowing an extra sparkle to 'There are more things in heaven and earth *Horatio* [or O ratio], / Then are dream't of in your philosophie',[32] reason and its limits being a repeated concern of the play (sixteen occurrences of the word and its cognates, the most of any Shakespearean play). Such classicizing names, names which in themselves might sound as if the parents who gave them were trying to set precedents for the lives of their children, seem to have been popular even further down the social scale of Danish households, for 'Marcellus' too is a Roman name, the name of a man celebrated for dying young and so potentially as misleading as 'Horatio'. For good measure, we have two soldiers with Italianate names (Barnardo and Francisco), two courtier-spies, Rosencrantz and Guildenstern, with decent Danish names which yet sound Germanic (and certainly sounded so to those responsible for the first Quarto where the names are mangled in a Teutonic direction, 'Rosencrantz' appearing as 'Rossenkraft'—German for 'horse-power'), and a third courtier, Osric, with an Anglo-Saxon name and Frenchified habits of speech. Denmark, it appears, was holding the presidency of the European Union when the events of this play took place. I merely mention the additional fact, of which James Joyce made so much, that 'Hamlet', one irreproachably Danish name

---

[31] *Hamlet*, V.ii.3826.   [32] *Hamlet* (Quarto 2, 1604), I.v.863–4.

in the cast-list, sounds very like the unusual name of Shakespeare's own son, Hamnet (born 1585, died 1596).[33]

I draw attention to this fricassee of French, Italian, Latin, Greek, German, Polish, Danish, and Anglo-Saxon because it contrasts so sharply with the usual practice of naming in revenge tragedies, both before and after *Hamlet*. Standard revenge-plays are usually set abroad, most often in notably Catholic countries on the European mainland, for preference Spain or Italy but sometimes France. All these countries are treated as much the same, and indeed are regarded as composing a single allegorical zone which we could call, by analogy with 'Disneyland', 'Popeland', for the standard revenge play has as a staple ingredient a prurient bigotry about Roman Catholicism, an attitude absent from *Hamlet*. In *The Spanish Tragedy*, for instance, Kyd seems so little concerned with anything specifically Spanish that when he includes snatches of foreign languages for local colour (another stock-in-trade of revenge plays which does not figure in *Hamlet*), his Spaniards sometimes speak Spanish and sometimes Italian, for no discernible reason. 'These dagoes are all the same.' The names in standard revenge plays signal two things— the ethnic foreignness of the characters, and their ethical status. The cast-lists of, for example, *Antonio's Revenge*, *The Malcontent*, or Chapman's *Bussy D'Ambois* are monocultural; the names are Italianate in the first two instances and Francophone in the third. This ethnic homogeneity is a counterpart of the ethical transparency of the names, their iconic quality—I mean such fine flowers of the bleeding-obvious as, for a heroine, 'Castabella' ('chaste and beautiful woman'), for a dunce 'Supervacuo' ('extremely inane'), and 'Cazzo' ('prick') for, well, a prick. None of the names in *Hamlet* were endorsed by Shakespeare on such an emblematic basis; the names of his play are strenuously un-Aristotelian: the philosopher, I repeat, was of the view that people in tragedies were *kinds* of people, identifiable categories or 'types'—such as the chaste, the vacuous, the prick—rather than individuals, and had proper names only by accident. Allegory adds to Aristotle's notion that characters are categories the handily simplifying convention that their names tell you which category they are—Error, or Nurse, or Castabella. Editors of *Hamlet* have sometimes puzzled why, for instance, Ophelia is called Ophelia, because she manages to give no one succour in the play, but

---

[33] James Joyce, *Ulysses*, ed. Jeri Johnson (Oxford: Oxford University Press, 2008), 181.

they are puzzled only because they assume that the 'name as signpost' rule is to guide us in understanding the names of the play, whereas the extreme variety of these names suggests rather that no one rule has governed naming in the play any more than it governs naming in the world we live in. Maybe Ophelia is called 'help' not because she gives it but because she needs it. In this respect, as in many others, *Hamlet* is a work of dramatic realism and therefore far indeed from being the same kind of play as a revenge play.

Ethnic homogeneity ('they're all frogs or dagoes') and ethical transparency ('they're all, or almost all, bastards') are two faces of the thin and violent world of revenge plays, a world related to that of Shakespeare's Hamlet the Dane principally by contrast, by the disdain Shakespeare's dramaturgy expresses for it. The revenge-play world is one of absolute monarchy (unlike the elective monarchy of Denmark), inhabited by sensation-seekers whose moral nature is rendered pellucid for the audience; a main part of the pleasure of these plays is that they provide lots of 'beautiful wickedness', as the Wicked Witch of the West calls it in *The Wizard of Oz*, while at the same time amply supplying moralistic alibis to salve the consciences of author and audience as they revel in sleaze and gore.[34] It is not necessary to read a revenge play to know what revenge plays are like; you merely have to skim a newspaper, say, the *Daily Mail* or *News of the World*, where a similar combo of finger-wagging and lip-smacking is still to be found. These plays also seethe with a cynicism about rulers and their conduct, from God downwards, a cynicism which had to be carefully cordoned off as, of course, applicable only to foreign potentates; these plays rarely mention England (there is a tellingly feeble exception in *The Spanish Tragedy*), unlike *Hamlet*, in which England is the most important 'offstage' country in questionable political alliance with—indeed, subordination to—the 'here' of Claudius's Denmark (see Act IV, scene iii, where England is to be Claudius's accomplice in the projected murder of Hamlet, our hero: 'Do it England').[35] Take the following soapy passage from Chapman's *Bussy D'Ambois*, a play which includes in its cast an English lady's-maid whose sole function in the work is to prompt reluctant acknowledgement,

---

[34] *The Wizard of Oz*, dir. Victor Fleming, screenplay by Noel Langley, Florence Ryerson, and Edgar Allan Woolf (Metro-Goldwyn-Mayer, 1939), based on the novel *The Wonderful Wizard of Oz* by L. Frank Baum.

[35] *Hamlet*, IV.iii.2730.

and from the King of France too, that the English, the English, the English are best:

> Henry.   ...the English court,
> Whose ladies are not match'd in Christendom
> For graceful and confirm'd behaviours;
> More than the Court where they are bred is equall'd.[36]

This contrasts sharply with what the Clown has to say in Act V of *Hamlet* about why it won't matter if Hamlet stays mad while in England, because 'there the men are as mad as he'.[37] I'll be giving more, specific comparisons and contrasts with revenge plays in what follows, but that's enough preambles.

> *Enter Barnardo, and Francisco, two Centinels.*
>
> *Bar.* Whose there?
> *Fran.* Nay answere me. Stand and unfolde your selfe.
> *Bar.* Long live the King.
> *Fran. Barnardo.*
> *Bar.* Hee.
> *Fran.* You come most carefully upon your houre,
> *Bar.* Tis now strooke twelfe, get thee to bed *Francisco*,
> *Fran.* For this reliefe much thanks, tis bitter cold,
> And I am sick at hart.
> *Bar.* Have you had quiet guard?
> *Fran.* Not a mouse stirring.
> *Bar.* Well, good night:
> If you doe meete *Horatio* and *Marcellus*,
> The rivalls of my watch, bid them make hast.
>   *Enter Horatio, and Marcellus.*
> *Fran.* I think I heare them, stand ho, who is there?
> *Hora.* Friends to this ground.
> *Mar.* And Leedgemen to the Dane,[38]

The play begins in the middle of the night, a special effect in the daylit, open-air Shakespearean theatre, so special that Shakespeare had tried it previously only in *A Midsummer Night's Dream*, which may, if scholars are right to think it was first intended for an aristocratic wedding, have been performed indoors and of an evening. Another aspect of Shakespeare's dramaturgy in creating Act I, scene 1 to precede—in

---

[36] George Chapman: *Bussy D'Ambois* (London: Eliot's Court, 1607, modernized), I.ii.5–8.
[37] *Hamlet*, V.i.3344–5.   [38] *Hamlet* (Quarto 2), I.i.3–21.

some informational respects 'unnecessarily'—Act I, scene 2 is this daring requirement from his audience that they 'understand' or 'imagine' what they see before them as taking place at dead of night. Had the play begun with the courtly procession of Act I, scene 2, the audience would have had less work to do in orienting themselves with regard to what they see. Orienting and reorienting yourself in the light, or darkness, of new developments is a task which often falls on characters within the play, many of whom might take as a motto Ophelia's 'O woe is me / T'have seene what I have seene: see what I see';[39] the play requires of its audience many comparable—though less painful—adjustments. The stage direction '*Enter Barnardo and Francisco, two Centinels*' conceals a further difficulty Shakespeare set, this time for his troupe, with this opening, because the fictional situation requires not that they both enter at the same time (as do Horatio and Marcellus) but that one of them (Francisco) be 'discovered' on stage and the other (Barnardo) 'enters to' him and, oddly, it is the man who enters, not the man on guard, who utters the formula 'Who's there?' *Hamlet*, you might say, begins as a radio play; a voice comes from one in the dark and to one in the dark. That is why the first sense emphasized is hearing: 'I thinke I heare them.'

The distinguished radio dramatist, Spike Milligan, wrote a fine, apparently *Hamlet*-like moment in one of the Goon Shows. Seagoon was in a pitch-dark dungeon and his ears told him he was not alone: 'Who's there?' he cried, and the voice of Eccles came in reply with the deathless words: 'Oh, the hard questions first, eh?'[40] It does indeed seem apt that *Hamlet*, which has often been fervently imagined as a founding text of modern scepticism, of self-doubt and of the individual self as distinguishing itself just *by* doubt, should have as its prime question 'Who's there?', a question which readily prompts considerations about personal identity, what it is to be a self and be given a name by others. The second line, with its 'unfold your selfe', also seems to dangle a metaphysical bait: to 'unfold' is to 'ex-plicate', and self-explication is a task on which Hamlet the Prince often embarks and of which he as often despairs. In the centuries which followed his first appearance, the Prince has not been short of experts of various persuasions, all of

---

[39] *Hamlet*, III.i.1816–17.
[40] Spike Milligan, 'The Last Goon Show of All', *The Goon Show*, BBC, first broadcast on 5 Oct. 1972.

whom are confident that they can explicate him better than he can unfold himself. The first such expert, Polonius, comes to a sticky end, but this has not deterred his innumerable successors, up to and after Freud, each of whom believes he has a special technique for getting to the bottom of Hamlet, and all of whom seem innocent of the fact that what matters about *Hamlet*, and therefore about Hamlet, is not hidden depths but hidden surfaces, surfaces hidden from us by what one of Beckett's figments tartly calls 'the stupid obsession with depth'.[41]

Let me explain what I mean by 'hidden surfaces' at least as far as concerns the opening exchange: 'Who's there?' / 'Nay, answer me. Stand and unfold yourself.' The play *does* return, repeatedly and pointedly, to the word 'selfe'—a mere selection from more than thirty occurrences: '*Horatio*, or I do forget my selfe'; 'to thine own selfe be true'; 'You doe not understand your selfe'; 'hath put him / So much from th'understanding of himselfe'; 'Poore *Ophelia* / Divided from her selfe'; 'she drowned her selfe in her own defence'.[42] I don't doubt that self-understanding and self-estrangement are big issues in the play, and yet the philosophical aura of 'Who's there?', understood in the manner of Eccles/Milligan, is a will-o'-the-wisp, a trick of the dark in which the words are said, for the point of the question 'Who's there' in Act I, scene I, line I is not 'Can you tell me the name and nature of your individuality?' but 'Are you a friend or an enemy?', as we can hear from the fact that 'Long live the King' is the answer to that question. The note of interrogation on which *Hamlet* begins is primarily one of embattled, political suspicion rather than of existential angst (not that these two states are mutually exclusive). It is, of course, possible, indeed easy, to make these opening lines profound with a capital 'P' by, for instance, treating them as epitomizing Hegel's account of self-consciousness as a process of mutual recognition between two consciousnesses which become themselves, unfold their actuality, just in such a process of question and answer.[43] You can in fact trundle any intellectual system you fancy behind Barnardo and Francisco at this moment, so that they stand in front of it as before a cyclorama and

---

[41] Sigmund Freud, *The Interpretation of Dreams* (1899), trans. Joyce Crick, ed. Ritchie Robertson (Oxford: Oxford University Press, 2008); Samuel Beckett, *The Unnameable* (1953), ed. Steven Connor (London: Faber & Faber, 2010), 3.

[42] *Hamlet*, I.ii.347; I.iii.543; I.iii.562; II.ii.1028–9; IV.v.2021–2; V.i.3195–6.

[43] Georg Wilhelm Friedrich Hegel, *Phenomenology of Spirit* [1807], trans. A. V. Miller (Oxford: Clarendon Press, 1977), 105–39.

seem to 'illustrate' the philosophical or psychoanalytical or what-have-you issues you have projected as a backdrop, and against which their apparently simple words can begin to loom with portent and insight. Do feel free to do this if you have nothing better to do with your spare time; many, many, more or less distinguished writers have done so. But any such easily summoned depth you conjure up should not blind you to the surface realities of their exchange, to the illocutionary force of 'Who's there?' from Barnardo, just arrived on these chill midnight battlements, to a Francisco whose watch is ending and who replies: 'Nay, answer me.'

Nor should metaphysical grandeurs make you deaf to the special twist Shakespeare has given the opening exchange by transferring the formulaic challenge of a sentry on guard, 'Who's there?', from the sentry who actually is on guard, Francisco, to the one just arriving to take up his watch, Barnardo. The man on guard would ask 'Who's there?' as a matter of dutiful course, but the man arriving asks it perhaps with more urgency of surprise, as if he had been startled by a sound or sight he had not expected. In my ideal production of the play, the first scene would take place on a black wall, so steeply raked that the actors would need spikes in their boots to stand on it; there would be no light at all on the stage. Then Francisco would light a cigarette or maybe yawn; Barnardo, who has not realized, so dark it is, that he has got near the sentry-post spins round, jumpily, and shouts nervously 'Who's there?', to which Francisco replies with the calm authority of the office-holder, 'Nay, answer me'. This is what I mean by a 'hidden surface' to the words, to their slight shift of 'Who's there?' from the man on guard to the man arriving; that little shift implies a world which it is the job of rehearsal to make surface from the depths of the page where it is implicit onto the stage.

I just mentioned the 'illocutionary force' of the opening line. This term, invented by the philosopher J. L. Austin, stands for 'what is meant by' an utterance of a word or words on a particular occasion.[44] For example, 'fire' has one illocutionary force when uttered in reply to the question, 'what does "le feu" mean?', another illocutionary force when screamed by a crowd pouring out of a smoke-filled lecture-hall, and yet another illocutionary force again when shouted by the officer in

---

[44] J. L. Austin, *How to Do Things With Words* (1955), ed. J. O. Urmson and Marina Sbisà, 2nd edn. (Oxford: Oxford University Press, 1975), 100, 148.

charge of an execution-squad; the same word 'fire' can be a piece of information, a warning, or an order. Shakespeare was acutely conscious of the phenomenon of illocutionary force, though he did not know the term any more than he knew the term 'soliloquy' or indeed 'play-wright'. He would have felt illocutionary force (or the lack of it) every time he heard his lines delivered by an actor, every time he was delighted by how well they sounded, every time he wanted to object 'for God's sake, say it as if you meant it' or—in cases such as that of Iago—'for God's sake, say it as if you didn't mean it'. As a dramatist, his speciality was the things that people do with words and their varying illocutionary force, such things as: swear vows; break promises; cajole; change the subject; poison someone else's mind; forgive. 'Who's there?' at the opening of *Hamlet* is a challenge before it is a question, though it is also a challenging question. A principal weakness of much com-ment on Shakespeare's plays is that the commentators pay little attention to what a figure in a play is doing by uttering *these* words at *this* point; commentators are often preoccupied rather with such things as imagery, or with what they take to be the philosophical suggestiveness of what is said, as if it were a secondary consideration who says what when and where to whom, whereas it is not secondary, not at all, but rather the drama itself. Some commentators are so concerned with putting across how deep the plays are that they have no energy spare to describe how they are deep, but they are deep because of, *through*, their surfaces. Let me try to clarify this point by describing the words which open out the night of *A Midsummer Night's Dream*:

> *Enter Theseus, Hippolita, with others.*

> *Theseus.* Now faire Hippolita, our nuptiall houre
> Drawes on apace: four happy daies bring in
> Another Moon: but oh, me thinkes, how slow
> This old Moon wanes; She lingers my desires
> Like to a Step-dame, or a Dowager,
> Long withering out a yong man's revennew.
> *Hip.* Four daies wil quickly steep themselves in nights
> Four nights wil quickly dreame away the time:[45]

A usual comment on this opening exchange picks up the mention of the moon, and proceeds from there to list the many other lunar references

---

[45] *A Midsommer Nights Dreame*, I.i.1–8.

in the play, pointing out that the moon in some aspects signifies fertility while also in other aspects signifying chastity. Fair enough, but such commentary neglects the fact that Theseus's words form part of an interaction with Hippolyta, and considers scantly, if at all, that his words are only part of a larger unit of discourse in which what she says also counts, and therefore fails to give weight to the fact he is talking to her and she replying to him. The commentator is unsurprisingly put in mind of the moon by these opening words and proceeds to descant on that theme, but the commentary is not concerned with how the notion of the moon was floated here—as a focus of disagreement between a bridegroom- and a bride-to-be—and not concerned with how the moon figures in the minds of those who are here and now speaking of it. In such commentary, it is as if the words had been said by nobody to nobody in an atmosphere which exercises no pressure on what is said, or as if they had been whispered by Shakespeare himself directly into our collective ear without the tiresome intermediaries of Theseus and Hippolyta. And this is the explanation of the curious fact that so many essays about Shakespeare's plays make him sound as if he had been occupied in writing essays rather than plays. My claim is that Shakespeare's material as an artist *is* interaction, interaction of two kinds—between the figures on the stage, and between the figures on stage and the audience. These interactions are what he composes, and to neglect them is to neglect an essential of his art. Most commentaries on Shakespeare seem to me like treatises on sculpture which never deign to mention stone.

What, then, is missing from an account of this opening which doesn't attend to how their speeches respond to each other? One thing missing is an interest in the fact that she contradicts him. He says, 'it's a bloody long wait until we get married and I can bed you'; she replies, in effect though with diplomatic suavity, 'doesn't seem that long a wait to me'. If you look at Hippolyta's responses to Theseus throughout the play, you soon see that this opening rebuff is a keynote: she continues to contradict him, indeed, she says very little to him that is not in some way a repudiation of what he has said (think, for instance, of how incisively she refutes his prattle about imagination at the beginning of Act V). The 'illocutionary force' of his opening lines is, I would say, that of a hand placed invitingly on a knee; the illocutionary force of her reply is gently but firmly to remove that hand. She does not seem to want marry him as much as he wants to marry her; we will shortly be told that he captured her by force to be his bride. She was an

Amazon, a female separatist, before he got his hands on her. From my point of view, moon-imagery and the like are mere cake-decoration in comparison to the nub of their interaction, and that nub is forced marriage, a nub which is immediately returned to in the ensuing scene with Hermia and her domineering father (note Hippolyta's highlit silence through most of that wrangle) and which returns in subtly varied ways at many levels of the plot—Oberon and Titania first appear engaged in their lyrical version of Theseus and Hippolyta's 'oh yes it is' / 'oh no it isn't'. Which is not to say that—especially in the context of an impending marriage—cake-decoration doesn't have its importance too.

So too, at the opening of *Hamlet*, though I sympathize with those who find the play involved at once with piercing philosophical questions, the *Shakespearean* character of that philosophical involvement seems to me the way it arises out of human interactions, as here, a nocturnal challenge between two sentries on duty. It is not difficult to write a play which kicks around large ethical or metaphysical issues; after all, Tom Stoppard has done that many times and to loud applause. It is more remarkable to write a play in which 'debate' occurs not through ruminative prosings but through event and interaction, in which thought *occurs* to and between people. This is what happens in *Hamlet*, thinking *happens*, and this is one reason why I present these observations about the play in an order which follows the order of events in the play, for thoughts are the 'cast' of *Hamlet* (the Prince speaks of the 'cast of Thought'),[46] and a cast is best listed 'in order of appearance'.

The first sixteen lines of the play establish that it is just after midnight (time), that we are in a fortified location which fears attack (place and political situation), even the temperature (bitter cold). These lines imply a state with a notable degree of military organization, because there is evidently a rota of watches, an organization which is functioning efficiently although it doesn't run quite like clockwork (Francisco notes that Barnardo is punctual—'You come most carefully upon your houre'—but the fact that he considers this worthy of notice shows that time-keeping is not invariably perfect here; these sentries are not robots). In line 16 we learn the name of this place; by inference from 'the Dane', we are in Denmark. Note that we locate ourselves by understanding

---

[46] *Hamlet*, III.i.1739.

the grammar of a political term, 'Leedgemen'; at the same moment we know where we are, we know the political constitution of the place—it is a state with at least the remains of vassalage, most likely a monarchy. The economy and atmospheric power of this quickfire exchange have been often and rightly praised. As they were praised with blowsy over-statement by Coleridge: 'The preparation *informative* of the audience [is] just as much as was precisely necessary.'[47]

Yet this little scene does more than tell us exactly what we need to know; it also tells us something we have no need to know at all: 'For this reliefe much thanks, tis bitter cold, / And I am sick at hart.' What's the matter with Francisco? We shall never know, as biographers like to intone; we hear no more about his problems (though we will hear, if we have good memories, something curiously turned from his words 'cold', 'sick', and 'heart' in conjunction, much later in the play, when Laertes says: 'It warms the very sicknesse in my heart').[48] Maybe Francisco is underpaid, unlucky in love, or mourning his own recently deceased father. Who knows? Who cares? Three lines later, he takes his particular misery, whatever it is, off the stage with him down the cor-ridors of Elsinore, where none of us can follow him. His is the first heart-sickness we hear of in the play, long before Hamlet in 'To be or not to be' descants generally on 'heart-ache', but we hear no more about Francisco's specific form of affliction. The play abounds in these hints of unrecounted lives, like snatches of conversation overheard in the street, inviting speculation, with the poignancy of scenes glimpsed from a passing train, scenes we are not allowed the time to dwell on. Francisco's heart and its sickness are the first of many things we catch sight of but can't stop for in what follows, and as such they indicate the depth-of-field, as it were, with which Shakespeare has written his play. They create what Johnson called its 'variety', though a variety that can baffle and pain as well as entertain.

Francisco's six monosyllables, 'And I am sick at hart', are slightly highlit by the fact that they are the play's first clearly hypometrical line. It takes a moment or two before we can be confident that this scene is in blank verse; we should hear that at 'You come most carefully upon your houre. / Tis now strooke twelfe, get thee to bed *Francisco*. / For

[47] Samuel Taylor Coleridge, 'Notes on the Tragedies', in *Shakespearean Criticism* (1811–12), ed. Thomas Middleton Raysor, 2 vols., 2nd edn. (London: Dent; New York: Dutton, 1960), vol. 1, p. 18.

[48] *Hamlet*, IV.vii.3065.

this relief much thanks, tis bitter cold', because these are the first
consecutive blank-verse lines of the play as the sentinels relax into pattern
after the nervily clipped speech of the opening challenge. Immediately
the tune has established itself in our ears, Shakespeare changes it:
'And I am sick at hart'. We hear the sound of some things missing—an
explanation of this heart-sickness, and four syllables. Not that Barnardo
gives a toss about Francisco's heart, it seems, for he immediately changes
the subject—'Have you had quiet guard?' Perhaps he knows all too
well what Francisco would say if he were to ask solicitously 'Oh, what's
up?' having listened long into other nights to the story of how Francisco's
wife doesn't understand him or his corns give him gyp when the wind
is in from the north north-west. Changing the subject is another thing
which people can do with words, another speech-act, which Shakespeare
often dramatized. He does so at a sticky moment in the first scene of
A Midsummer Night's Dream, when Theseus notices a perhaps ominous
silence in his bride-to-be:

> For you faire *Hermia*, looke you arme your selfe,
> To fit your fancies to your Fathers will;
> Or else the Law of Athens yeelds you up
> (Which by no meanes we may extenuate)
> To death, or to a vow of single life.
> Come my *Hippolita*, what cheare my love?
> *Demetrius* and *Egeus* go along:
> I must imploy you in some businesse
> Against our nuptiall.[49]

For Hippolyta, the ravished Amazon, thoughts of a 'vow of single life'
may not be as daunting as they are meant to be for Hermia; Theseus
perhaps catches sight of the fact that her mind is elsewhere just as he
mentions 'single life', a life in which she would have 'to abjure / For
ever the society of men',[50] and tries to include her in the conversation
(nobody has paid her any explicit attention for 101 lines up to this point
where Theseus asks her what's up). When met with only silence from
her, he suddenly remembers that he has important matters to deal with
and rushes offstage with his buddies.

Life-expectancy has risen in a cheering way since Shakespeare's day,
though life is still probably too short to count the syllables in every line

---

49 *A Midsommer Nights Dreame*, I.i.126–34.
50 *A Midsommer Nights Dreame*, I.i.74–5.

of *Hamlet*, especially given the waywardness of the texts in the matter of lineation. But the tune of the play should not escape us, or rather the tunes, for the play's verse deserves, as much as the play itself, the 'praise of variety'. (And don't despise counting: your fingers can be a great help to your ears.) For instance, there are thirty-three hypometrical lines in the 174 lines of Act I, scene 1, whereas there is only one hypometrical line in the first 164 lines of Act I, scene 2. It comes when Hamlet breaks off his words in disgust at his mother's conduct:

> A little month or ere those shooes were old
> With which she followed my poore fathers bodie
> Like *Niobe* all teares, why she
> O God, a beast that wants discourse of reason
> Would have mourn'd longer.[51]

'Like *Niobe* all teares, why she' is only two syllables short, but that, along with the syntactical abruption, the huge swivel from 'she' to 'O God' and then to 'a beast', is long enough to hear the sound of something being bitten back. That Act I, scene 1 has thirty-three short lines and Act I, scene 2 only one in roughly the same span matters only in so far as the difference characterizes the way people speak in the two scenes—tense, rapid, and yet candid in Act I, scene 1; measured, indeed wary, ceremonious though perhaps forced, in the first half of Act I, scene 2. The distinct styles of speech in the two scenes correspond to two of the many diverse ways of life which Elsinore encompasses; it is an odd castle because, reflecting on the contrasting kinds of talk in the first two scenes, we might say that it is colder on the inside than on its walls.

---

[51] *Hamlet* (Quarto 2, 1604), I.ii.331–5.

6

Inferno 32 and 33

Soon after Dante died, in 1321, and went we know not where, the Florentines were running series of lectures in which the poem was explicated canto by canto. Two of his sons wrote commentaries, Jacopo once in 1322 and Pietro three times between 1340 and 1364. Boccaccio gave a series of lectures on the *Commedia* in 1373. There were no handouts at these early lectures because techniques for mechanically reproducing writing had not yet been discovered in the West; the lecturers served an elementary need by reading the poem aloud to their auditors, few of whom would have seen, let alone owned, copies of the text. The basic task of helping people get acquainted with the poem supplied an extra rationale for the form of line-by-line commentary which was adopted then, although the commentators would have naturally gravitated towards this pedestrian kind of glossing, because it was a method of dealing with texts they were familiar with; it was standard practice with respect to the Scriptures and to any other texts studied in universities, Aristotle for example. As it happens, this is a method particularly suited to Dante, because the *Commedia* is a pedestrian poem, in the sense that, at least for two-thirds of the time, it's a poem about someone walking, first down dale and then uphill; it understands itself as a pilgrimage, undertaken, like many pilgrimages, for penitential reasons, and regards its central figure, the 'I' unnamed till late in *Purgatorio*, as a pilgrim. The inching through writing of the early commentators has now largely disappeared, partly because the availability of text in printed or electronic forms removes some of its point, but also because we live in brisker times.

The audience at those early lectures brought to the poem an interest not typical of those who go to lectures about it today. Then it was nobody's set text, figured on the curriculum of no institutional course;

it was becoming famous rather than being a settled regular on lists of the Hundred Best Books. The appeal of going to early lectures about Dante was nearer to the draw exercised by indie music in a small club than to the pull of Madonna in a stadium or the hearty familiarity of the Last Night of the Proms. The poem, like an indie band, was a curiosity and so inspired curiosity; it had rarity value, odd and cranky ways, which was why so much of it needed explaining; it was edgy, in the sense that it was reputed to say rude things about establishment figures, as indeed it does. For some, then, Dante was a Johnny Rotten, but for others he was more a Mrs Thatcher, in that he had once held high political office and very definitely had a mind of his own about the conduct of politics, though by the 1320s few under the age of 35 would have had more than a fairytale memory of him, as few under the age of 35 now can remember with any precision or balance the woman who left Downing Street in 1990; like the Baroness Thatcher, he was a love/hate figure, and early commentaries on his greatest work are therefore, unsurprisingly, marked by the partisanship, the factionalism, which is close to the heart of the subject and the manner of the poem itself. As he had been sent into exile by the powers that were in Florence, and returned their favour with bristlingly candid assessments of the Florentines, he also had about him some of the appeal of Alexander Solzhenitsyn for the Soviet reader of the 1960s: he was slightly samizdat; he had suffered for his beliefs; he spoke out where it was wiser to be mealy-mouthed or, indeed, silent; he had a powerful conviction, reinforced by official hostility, of his own rightness and righteousness. Although we must remember that the authorities, secular and ecclesiastical, of Dante's time were incomparably less powerful than the institutions we are used to, all organizations in those days being much less organized, more ricketty, less joined up, than their successors today (including the organization of the celestial bureaucracy in Dante's hell, purgatory, and paradise, where it often surprises modern readers that functionaries like Minos or Cato seem to have been left uninformed by head office of Dante's special status). In response to these several varieties of charisma, the fourteenth-century lecturers and commentators took time spelling out patiently the many passages in the poem which were found obscure, defending its novelties by reference to Virgil and Ovid, and so on; but they also had spicier things to say—there were all the hints and rumours about skulduggery in high places to be fleshed out, claims and counter-claims about who had done what to whom to be sorted, so that the commentaries at times came to resemble a trawl through the archives of a medieval *Hello* magazine.

I will go through *Inferno* 32 and 33 in the order in which the lines come, but I'll be moving out from the particular lines across the poem backwards and forwards in order to show some ways in which Dante's writing of these two canti is characteristic of his writing in the poem as a whole. I'm not offering an explanatory commentary or line-by-line gloss on *Inferno* 32 and 33, but treating them as samples from which to offer a preliminary sketch of how Dante writes. That's enough throat-clearing from me, here's some throat-clearing from Dante:

> S'io avessi le rime aspre e chiocce,
>   come si converrebbe al tristo buco…
> io premerei di mio concetto il suco
>   più pienamente; ma perch'io non l'abbo,
>   non senza tema a dicer mi conduco;
> ché non è impresa da pigliare a gabbo
>   discrivir fondo a tutto l'universo,
>   né da lingua che chiami mamma o babbo.

If I had harsh, creaking rhymes, such as would suit the sad hole [of lowest hell], I would press out the juice from my faculty of conception more fully; but since I don't have them, I bring myself not without fear to speak; for it's no joke to describe the lowest point of the whole universe, especially not with a tongue that calls out 'mummy' and 'daddy'.[1]

Most of what Dante writes about is no laughing matter, whether because his subjects are thought beneath or above humour, so it seems reasonable to wonder what kind of comedy his *Commedia* is supposed to be. One kind of comedy he probably did not himself suppose it to be is a 'divina' *Commedia*: there is no evidence that he called the poem this or thought of it so, the first occurrence of 'divina' in relation to the *Commedia* is in a Venetian publisher's blurb from 1555, where it means something like 'fabulous poem, darling, loved it loved it loved it' or 'must-buy *Commedia*'. The name under which the poem now labours is a misnomer, or at least misleading, because it is ambiguous about whether it means 'the comedy, the story with a happy ending, which is produced by divine means, by God's operation' or whether the poem

---

[1] Dante, *The Divine Comedy: Inferno, Purgatorio, Paradiso*, trans. and ed. Robin Kirkpatrick (London: Penguin, 2012), *Inferno* 32, ll. 1–2, 4–9, p. 144. The translation given above differs slightly from Kirkpatrick's.

itself is to be thought of as one of those divine things which it tells us about. This leads to a confusion between the workings of Dante and of God which, though the poet was, as he tells us, an extremely proud man, is not a confusion he was himself much prone to, so far as I can tell. On the contrary, he was theologically well educated and not only knew that he was not God but knew in a conceptually sophisticated way the difficulties there are in speaking of divine realities in human terms, because, as Beatrice points out to him in *Paradiso* 4, ll. 41–5: 'it is only from what is taken in by your senses that you can form notions suitable to your intellect. For this reason, Scripture comes down to the level of your understanding and speaks as if God had hands and feet, though it means something quite other.'[2] The opening lines of *Inferno* 32 are a reminder for the reader from Dante among the lost people of such discrepancy between terms and their referents, as Beatrice's words in *Paradiso* 4 will be a reminder from his final guide among the blessed for the poet. He speaks about not having screechy rhymes in words which, by Italian standards, are about as screechy as can be, and this is part of the intricate tease which runs through the lines: they make out that Dante might possibly have a language more appropriate to lowest hell (Dutch, say), he just happens not to have one, but no human language, learned and deployed and understood in time through exercise of the senses, can be fully congruent with the eternal realities which he encounters in hell just as much as in heaven—there is no time in heaven any more than there is hell, and nor is there hope or faith in heaven any more than there is in hell, though for different reasons.

People sometimes say that language is 'inadequate' to Dante's vision (or to expressing anything else they find ineffable, such as their own ideas or feelings) but this is an unhappy expression, as if we had taken a perfectly clear measure of that vision and then found language didn't fit it or live up to it. But we cannot have measured it without a language, where 'language' means 'any of our ways of measuring', not only the verbal ones; the difficulty Dante is talking about is not like the difficulty of describing a shape or a smell or a tune in words; it is more like describing a kind of intelligent life that has developed on another planet in ways radically different from ours; or, you could say, it's like getting inside a cat's world while keeping all your human faculties. These are just analogies, of course, but for Dante, theology is primarily

---

[2] Dante, *Paradiso* 4, ll. 41–5, p. 335.

an exercise in analogies, and in caution about them; the indispensable role of analogy in theology is one reason why his similes are often so deep. The terms we have don't properly apply to the divine realities, but we should not assume some other terms *we* could have would apply better, as if our difficulties here were merely technological (if we could upgrade to broadband, all would be well). The terms we have are, for us, inevitable; having these ways of thinking is part of what it is for us to be the kind of creature that we are. Caution like Beatrice's about extending concepts learned in our empirical world to the divine realities is known as 'negative theology' or, for those who like a nice, out-of-the-way Greek term once in a while, as apophatic (as contrasted to cataphatic) theology. One of the main sources of such theology in Christian tradition is the quaintly named Pseudo-Dionysius, a fifth- or sixth-century writer. Dante gives him an exalted place in heaven in *Paradiso* 28, l. 130, and this admiration was not an idiosyncrasy of the poet's—Aquinas quotes his writings some 1,700 times and he had been given official approval at the Fourth Lateran Council in 1215. What stirred up all this admiration is a passage like the following where he writes about how the human mind can grow in sophistication and carefulness about applying the terms which come naturally to it, which make it a *human* mind, to God:

as we climb higher we say this. [The supreme Cause] is not soul or mind, nor does it possess imagination, conviction, speech, or understanding. Nor is it speech per se, understanding per se. It cannot be spoken of and it cannot be grasped by understanding. It is not number or order, greatness or smallness, equality or inequality, similarity or dissimilarity. It is not immovable, moving, or at rest. It has no power, it is not power, nor is it light. It does not live nor is it life.[3]

We are not supposed to infer from this that he thinks it would be better if we said God is mindless, unimaginative, mute, impotent, and dead. Each of those terms is just as unsatisfactory when applied to God as its affirmative counterpart. The point is not to stop us characterizing God as loving and just and start us characterizing him as hateful and unfair, but to slow down the process by which we characterize him in any way at all and to help us become more self-conscious about how much

---

[3] Pseudo-Dionysius, *The Mystical Theology*, in *Pseudo-Dionysius: The Complete Works*, trans. Colm Luibed and Paul Rorem (London: SPCK, 1987), 141.

our own character shows through in our characterizations of him. He writes in another of his works:

> we have a habit of seizing upon what is actually beyond us, clinging to the familiar categories of our sense perceptions, and then we measure the divine by human standards and, of course, are led astray by the apparent meaning we give to divine and unspeakable reason.[4]

'Seizing upon what is actually beyond us' is a phrase which happily commits something like the intellectual mistake it criticizes, for if what we seize really were 'beyond us', we would not be able to seize it. It is as if we began to detect an outline from the many ways in which something eludes our grasp. As Dante climbs lower in hell, he continues to talk about his encounters with the lost in terms which he himself has told us are not right: nobody in hell apart from Dante has a body, and yet he can kick people in the head or pull their hair, and one lost person can prey upon another disembodied shadow's skull. An explanation for these paradoxes in virtual reality is given much later in *Purgatorio*, but, as is characteristic of the *Commedia*, the explanation comes only long after we have been through experiences which should puzzle us to find terms for. These paradoxical occurrences dramatize as narrative incident what negative theology teaches about logical discretion in the analogical extension of our empirical terms, just as the stylistic remark with which *Inferno* 32 begins pretends that there could be a style which could fully answer to what is actually beyond any style.

I come back to the question: what sort of comedy is the *Commedia* supposed to be? It is supposed to be a comedy in the perhaps slightly disappointing sense that it is a poem whose central protagonist is a non-grand, non-heroic person, Dante, who not only does not think he is God but knows he is not even Aeneas or Saint Paul (*Inferno* 2, l. 32), a poem written about such an unimpressive soul in an appropriately non-grand manner, in the *sermo humilis*, the low or humble style, considered inherently comic as contrasted to the sublime, elevated manner of tragedy or epic.[5] I recommend to you Erich Auerbach's fine pages on the *sermo humilis* for an account of this stylistic matter which brings out in how complex and vital a way the humbleness of

---

[4] Pseudo-Dionysius, *The Divine Names*, in *Pseudo-Dionysius: The Complete Works*, 106.
[5] Dante, *Inferno* 2, l. 32, p. 8.

style in the poem interacts with its concern for the histories of paganism and Christianity.[6]

The *Commedia*, that is, is a 'comedy' in being about, say, the Royle Family or Gavin and Stacey, written in a style plausible for people of their status, but without any commitment to finding them funny. Not that the poem has a single level of style, but that it allows itself to go much further downmarket than suits some conceptions of tragic or epic dignity (and these low reaches of its language were one cause of its unpopularity among the neoclassicizing humanists of the Renaissance). In his treatise on eloquence in the common tongue, *De vulgari eloquentia*, Dante mentions as unsuitable for the high-falutin' genres such words as *mamma* and *babbo*, unsuitable because they are 'puerilia', childish terms, 'propter sui simplicitatem', on account of their lack of sophistication, because they are not sufficiently learned, the words which he uses at the opening of *Inferno* 32 to characterize his own tongue as one which 'chiami mamma e babbo'.[7] He also excludes there, on the grounds that they are too coarse and rustic, other words which make their way into the *Commedia*, words like *greggia*, a flock, which appears five times in the poem, even as high up as *Paradiso* 10, l. 94.[8] When he says that a tongue, such as his own, to which words like mummy and daddy come naturally, is not fit to cope with the lowest depths of the universe, he means in part something like what Pseudo-Dionysius meant when he cautioned against applying terms learned in this world to the divine realities—and this point would apply equally to any and every natural language. But Dante had also a more homely, a less abstract sense of the frailty of his own language, a sense specific to him as a native speaker of what we now call Italian, because Italian was nearest of all the vernaculars to Latin and yet this proximity awoke in Dante an acute sense of 'near miss' about his mother tongue and its relation to the literary, the official, the international, the ecclesiastical, even the sacred language of Latin, which he usually called not Latin but *gramatica*, grammar. Like all educated men in those days, he was brought up bilingually—speaking one language, in his case Tuscan, at home and in

[6] Erich Auerbach, '*Sermo Humilis*', in *Literary Language and its Public in Late Latin Antiquity and in the Middle Ages* (1958), trans. Ralph Manheim (Princeton: Princeton University Press, 1993), pp. 25–82.

[7] Dante, *De vulgari eloquentia* (*On Eloquence*), trans. and ed. Stephen Botterill (Cambridge: Cambridge University Press, 1996), 2.7.

[8] Dante, *Paradiso* 10, l. 94, p. 366.

the street, speaking Latin at school, in church, on some state business, and so on. Descartes imagined a demon sitting on his shoulder saying 'Oh really?' in sarcastic tones whenever Descartes claimed to be sure of something that, actually, he didn't have grounds for certainty about.[9] On Dante's shoulder there sits a more benign creature, but still a daunting one, the figure of everything implied by Latin, a guardian angel of sorts, call it Beatrice or *gramatica* as you prefer, which says in searching tones, 'Is that quite right?' whenever Dante opens his mouth. Now that the notion of correctness has become unpopular among linguists, and now that, more generally, we are repeatedly assured by the kindly ones on radio and TV that each of us has a right to his or her own opinion, to which no quality control applies, this perpetual, intimate sense in Dante that there is a wisdom higher than his own, a sense consolidated in the self-consciousness of style which comes from endless comparison between his mother tongue and the educated idiom, may strike us as very gloomily haunted, as of someone always worried he's about to be caught out in error, but that is only at most half the story of what *gramatica* does for Dante, for through *gramatica* he also finds his own words uplifted, translated beyond what he could hope for or even grasp, wondrously sustained.

He says he brings himself to speak of these lowest depths 'non senza temer', 'not without fearing'. It would be fair to say that the *Commedia* is a poem full of fear, not particularly because it describes grisly things which make the reader afraid (it is much less grisly than people think it is, or than many illustrators have made it look), but full of fear about speech, full of the writer's fear that he might write badly, something he can still rationally fear even though everything he writes will be, to the eyes of apophatic theology, wrong. Such fear is with Dante right from the start:

> Ahi quanto a dir qual era è cosa dura
> esta selva selvaggia e aspra e forte
> che nel pensier rinova la paura!

Oh woe, how hard a thing it is to say what it was like, this wild wood, so harsh, so potent that even thinking of it renews the fear![10]

---

[9] René Descartes, *Meditations on the First Philosophy* [1641], in *Meditations on First Philosophy with Selections from the Objections and Replies*, trans. Michael Moriarty (Oxford: Oxford University Press, 2008).

[10] Dante, *Inferno* I, ll. 4–6, p. 3.

As he steps onto the ice of the last circle, he mentions again the linguistic tremor which he had spoken of at the start of the poem before hell was on the agenda. *Inferno* begins in an earthly wood and during a midlife crisis, such as anyone can go through. But though we hear of the fear in *Inferno* 1 before we learn about the fear in *Inferno* 32, the fiction of the poem is such that the fear of *Inferno* 32 happened to Dante before he wrote the lines about fear in *Inferno* 1—he has the midlife crisis, he is sent on the penitential journey of discovery; returned from the journey, he writes the poem which tells the story of the journey. Notice that it is not only the general thought of trepidation about how to put things which recurs between the two canti, but the particular word 'aspra', pluralized to 'aspre' in *Inferno* 32. *Inferno* has the structure of one of those nightmares during which something terrible is about to happen and you wake up sweating in relief and start telling someone about your bad dream, only to realize that you have dreamed you woke up, that your confidant is in the nightmare with you, and that the terrible thing is still about to happen. It has this structure narratively in that, climbing down Satan's haunches, Virgil turns head over heels and begins climbing in reverse, 'so that I thought we were going back into hell again'—this is one of those moments in which Dante's intense fascination with natural science, as it was pursued in those days, shows up.[11] It also has this structure lexically, being an astonishing cat's-cradle of Möbius strips on which words are wound around each other, grow into arches, return as if traumatic memories or stick with you through thick and thin like faithful friends.

This architectonic density in the poem was something harder for its original readers to get the hang of than it is for us now, and it is something a canto-by-canto explication tends to cast into the shade by its concentration on individual passages rather than on the network of their interconnections. Whereas a great thing about Dante as a poet is what a patient and imaginative networker he is. It was harder for the original readers because they mostly didn't have copies of the text; the few who did have access to a text were dealing with a more cumbersome thing than the handy, flickable creatures we know as books; and even readers with books are at a disadvantage compared to readers with internet access, because you can now find search-engines which enable you to take initial impressions and wonderings such as 'haven't

---

[11] Dante, *Inferno* 34, l. 81, p. 156.

I heard "aspre" somewhere importantly similar before?' and quickly bring them into focus or discount them. So, for example, I have known for some time, and without resort to a search-engine, that the word 'dura' in 'Ahi quanto a dir qual era è cosa dura' is a word that importantly returns in the poem with reference to difficulties of expression or understanding. When, in *Inferno* 3, Dante reads the words over the gate of hell, in which hell claims 'io etterno duro' ('I last for ever'), he is troubled by them: 'Maestro, il senso lor m'è duro' ('Master, their meaning is hard for me'), and the pun, the *rima equivoca*, on the 'duro' of eternal duration and the 'duro' of difficulties for human comprehension tells us something about Dante's attitude to the doctrine of eternal punishment.[12] Relying only on my memory, I can retrieve other occurrences, like Ugolino's anguished cry 'ahi dura terra' ('ah hard earth'), when he asks why it didn't swallow him and his starving children.[13] But I wouldn't have known from memory alone that his cry is the last occurrence of the word in *Inferno*, nor would I have remembered that it is not only *aspra/aspre* which links *Inferno* 1 and 32 but also *dura/duro*, because the frozen lake like the harsh wood is 'loco onde parlare è duro' ('the place where speaking is hard', *Inferno* 32, l. 14), meaning, with characteristic density, that it is hard to speak there (your breath turns to ice), hard to speak about there (an eternity which his words cannot grasp), and that everything said there is a hard saying, because the people there are frozen together in the permanent alienation of hatred, a hatred which comes over Dante himself as he travels through this lost zone.[14] Nor would my memory have told me that the frequency of occurrence of 'duro' and its cognates decreases as you move from *cantica* to *cantica* (27 in *Inferno*, 16 in *Purgatorio*, 8 in *Paradiso*), let alone that the meanings of 'duro' which have to do with duration and lasting come to preponderate over the meanings of 'duro' which have to do with refractoriness and pain, although it is of course entirely rational that this should happen as we move from hell to heaven. The *Commedia* is an eminently rational poem, and the search-engines wonderfully speed up the process of grasping the rationale of its verbal organization. Poems are organizations of words, though many people don't like admitting this because the admission requires you to pay

---

[12] Dante, *Inferno* 3, l. 8 and l. 12, p. 12.

[13] Dante, *Inferno* 33, l. 66, p. 151.

[14] Dante, *Inferno* 32, l. 14, p. 144.

them close and patient attention, and we are all busy people with many, many less important things to do than paying attention to poems.

Spotting these patterns of verbal texture in the *Commedia* is not only an innocent pastime, like spotting trains, it also helps clue you in to Dante's frame of mind. For example, though I am talking principally about *Inferno*, I have not yet used the words 'damned' or 'damnation'. I have, though, referred four times to 'the lost', 'lost people', 'lost zone', and the like. This is because I am trying, in this respect at least, to keep my words in tune with Dante's. 'Dannato' and its cognates occurs only four times in the *Commedia*; the word Dante characteristically has in its place is 'perduto'. I don't want to make a meal of that small fact, and I agree that it could be interpreted in various ways, but coming across a fact of whatever size in the wastes of literary criticism is such a welcome change that I rejoice in it and cherish the little rascal. A further fact: these arches of lexical recurrence, this extraordinary memory for words over vast spans of poetic composition, are key features of the *Commedia*. Many of Dante's most characteristic verbal behaviours arise because of his vivid and subtle concentration on the details of his story and how he thinks best to tell it. I'll give you some examples.

Cross-talk between sayings works on a small scale as well as on the largest spans as with 'aspro' and 'duro' over thirty cantos. Take the expression 'io premerei di mio concetto il suco / più pienamente' ('I'd press out the juice from my faculty of conception more fully') from the start of *Inferno* 32. Footnotes will tell you this is an elaborate periphrasis for 'I'd express myself more completely', and, in a sense, that's right—though Dante had quite a few odd views, he did not have a bizarre theory about squeezing meaning from his brains like juice from an orange. But what footnotes don't tell you, because they don't bother to ask, is why he lit on this particular poetical circumlocution here, rather than another, such as 'I'd knit my thoughts together more intricately' or 'I'd lick the last drops from the vodka-bottle of my imagination'. I think the decorativeness of this phrase coheres with the central narrative destination of this canto, that is, the sight of Ugolino with his teeth sunk into the archbishop's nape, as if he were eating the prelate's 'cervel[lo]' (l. 129), though Dante doesn't say anything quite so explicitly Hannibal Lecterish as that he was eating his enemy's brain.[15] That sight of violence in the region of the brain grotesquely literalizes

---

[15] Dante, *Inferno* 32, l. 129, p. 147.

the fancy phrasing about squeezing your powers of conception. This
instance would not be convincing if it weren't one of an extremely
frequent kind in Dante. That kind is: occasions when expressions from
the narrative frame of a canto are literalized in the speech of someone
Dante meets or vice versa; occasions where Dante is mirrored in the
sinners whom he meets, on whom he reflects, as this canto makes
explicit when one of the lost shouts at him 'Perché cotanto in noi ti
specchi?' ('Why do you gaze at us so much like someone gazing in a
mirror?').[16] These carry-overs between the stories the lost tell and
Dante's own storytelling are an integral element of the poem's penitential character, something quite distinct from the censorious and
vindictive rant which careless readers have made of it, careless readers
like Nietzsche, who described Dante as 'the hyena who poetizes on
graves'.[17] So, for instance, when at the start of *Inferno* 32 he rounds off
his lament about how far his language falls short of the final grimness
he is walking through, he does so with what might at a first glance read
like a standard-issue invocation of the Muses:

> Ma quelle donne aiutino il mio verso
> ch'aiutaro Amfione a chiuder Tebe...

But may those women lend assistance to my verse who lent assistance to
Amphion when he closed up Thebes...[18]

Footnoters such as the excellent Natalino Sapegno rightly tell you that
Amphion 'closed up' Thebes in the sense that he built its protective
circle of walls by playing his lyre, to the sound of which, with the help
of the Muses, stones assembled themselves in the desired order, and
they refer you to Horace and Statius for parallel passages.[19] Marvellous,
give that boy a bun, but the question remains, 'why single out this one
of the Muse's many helpful acts to mention here?' and it remains
unanswered because unasked in footnotes. The answer once again,
I think, is that the framing discourse—what Dante says about his own
task of writing as contrasted to the tale he tells and the tales others tell
him within that tale—is subtly and alertly responsive to what it frames.

[16] Dante, *Inferno* 32, l. 54, p. 145.

[17] 'die Hyäne, die in Gräbern *dichtet*.' Friedrich Nietzsche, *Götzen-Dämmerung* (*Twilight of the Idols*) [1889], in *Werke*, ed. K. Schlechta, 4 vols. (Munich: C. Hanser, 1954–65), vol. 2, p. 991.

[18] Dante, *Inferno* 32, ll. 10–11, p. 144.

[19] Dante Alighieri, *La Divina Commedia*, ed. Natalino Sapegno (Milan: Ricciardi, 1955–7).

This is not the only reference in *Inferno* 32 to the protective walls of a city, so massively important in Dante's time—they were integral to the defensive system, like nuclear submarines today—and which bulk so large in his poem, because at *Inferno* 32, ll. 121–3, a reverse-Amphion is named: '...e Tebaldello, / ch'aprì Faenza quando si dormia' ('...and Tebaldello who opened up Faenza while it slept');[20] 'aprì' here reverses the 'chiuder' of the Amphion passage as Tebaldello betrayed the city of Faenza by, so to speak, circumventing its walls (he opened the city gates at night to the Bolognese enemy), whereas Amphion protected Thebes in erecting its walls. Both Amphion and Tebaldello are relevant to the central case of *Inferno* 32 and 33, the case of Ugolino, because, as Dante brings out towards the end of the count's story, Ugolino was accused of having betrayed Pisa by damaging its defensive network: 'Che se'l conte Ugolino aveva voce / d'aver tradita te de le castella' ('Even if Count Ugolino was said to have betrayed you by handing over your castles').[21] All this interaction between the story and Dante's conduct of that story is concentrated at the great moment when Ugolino says that he did not weep but turned to stone inside (l. 49)—a long history of defensiveness from ancient Thebes to contemporary Pisa, humans within their circles of stone, implodes into the figure of the petrified father who couldn't defend his own children (note the echo of Dante's appeal, 'Ma quelle donne m'aiutino', in the futile plea of little Gaddo, 'Padre mio, ché non m'aiuti?', 'You're my father, why don't you help me?'), walls within walls and at the heart another wall of stone.[22]

Another very characteristic happening in the poem comes a few lines further into *Inferno* 32:

> dicere udi'mi: 'Guarda come passi:
> va sì, che tu non calchi con le piante
> le teste de'fratei miseri lassi.'

I heard it being said: 'Watch out how you pass by: walk in such a way that you don't trample down with your feet the heads of brothers who are wretched and tired.'[23]

But who said this? We never find out; it might have been Virgil or one of the brothers (and just whose brothers are they? They are those who

---

[20] Dante, *Inferno* 32, ll. 121–3, p. 147.
[21] Dante, *Inferno* 33, ll. 85–6, p. 151.
[22] Dante, *Inferno* 33, l. 49 and l. 69, pp. 150–1.
[23] Dante, *Inferno* 32, ll. 19–21, p. 144.

were treacherous to their kin, and yet this voice seems to claim for them a solidarity with each other and perhaps with Dante), or it might even be some bit of Dante, some bit more mindful and less vindictive than he is for much of cantos 32 and 33. The characteristic happening I'm thinking of is the way that the reader, and perhaps Dante on his journey, is surprised by speech. The voice comes out of nowhere, it is never located, and no comment is made explicitly on what it says. The *Commedia* is a travelling chat-show; its two hosts, Virgil and Dante, and in the later stages of the run, Dante and Beatrice, go round meeting and interviewing people, who more or less reluctantly do little *This Was Your Life* spots. The shape of *Inferno* 1—setting of Dante, meeting with guest, dialogue, coda or 'wrap' as they say in the media—is the shape of most canti in the poem, but the variants played on this basic shape are many: sometimes the guest comes on all coy and has to be cajoled or bullied into speaking; sometimes there are two, who back each other up or bitch at each other; an occasional interview has to be conducted in a foreign language; some guests are given an intro and come down the stairs in the recommended manner, but some, as here, just pop in and out unannounced. The reason why this feature matters is that the presentation of the encountered figures varies with Dante's attitude to them, so that to develop a rounded sense of how the poem stands with regard to its individuals—and that is in essence how it embodies its drifts, ethical, political, and credal—you need to attend to how Dante interacts with those he meets as well as to what he says about them. In this respect, the *Commedia* is a dramatic poem: you have to respond to what people do to each other, how they move around one another, how they listen or fail to listen to one another, as well as to what they say. Just like Shakespeare, really. And moments like this sudden eruption of a voice that is nobody's in particular from no specific place (there are other such eruptions, as for instance Farinata's first words in *Inferno* 10) were even more vivid in the early text, because the manuscripts of the *Commedia* precede the invention of inverted commas, so a reader then was taken as unawares by Farinata's 'O Tosco', which doesn't have even the minimal 'dicere udi'mi' of this passage, as Dante was surprised by it when he heard it in the story. Nothing prepares the reader any more than anything prepared Dante for the haughty buttonholing that breaks in on the poet and the poem at this moment.

Whoever urges Dante to watch his step, the advice is needed just because it is not heeded; about fifty lines after he's told to watch out:

'passeggiando tra le teste, / forte percossi 'l piè nel viso ad una' ('strolling between the heads, my foot struck one of them violently in the face').[24] *Inferno* 32 and 33 are much preoccupied with strength, hardness, violence, all the implications of being 'forte', a term kin to the 'duro' I've already discussed. There are the two traitors at canto 32 (l. 46 onwards) glued together so tightly by their frozen tears that 'clamp never bound a board to a board so tightly' ('forte così'), then this 'forte percossi' and, at the end of Ugolino's tale, the climax of all the clenched, hate-filled togetherness (the canti turn three times to the word 'insieme'), the count's teeth fixed hard on the archbishop's skull, strong as a dog's on his bone: 'denti, / che furo a l'osso, come d'un can, forti' (*Inferno* 33, ll. 77–8).

But note also, amid all this impacted conflict and mutual recrimination, the relaxed and breezy verb 'passeggiando' which Dante alights on to describe the way they pick between the skulls protruding from the ice, and which the sterner among you may feel I translate loosely and laxly as 'strolling'. You would be wrong to feel this, my translation is in tune with the humble style of the poem and its frequently non-grand subject matter, though if you are a Renaissance humanist or a prig you will avert your decorous eyes from such realities. The Italian custom of the *passeggiata*, the stroll about sunset to parade round town and eye up the others on parade, was already in vigorous life in Dante's time, and, judging from what Beatrice says to Dante, he was all too keen on such preening and ogling. She reproves him when at last they meet in the Earthly Paradise for having been unfaithful to her memory by showing off to others who had no special merits such as might have compelled him to flirt with them:

> E quali agevolezze o quali avanzi
> ne la fronte de li altri si mostraro,
> per che dovessi lor passeggiare anzi?

And what charms or what traces showed on the foreheads of others such that you just had to stroll about in front of them?[25]

'Passeggiare' here has the full sense of the customary dalliance and swagger which you can still watch the *ragazzi* perform in public squares as the sun goes down. It is the climactic word of her accusation against him, that he so loved showing off in front of the girls (and in

----

[24] Dante, *Inferno* 32, ll. 77–8, p. 146.   [25] Dante, *Purgatorio* 31, ll. 28–30, p. 305.

front of the boys too, because 'li altri' here includes both sexes) he forgot what Beatrice had meant to him. The sublimely comic embarrassment which *Purgatorio* 31 spins from 'passeggiare' recalls the louche callousness with which Dante uses the term in *Inferno* 32, just as *Purgatorio* 31 is in its turn recalled in *Paradiso* 31, when Dante himself has the term again to describe how he looked around and marvelled in the Empyrean after he had seen the white rose formed by the souls of the blessed:

> E quasi peregrin che si ricrea
>   nel tempio del suo voto riguardando,
>   e spera già ridir com'ello stea
> su per la viva luce passeggiando,
>   menava io li occhi per li gradi,
>   mo sù, mo giù e mo recirculando.

And like a pilgrim, enjoying a treat in the shrine he vowed to visit, looking all round, already full of hopes about how he'll recount what it was like, I took my gaze for a stroll, ascending on the living light through all the ranks, now upwards, now downwards, and now promenading round and round.[26]

That 'passeggiare', which Beatrice used to goad Dante into confession and repentance, should return from his mouth to describe with wry self-consciousness his state of mind in heaven operates on the level of style a demonstration of what it is like to believe your sins have been forgiven—he does not forget his earlier foibles, but he is not afraid of them, doesn't need to tidy them out of sight or pretend they never happened, he can even draw them to our attention and to his own, so thoroughly is he assured that he has been accepted entire as the person he is. One answer to my question 'what kind of comedy we can expect to find in the *Commedia*?' would be: the kind of comedy shown here—a comedy more earthy than 'divine', in the sense that it arises from a keen, uncensorious humour about human backsliding and half-heartedness. He imagines himself in heaven as like someone who has made, say, the journey to Santiago de Compostella, to the shrine of Saint James, 'that great lord for whose sake...people pay visits to Galicia' (*Paradiso* 25, ll. 17–18), the extreme western edge of southern Europe and in those days one of the ends of the known world, a pilgrim now sitting in the basilica, after hearing Mass maybe, quite pleased with himself for having managed to get there, nodding amicably to passing nuns as they go

---

[26] Dante, *Paradiso* 31, ll. 43–8, p. 469.

polishing and sweeping by (he feels quite one of the holy Galician in-crowd now), making a list of the pious souvenirs he must buy before starting home, and already picturing himself holding the floor on his return with many tales of devotion and adventure related to a crowd of stay-at-home admirers 'well, I never'-ing at his every anecdote.[27] And all this, remember, he says was what he was like while experiencing the beatific vision. It is a startling admission and entirely characteristic of the poem in its honest amplitude about the varieties of religious experience; to sense its humour, imagine someone wearing an 'I went to heaven and all I got was this lousy T-shirt' T-shirt and meaning what was written there. Such realism about the mixed motives which lead to pilgrimage and the intermittences of devotion in the pilgrim's heart is typical of the poem and contributes to its status as one of the splendours of Christian anthropology, whatever its status as a theological enterprise. The shape of a pilgrimage—leaving home for religious, usually penitential, reasons to make a journey to a distant shrine, a journey which will take you through many experiences which would not be called 'religious' in a strict sense, and then, having arrived at the shrine, turning round again and returning home, returning to your former life with a new orientation gained from your absence—is the shape of the *Commedia*. Evidently, at the level of literal narrative: he is in a mess, he is taken out of himself and led through the other world, and then returned to this world with the task of writing the story of how he was put into better shape through his vision; but also stylistically, as the linguistic home, the mother tongue, of Tuscan is brought into comparison with the Latin of previous epic poetry and religious practice, and then rediscovered through that comparison. This essentially boomerang contour to the poem on so many levels is part of the reason why one of Dante's favourite verbs is 'volgere', to turn.

I can show you what I mean by going back to the words the anonymous voice cried to him out of nowhere in particular, warning him to be careful whom he hurt as he strolled by:

> '...le teste de'fratei miseri lassi.'
> Per ch'io mi volsi, e vidimi davante
>   e sotto i piedi un lago che per gelo
>   avea di vetra e non d'acqua sembiante.

[27] Dante, *Paradiso* 25, ll. 17–18, p. 438.

'...the heads of brothers who are wretched and tired.' Then I turned myself round and saw in front of me and beneath my feet a lake which, because it was frozen, looked more like glass than it looked like water.[28]

The sudden unfolding of the lake, where the last we heard about the landscape it was all mist, walled Tuscan cities like Montereggione or the town centre of Bologna (the Garisenda tower of *Inferno* 31, l. 136, mentioned in a simile, was the last place we heard of), is one of the great conjuring-tricks of the poem, especially as the syntax of these lines suspends the fact the lake is frozen, so that for a moment he seems to be walking on water: 'and I saw before me and beneath my feet a lake—and only then: which because of the ice...' Dante specializes in these sudden effects of spectacularly changed horizons or leaps around the global clock, as when, at the end of *Purgatorio* 4, Virgil in an instant shifts Dante's mind and our minds from a jokey conversation about why you might as well be a couch-potato to an evocation of vast expanses: 'come on now: see, the sun has touched the meridian, and night already covers with its foot Morocco.'[29] But the more characteristic element of Dantescan sublimity is not the huge or the exotic but the intimate and arduous, and the turnings which most concern him are usually not physically sweeping but personally taxing, for they are turns of mind or heart or spirit, as when the exasperated Filippo Argenti in *Inferno* 8 turns on himself with his own teeth, or when the disdainful angel of *Inferno* 9 turns away to deal with higher business, or when the Virgin Mary says 'Behold the handmaid of the Lord', accepting the Incarnation already taking place within her, and with those words 'turned the key which opened the world to supreme love' (*Purgatorio* 10, l. 44), or when the Emperor Constantine turned the flight of the imperial eagle from West to East (*Paradiso* 6), or Beatrice's lovely eyes, to which he returns his own (*Paradiso* 22) and which at last she turns from him and to the fountain of eternity (*Paradiso* 31).[30] The *Commedia* has so many turns because 'volgere' is the eloquent common parlance for conversion, repentance ('convertere', 'metanoia' in the language of *gramatica*). The story is: Dante was so far gone astray he had to be granted his vision and the task of writing the vision down in order to bring him round. Virgil explains to Cato as they move towards the mount of Purgatory:

[28] Dante, *Inferno* 32, ll. 22–4, p. 144.   [29] Dante, *Purgatorio* 4, ll. 137–9, p. 177.
[30] Dante, *Purgatorio* 10, ll. 40–5, p. 203.

> Questi non vide mai l'ultima sera;
> ma per la sua follia le fu sí presso,
> che molto poco tempo a volger era.

This man never saw his last night but his craziness brought him so close to it that very little time indeed was left for turning.[31]

The entire poem performs at the level of how it is written this act of urgent 'turning', of conversion, an act which it records in its story. It is this dramatic and historical process of changing the self and its world, rather than any especial involvement with theological doctrine, which makes the poem 'sacro'—Dante calls it the 'poema sacro' in *Paradiso* 25—'holy' in a way which God, because he does not change, cannot be holy, and therefore 'holy' in a way which makes it elementally wrong to call the *Commedia* 'divina'.[32]

---

[31] Dante, *Purgatorio* 1, ll. 58–60, p. 161.   [32] Dante, *Paradiso* 25, l. 1, p. 438.

7

French as a literary medium

The sixteenth century was a changeable time for French, as for most modern European vernaculars; just as English underwent a massive expansion of its vocabulary in this period, so too did French. About 20 per cent of the words now current in French entered the language in the sixteenth century (nearly double the average rate for new lexical acquisitions in the three centuries before and the three centuries after the sixteenth).[1] And many more entered the language and then dropped out, so that there were three forms of sadness in Old French:

> tristece [< tristesse]; tristor [*obsolete*]; tristance [*obsolete*]

and four kinds of blindness:

> avueglece [*obs.*]; avuegleüre [*obs.*]; avuegleté [*obs.*]; avueglement [< aveuglement].[2]

In Racine, as nowadays, there is only the one sadness of 'tristesse', only the one blindness of 'aveuglement'. This is a small (but perfectly formed) instance of other changes which came over French in the years between Montaigne and Racine. In sixteenth-century France, as in sixteenth-century England, they were expanding their vocabularies as if there were no tomorrow—there was, for instance, a fad for Italianate words, which arose because of Catherine de Medici's powerful influence at court but was, more generally, a consequence of the great cultural prestige Italy exercised at this time as a result of having invented the Renaissance. Many of the sixteenth century's borrowings

---

[1] R. Anthony Lodge, *French: From Dialect to Standard* (London: Routledge, 1993), 137.
[2] Peter Rickard, *A History of the French Language*, 2nd edn. (London: Routledge, 1989), 57.

from Italian are now thoroughly naturalized French words and turn up in Racine: 'attaquer', 'briller', 'manquer', 'brave', and so on.[3] The word 'appartement' crossed the Alps at this time, and so did the architectural phenomenon it named: it had previously been usual to build palaces with one room opening into the next, so that no room was absolutely 'apart from' any other and, consequently, nobody could 'go to his room' or her room, shut the door, and feel safely private. The Italians had the idea of building corridors off which individual rooms opened, spaces apart into which a person might retreat to be alone in the locked domain of the self. *Andromaque* was first performed in the queen's apartments at the newly aggrandized Louvre. This fact from the history of interior design may go some way to explaining why Racine's favourite adjective is 'seul' (with 'grand' and 'cruel' as runners-up taking the silver and bronze); Corneille, on the other hand, prefers 'grand', with 'seul' coming in second. There's quite an allegory you could spin on the basis of this statistic about the intricate relations between prestige and loneliness in these writers, between the 'grand' and the 'seul', about what Racine called 'tristesse majestueuse', majestic sadness but also the sadness *of* majesty, of those who can afford massive apart-ment.

In the twentieth century, French linguistic purists went miffed about 'le weekend', 'le parking', and so on; they thought such terms 'bizarre' and not properly French, though actually 'bizarre' had been borrowed into French from Italian in the sixteenth century, when it was Italian which invaded the French lexical field. Then as now, there was not just one attitude to the phenomenon of linguistic borrowing (human soci-eties are rarely characterized by unanimity, despite those supposedly helpful and actually misleading books about 'the Elizabethan world-picture' or 'the Victorian frame of mind'; it is therefore a mistake to use brisk phrases such as 'Racine's seventeenth-century God-fearing audience': plays are forms of fictional debate, they get their energies in part from disagreements in the audience). So, as regards the lexical exuberances of the French sixteenth century, there were those like the poet Ronsard who delighted in the expansion—'plus nous aurons de mots en nostre langue, plus elle sera parfaitte' ('the more words we have in our language, the more perfect it will be')—while there were of course others who disapproved of it, and sought a more restrained

[3] Rickard, *A History of the French Language*, 89.

and measured vocabulary.[4] There was a generation shift between Ronsard, who died in 1585, and Malherbe, who became the official poet of Henri IV and Louis XIII from 1605 onwards and who stood out against linguistic fancy-pants-ism of all kinds—archaisms, neologisms, loan-words, dialect, expert technical terms. French—at least the 'high' French of literature—underwent in the early seventeenth century the kind of linguistic sobering-up which the binge-culture of English didn't experience until the last decades of that century. And Racine is a model child of the new attitudes; he does not often engage in word-play like Shakespeare, he avoids puns and lexical display, he has a very restricted vocabulary in his verse, and, though he does permit himself some inversions of word order and other such poeticisms as would not normally have been heard in the speech around him, his language is actually not remotely formal, far-fetched, monumental, though it is 'polite' in the sense of 'self-consciously well-mannered, such as is spoken in "good society"', which does not mean that it is not also alert, biting, cruel, and dramatic.

These facts about the recent changes French had undergone in the years before Racine started writing matter to his plays because such shifts in the language of literature were part of a much broader process of state-formation—of the centralization of power around the king, of more refined codes of conduct, of the growth of what might be thought of as a 'cultural establishment'. One reason why you need to learn to listen in responsively to Racine's style is that 'style' was such a substantial consideration for the political world of his day. Malcolm Bull mentions an emblematic fact, a fact about emblems, as regards the regime in which Racine lived and worked:

unlike his predecessors, Louis [XIV] was not a part-timer: the sun rose when he got out of bed in the morning, and set when he went to sleep. The artistic expression of this total identification between king and sun-god was Versailles, where the Salon d'Apollon (with Charles de la Fosse's ceiling of the sun-god coursing across the sky) was also the throne-room. It was probably the first time Apollo rather than Jupiter had presided over the throne, and the change highlights the way in which sovereignty, which had once been expressed as Herculean strength and then as Jovian omnipotence, was now conceived in terms of Apollonian splendour. The sequence is an acknowledgement that rulership required more than an ability to fight off the enemies of the state,

[4] Pierre de Ronsard, *L'Art Poétique; Cinq Préfaces*, ed. Jean Stewart (Cambridge: Cambridge University Press, 2013), 'Abrégé de l'Art poétique François', 20.

or achieve a monopoly of power within it. Power also had a cultural dimension: the visible proof of the sun's ability to co-ordinate its numerous satellites was its ability to outshine them.[5]

In the opening line of Racine's *Iphigénie*, a heavy weight of implication rests on the simple fact that the play begins with the king, Agamemnon, waking up one of his courtiers before dawn, thereby reversing the polite order of things, in which the courtier came to attend on his lord as he arose.[6] The audience at that moment recognizes its own world in the world of ancient Greece, but its own world estranged; Agamemnon both is and is not Louis XIV—the ancient and the current king are like each other, the hinted resemblance implies, in so far as they are semi-divine, super-groovy, amazingly devoted to the welfare of their community, martyrs to their sense of duty, etc., etc., but the analogy has to be handled with kid gloves or it will soon begin also to suggest: 'alike also in that they are both doomed to be murdered in the bath by their wife and her lover' and various other unwelcome possible implications of a resemblance to Agamemnon. With analogies as with kings, it is important to know how far it is safe to go. Professor Bull is too brisk when he moves from the resemblance between Louis's tireless day and the sun's endless round to his claim that there was a 'total identification between king and sun-god', because people in the French seventeenth century knew the difference between the sun and the sun-god, which Professor Bull seems momentarily to have forgotten; one notable difference between them is that most people in France in the seventeenth century believed that the sun existed, whereas they mostly believed that the sun-god did not exist. It is importantly true that official hype of Louis XIV centred on a pretence that he was 'sort of' Apollo, and that this iconic significance of Apollo rather than Hercules or Jupiter for the regime shows its style-consciousness, its preoccupation with the 'splendeur' and 'gloire' so important in Racine's plays. The pagan world may be a mirror in which Racine's society sees itself reflected, not reflected plain, though, but as in a visibly distorting, concave or convex, glass in which his world does indeed recognize itself, but with more or less scary, more or less titillating differences.

---

[5] Malcolm Bull, *The Mirror of the Gods: Classical Mythology in Renaissance Art* (London: Allen Lane, 2005), 340–1.

[6] 'Oui, c'est Agamemnon, c'est ton Roi qui t'éveille.' Racine, *Oeuvres complètes*, 2 vols., ed. Georges Forestier (Paris: Gallimard, 1999–), vol. 1: *Théâtre—poésie* (1999), p. 703.

As we in turn can recognize in seventeenth-century France our world and its investment of political thrill and substance in 'image' and 'perception'.

Two books by Norbert Elias—*The Civilizing Process* (1939) and *The Court Society* (1969)—offer long and searching studies of the cultural changes imaged by such promotions of Apollo to the role of top god; they are amongst the most thought-provoking things to read on Racine. Such things as the supremacy of Apollo, sobriety of verbal style, the changes in interior design which produced the 'appartement', were new or new-ish anyway around Racine, he had grown up with them. They help configure much in his work, such as the role of Pyrrhus in *Andromaque*, who is trying to be a 'new man' but can't forget or escape the massacres at Troy on which his current 'gloire' is based, a figure whom Racine said, in a preface to the play, the writer tried to 'adoucir' (make gentle, tone or calm down) as Pyrrhus tries to 'adoucir' himself— though neither manages the process with complete success.[7]

It is easy to be over-impressed by the icons of stability and power which were produced in such abundance around Louis XIV as he strove to take firm hold of his kingdom, easy to mistake those projections of regal glamour for records of an actual and achieved state of assurance. They were designed to over-impress. They are devices aimed at bringing about that solidity of government which they pretend has already been secured, to make things become so by pretending they already are so. Louis XIV's control over most of his subjects was weaker than he liked to let on, and much less pervasive than that exercised by the central authorities in our own free world. The king and the official imagery which surrounded him are better understood as the seventeenth-century French equivalent of Eric Cartman's repeated cry 'RESPECT MY AUTHORITY',[8] which is not something that someone who unshakeably *has* authority needs to cry. Similarly, it is easy to be over-impressed by the supposed 'regularity' in Racine's plays, to exaggerate their decorum or monumental poise. His plays don't, as I mentioned before, engage in the linguistic and generic time-travelling so typical of Shakespeare— there are no jokes about old-fashioned acting, outmoded ways of talking, hardly any revivals of archaic theatrical devices as in Time's speech from *The Winter's Tale* (though there are such jokes in other French

---

[7] 'Toute la liberté que j'ai prise, ça été d'adoucir un peu la férocité de Pyrrhus'. Racine, 'Virgile au troisième livre de l'Énéide', *Andromaque*, in *Oeuvres complètes*, vol. 1, p. 197.

[8] In the American animated sitcom, *South Park*.

writers contemporary with Racine). Racine's plays are spick and span in these respects, 'cutting edge', you might say, if you allow the phrase 'cutting edge' to mean both that they are self-consciously in a new approved manner and also that they are acutely aware of their own riskiness. His plays may have, at one stylistic level, the projected self-confidence of a new regime, but—and this is a big but—they frequently depict, as *Andromaque* does, a society struggling to establish in fact the new and smoother order which the plays carry through in imagination at the level of style. They are haunted, as *Andromaque* is haunted, by a rough and nightmarish past which they have not escaped, cannot quite escape. Many of them, like *Andromaque*, concern the labour-pains of a new political dispensation struggling, more or less successfully, to be born; this is true of his next two tragedies, *Britannicus* and *Bérénice*, as also in differing ways of later plays such as *Phèdre*, *Esther*, and *Athalie*.

Racine's plays show at the level of style and structure the manner of a new dispensation, but at the level of subject they turn with a fascinated horror to what has had to be overcome in the civilizing process of which they form a part—they are aware of the process by which they became as polished as they are, of the effort it takes to keep up actual civility. For instance, there are twelve occasions in *Andromaque* on which a character speaks of 'gloire'. This is so central and variously potent a word in Racine and in his world that it is tricky to translate. Louis XIV told his son that the ruling passion of his life had been concern for his own 'gloire'; in English, 'gloire' might be rendered as 'self-esteem', 'standing in the eyes of others', 'reputation', 'narcissism', 'celebrity', 'chic'. Of those twelve usages in *Andromaque*, ten are either from or about Pyrrhus or Hermione; six of the twelve occurrences of the word come from Hermione herself, sometimes talking about her own 'gloire' (as at line 413)[9] but more often revelling in the 'gloire' of Pyrrhus, in which she hopes to bathe when married to him. Pyrrhus's 'gloire' derives chiefly from the role he played on the night Troy fell. Phoenix, Pyrrhus's old tutor, disapproves of all his rigmarole with Andromaque and is glad to see him angry with her; he reminds him what his reputation is based on:

> ce juste courroux
> Ainsi qu'à tous les Grecs, Seigneur, vous rend à vous. [...]
> Ce n'est plus le jouet d'une flamme servile.

⁹ Georges Forestier, *Jean Racine* (Paris: Gallimard, 2006), 212.

C'est Pyrrhus. C'est le Fils, et le Rival d'Achille,
Que la Gloire à la fin ramène sous ses lois,
Qui triomphe de Troie une seconde fois.

PYRRHUS

Dis plutôt qu'aujourd'hui commence ma Victoire.
D'aujourd'hui seulement je jouis de ma gloire.

your justified anger, my lord, brings you back in line not only with all the
Greeks but also with yourself… You're no longer the plaything of a slavish
ardour, you're Pyrrhus, you're the son, indeed the rival, of Achilles, whom
self-esteem has at last reclaimed as subject to its laws, and who now tri-
umphs over Troy for a second time.

PYRRHUS

Say rather that today is the first day of my triumph, that only from today do
I taste the sweetness of my reputation.[10]

Though I said that Racine has less by way of word-play than Shakespeare
does, that doesn't mean he wasn't a thoughtful and even a tricksy
writer—as in this passage, where Phoenix's goading word for what
Pyrrhus has become since he fell under Andromaque's influence, a
'jouet', a 'plaything', as if to say 'you're no hero, you're just a toy-boy',
is taken up and retorted on by Pyrrhus in his 'jouis', 'I come into pos-
session of', 'I delight in' and even 'I experience orgasm on account of',
for in Racine's French you could 'jouir d'une femme' (physically enjoy
her favours); when Molière speaks of a 'jouissance', he can mean a
consummated sexual desire. So that, in the moment when Pyrrhus
resolves to give up courting Andromaque and show her who's boss, he
experiences a pleasure like that he had long imagined he would enjoy
if she gave herself to him; he enjoys, you might say if you wanted to
push the point, his 'gloire' as if it were her genitals.

The particular jewel in the crown of Pyrrhus's reputation was that
to him fell the glory of having killed old Priam, the king of Troy,
not that this was a feat of physical heroism—on the contrary—but on
account of the symbolic distinction, as in chess, of taking the king,
weak though that piece is in itself. When Hermione is finally exasperated by Pyrrhus, she refers sarcastically to the celebrity he gained 'Du
vieux Père d'Hector la valeur abattue' ('from having slaughtered the
mighty prowess of Hector's old father').[11] The verb she uses here as

---

[10] Racine, *Andromaque*, II.v.627–34, *Oeuvres complètes*, vol. 1, p. 219.
[11] Racine, *Andromaque*, IV.v.1333, *Oeuvres complètes*, vol. 1, p. 245.

a participial adjective, 'abattue' from 'abattre', 'to butcher', 'to lay low', is rare in mature Racine; this is the first time we hear it in this play, and it will come only once again, with a grim power of retribution, as Oreste describes to Hermione how Pyrrhus dies, torn by infuriated Greeks, at an altar, just where he himself killed Priam: 'Chacun se disputait la gloire de l'abattre' ('Every man claimed for himself the distinction of bringing him down').[12] Pyrrhus tries throughout the play to hang on to the rewards of his 'gloire', but also to start a new way of behaving which is not dependent on the violence of physical conquest; he does not wish to compel Andromaque into marriage or into his bed (as Racine well knew, this was exactly what Pyrrhus had done in the Euripides source, according to standard customs governing military 'gloire' in the ancient world, and in the not-so-ancient one). He is at last swallowed by his own 'gloire', becomes a second Priam in a second Troy, as he had defiantly dared the Greeks: 'Qu'ils cherchent dans l'Épire une seconde Troie' ('Let them come looking for a second Troy in Epirus').[13] So that, for all his efforts to become a new man, to start a way of living that will not be the mere aftermath of the destruction of Troy, he is collapsed back into the past, becomes the perpetual relic of his own butchery and 'gloire', a replayed Priam.

Pyrrhus's eventual experience of what a new, gentler refinement may cost shows throughout Racine's plays in innumerable features of their language. They are written in what Christian Surber calls the 'dialecte tragique', or 'dialect of tragedy', a conscious selection from the broader range of the language spoken at that time.[14] You will find 'vaisseaux' ('vessels') in Racine but not 'bateaux' ('boats'), you find the word 'entrailles' ('entrails') in Racine but not low 'synonyms' of that word such as 'tripes' or 'abats'; you find 'abattre' as a verb in *Andromaque*, as we have just seen, but nobody ever speaks of an 'abattoir': that is too messy a place to be mentioned. The non-appearance of such 'low' words does not mean that Racine was unaware of their existence, nor that his audience was not conscious they were listening to a stylized version of their own language; they knew there were other ways of talking from the way Pyrrhus talks, other ways of talking from the ways they themselves talked. Not all plays in Louis XIV's France were

---

[12] Racine, *Andromaque*, V.iii.1517, *Oeuvres complètes*, i. 251.

[13] Racine, *Andromaque*, I.ii.230, *Oeuvres complètes*, i. 205.

[14] Christian Surber, *Parole, Personnage et Référence dans le Théâtre de Jean Racine* (Geneva: Droz, 1992), 11.

like Racine's, not even all rhymes were like Racine's. In Richelet's
contemporary *Nouveau Dictionnaire des Rimes*, for instance, there's an
exhaustive list of jingles, including rhymes for Graeco-Roman names
which appear in Racinian drama: 'Achille' appears a dozen times in
Andromaque but Racine never rhymes his name with 'pédophile' as
Richelet suggests he might have done, he keeps decorously to 'asile',
'tranquille', and 'servile'; there's an 'Agrippine' in Racine's *Britannicus*
but her name is never rhymed in Richelet's manner with 'sardine', but
rather with 'ruine'.[15] The playwright knew that even his own name
was susceptible of a pun, containing as it does both the low 'rat' and the
decorously lyrical 'cygne' ('swan'), and wryly remarked that he had
dropped the less dignified rat from his coat of arms as unsuitable for a
swan-like bard. This does not stop his characters often sounding vicious
as cornered rats; indeed, one good way of describing Racine's plays
would be to say that their subject is 'the weasel under the cocktail cab-
inet', which is how Pinter described the subject of his plays, or the 'rat'
beneath the 'cygne', the aggression beneath or within the decorous,
lyrical polish, to put it in more Racinian terms.[16] Racine may have
wisely avoided the rhyme of 'Agrippine' and 'sardine', but plenty of
people around him made coarse jokes about his refayned protagonists,
such as the rude wag Fatouville who rhymed on the name of the leading lady in Racine's most restrained play, *Bérénice*, in his play *Arlequin
Protée*, where someone asks where is the 'reine Bérénice' and gets the
reply 'elle est là haut qui pisse' ('she's upstairs having a piss').[17] Racine
does not have the verb 'pisser' in any of his plays, but this does not
mean he was delusionally prissy, and believed that people never went
to the toilet. He was a courtier, spending long periods at Versailles
and in the Louvre (no pun intended), and so could not have failed to
notice the poor facilities in these palaces, where 'behind the doors and
almost everywhere one sees there a mass of excrement, one smells a
thousand unbearable stenches caused by calls of nature which everyone

---

[15] César-Pierre Richelet, *Nouveau Dictionnaire des Rimes* (Paris: Bilaine, 1667).

[16] Harold Pinter, quoted in John Russell Taylor, 'A Room and Some Views', in *Anger and After: A Guide to the New British Drama* (1962) (Abingdon: Routledge, 2014), 321–60 (p. 323).

[17] Nolant de Fatouville, *Arlequin Protée*, in Evaristo Gherardi, *Le Théâtre Italien de Gherardi, ou Recueil général de toutes les Comédies et Scènes Françoises jouées par les Comédiens Italiens du Roy, pendant tout le temps qu'ils ont été au Service*, 6 vols. (Paris: J.-B. Cusson et P. Witte, 1700), vol. 1, p. 101.

goes to answer there every day'.[18] In 1702, the Duchesse d'Orléans was still complaining that 'the people stationed in the galleries in front of our room piss in all the corners. It's impossible to leave one's apartments without seeing someone pissing.'

The superstitions about Racine and his world which prevent people from hearing his verse for the alert and biting medium it is, which flatten the dynamic between figures on his stage into a dull and stately parade, are all of a piece: they arise from a foolish belief that the age's PR for itself was the age's reality, that nothing but Racinian tragedy as standardly misconceived ever happened in the French seventeenth century, with the result that neither Racine nor his audience had any self-conscious perspective on these plays and their styles of conduct and utterance. This is just another version of that sad tendency people have to want to believe that in the past everybody thought just one thing until, by a wholly inexplicable process, they suddenly all changed their minds and ways of living and started thinking and doing something wholly different. People were, however, at least as diverse one from another in those days as they are now; it is not true, for example, that everybody in Racine's audience knew Euripides' play *Andromache*, not quite by heart perhaps, but extremely well. On the contrary, very few of his audience knew the play or any Greek, and this was one reason why they complained that Pyrrhus was a bit of a rough diamond, and why Racine is so demurely ironic about their complaints in the preface to his play; they had only the most pallid idea of how much rougher the classical past had been than they might have liked to think. The very subject of Racine's play, I mean the story of Andromaque, had been treated in a manner far from reverent and monumental a decade or so before his play appeared. Scarron's *Le Virgile travesti* (*Virgil Burlesqued*) was published in instalments between 1648 and 1662; it formed part of a great vogue for burlesques of the very works which neoclassicism so admired, including tragedies. Here's Andromaque in Scarron's version, meeting Aeneas as she tends yet again the cenotaph she's raised to Hector's memory:

> Elle faisait l'anniversaire,
> Avec un fort beau luminaire,
> Auprès d'un tombeau fait exprès,

[18] Anne Somerset, *The Affair of the Poisons: Murder, Infanticide and Satanism at the Court of Louis XIV* (London: Weidenfeld & Nicolson, 2003), 53.

Tout entouré d'un vert cyprès,
D'Hector (Dieu veuille avoir son âme!);
Et cette vénérable dame
Avait fait bâtir ce tombeau
Dans un bois, auprès d'un ruisseau,
Nommé Simoïs, du nom du fleuve
Qui les murs de Pergame abreuve.
Elle pensa mourir d'effroi,
Quand elle vit mes gens et moi,
Et nos armes à la Troyenne.
Elle cria: "Qu'on me soutienne!
Je me sens les jarrets plier."

She was performing the memorial, under tasteful lighting, beside a designer-tomb, completely framed with cypresses, of Hector—may God receive his soul!—and this noble lady had had this tomb built in a glade, by a stream, which she called Simois, after the river which laps at the walls of Troy. She nearly died of fright when she saw me and my men with our uniforms and weapons in the Trojan style. She shrieked: 'Assist, good friends! my legs have gone all wobbly.'[19]

Quoting Shakespeare's Cleopatra at the death of Antony—'Assist, good friends'—next to the *Carry On Camping* language of 'my legs have gone all wobbly', I try to bring out a disparity of style in Scarron's French, between the lavendered use of the subjunctive to issue a command or a request, 'Qu'on me soutienne!', and the occurrence of the 'low' word 'jarret'. There are no 'jarrets' ('shins') in Racine, but this no more means he thought the human body stopped at the knees than the fact that there are no octosyllabic lines such as Scarron's in Racine's plays till *Iphigénie* means that he discovered verse could be written in lines of less than twelve syllables only in 1674. So too, he was aware of a range of possible attitudes to the right way for a widow such as Andromaque to behave: he had not only read his sources in Virgil and Euripides, where there is no question of her remaining an indeflectibly chaste relict of Hector, because she has already been distributed along with the other booty of war as a concubine, but he also lived in a world where widows were powerful figures, whether they remarried or not, and where the Queen of France had been reluctantly a widow in all but name for years, having been abandoned by Louis XIV for

---

[19] Paul Scarron, *Le Virgile travesti* (1648–62), ed. Jean Serroy (Paris: Garnier, 1988), Livre 3, ll. 1059–107, p. 265.

a succession of mistresses. It was in about the year of *Andromaque*'s premiere in the 'apart-ments' of the bereft Marie-Thérèse, that Madame de Montespan became the King's mistress, bearing him seven children, who were legitimized after her marriage was annulled in 1674, for the King's convenience. Madame de Montespan never became queen (she retired to a convent in 1687 and eventually became its superior); that honour was reserved for Madame de Maintenon, herself a widow—as it happens, of the poet Scarron who wrote the lines I'm commenting on—since 1660, and eventually, though at first in secret, Louis's queen from 1684 on. You do not need to know these racy facts to recognize that Andromaque's relentless devotion to the dead Hector is a topic of debate in Racine, that the play is written in full responsive knowledge of the fact that people disagreed about how widows should behave. Racine's Andromaque is, as it were, halfway between the object of Scarron's sly digs about designer-grief and the luxurious chic of mourning and the Andromaque of Baudelaire, lyrically abandoned to a sorrow whose very futility is the mark of its distinction:

> Andromaque, des bras d'un grand époux tombée,
> Vil bétail, sous la main du superbe Pyrrhus,
> Auprès d'un tombeau vide en extase courbée…

Andromache, let fall from the arms of a noble husband, become a despised chattel under the hand of haughty Pyrrhus, bent double in an ecstasy of grief beside an empty tomb…[20]

Racine's verse is, as it were, halfway between the lush densities of Baudelaire and the comically hard-hearted octosyllabics in which Scarron blows the gaffe on her distress. Always remember, when reading *Andromaque*, the following emblematic facts about the actress who created the title-role:

In 1653 the twenty-year-old Thérèse Du Parc had come to Paris with Molière's troupe of actors, after being spotted performing acrobatics in the market square at Lyon. Later that year she had married a comedian in the company with the stage name of Gros René [Big Fat René], but she had attracted many other admirers, including the ageing playwright Corneille, whose advances she rejected. In 1664 she had danced before the King in a skirt split to the thigh, and the sight of her wonderful legs encased in silk stockings had excited

---

[20] Charles Baudelaire, 'Le Cygne' (1861), *Les Fleurs du Mal*, ed. Claude Pichois (Paris: Gallimard, 1996), ll. 37–9, pp. 126–7.

much admiring comment. Following the death of her husband in 1667, she had joined Racine's theatre company.[21]

She also became Racine's mistress at about the same time. Never forget while imagining the pious widow, Andromaque, that the actress who created the role was herself not only the widow of a comedian, Big Fat René, who sounds as if he's escaped from *'Allo'Allo*, but also a hoofer, always happy to show a king a bit of leg.

Racine's plays are written in the 'dialect of tragedy', as Christian Surber says. As with the dialect of any group or clique, the more alert members of that clique always know that they have a special way of speaking—that's what makes them chic: 'you say tomayto, but we say tomahto.' Those in the audience who watch protagonists speaking 'the dialect of tragedy' do not themselves speak that dialect, or at least not all the time—this is the crucial point: the audience is not confined to the 'dialect of tragedy' as the protagonists of the plays are. The same is true in reverse of comedy: in 1659, Molière had one of his earliest big successes with *Les précieuses ridicules*, a satire in colloquial prose of high-society affectations which was performed as an afterpiece to Corneille's magnificent verse tragedy of imperial Rome, *Cinna*. Though 'tragedy' and 'comedy' may now be subject to an intellectual and theatrical apart-heid, they were not so separated in those days, but regularly appeared on the same bill. In Molière's frisky piece, one of the pseudo-intellectual ladies at one point says, 'but darling, life outside Paris is absolutely not worth living', and you can tell from the context in the play that this was supposed to get a laugh from the Parisian audience. But the fact that the audience laughed doesn't prove that they themselves didn't sometimes talk like that—indeed, this attitude to Paris is still common among some would-be intellectual Parisians—it shows rather that the theatre is a place where people can sometimes stand aside from themselves, 'watch' or 'catch' themselves 'at it'.

There are many simple facts about the French of Racine's day which show that the dialect of his tragedies was not a universal language, and so, that the mirror his stage held up to his audience was a recognizably distorting one. I've mentioned the self-conscious selectivity of his vocabulary, but even simpler and more pervasive is the fact that the pronunciation of French was changing in ways which produced an

[21] Somerset, *The Affair of the Poisons*, 191.

ever-wider divergence between daily talk and tragic dialect.The so-called
mute 'e' was not mute at all in medieval French, but was falling silent
all around Racine, so lines which contain mute 'e's are heard as 'poetical'
at a miniscule level, they require a manner of pronunciation distinct
from that of common speech. So too, the liaison between terminal
consonants and following vowels which is required in French classical
verse had once been a more prominent feature of ordinary speech but,
from the sixteenth century on, there are records from grammarians
moaning about the disappearance of final consonants: 'The people
say...*plaisi, mestie, papie*'. But when Hermione speaks to Cléone—
'Prenons quelque plaisir à leur être importune'[22]—there are three
liaisons of a terminal 'r' into a subsequent open vowel—'plaisiRR-a
leuRR-etRR-importun', affording the actor an opportunity for a tiger-
ishly caressing drawl. Though, in fact, the uvular [r] now familiar in
French is a phonetic late-comer, and was not frequent in Racine's day
(it grew up around the time of the Revolution). Because writing only
outlines the acoustic realities of speech—pronunciation, but also pace,
intonation contour, pitch, and so on—it seriously under-represents the
informational richness of a vocal utterance. If you could see the script
from which I am now speaking, you would not see in that script an
indication of my accent or other tricks of my voice, or the fact that
I suddenly shouted the word 'shouted', though there could have been
a stage direction to that effect, but in fact there isn't. (There are no
such stage directions in any of Racine's scripts any more than in any
of Shakespeare's.) A script stands in the same relation to the speech
current around it that government PR such as Louis XIV's stands in
relation to the political actualities of the day—a script is a more or less
intelligent and self-conscious idealization of speech. And just because
Racine's scripts, like Shakespeare's, are not documentary records but
reconfigurations of the world around him, not transcripts of phonetic
realities but a projection of those realities into the dialect of tragedy,
the plays are not left behind by historical changes in pronunciation,
and you do not need to worry that people pronounced 'roi' differently
in those days, not as 'rwa' (with uvular) but as 'ré' (with post-alveolar),
so that you now hear Racine's lines, so far as you hear them at all, in a
phonological system different from the one they first sounded in. The
failure of French graphemes to record exactly French phonemes may

---

[22] Racine, *Andromaque*, II.i.442, *Oeuvres complètes*, vol. 1, p. 213.

be the despair of a historical phonetician, but it is a condition of the trans-historical survival of Racine's plays in the theatre. As the linguist Martinet wrote:

En français, les différences entre la graphie et la phonie sont de nature telle que l'on peut dire, sans aucune exagération, que la structure de la langue écrite ne se confond pas avec celle de la langue parlée.

In French, the differences between the language as written and the language as spoken are such that it can be said, with no exaggeration at all, that the structure of the written language is quite distinct from the structure of the spoken language.[23]

Though there is no need to be much concerned with the history of French pronunciation for our purposes, we do need to get real about some acoustic features of Racine's writing, and in particular about the alexandrine. In the first place, it was not the only kind of verse-line French people had ever heard of—Scarron wrote in octosyllabics, because those snappy little lines made a good mickey-taking contrast to the Virgilian hexameters he was travestying. (An alexandrine is *not* a hexameter; hexameters have six feet, alexandrines have no 'feet' at all, because a 'foot' is a defined sequence of syllables, long or short, and French verse is not written in such units; French alexandrines *always* have twelve syllables, classical hexameters do not have a fixed number of syllables but vary around about sixteen.) Alexandrines were comparative newcomers on the French poetic scene; they'd been around barely a century when Racine began his career. The sixteenth-century poet du Bellay never mentions alexandrines in his 1549 treatise about French as a literary medium, though he writes them in his *Les Regrets*. Ronsard was blamed by some twerpy prosodists for not having written his epic, *La Franciade*, in alexandrines, but he thought their complaints were ignorant and absurd; he explained why he hadn't written his patriotic poem in twelve-syllable lines:

il m'eust esté cent fois plus aisé... d'autant qu'ils sont plus longs, et par consequent moins sujets, sans la honteuse conscience que j'ay qu'ils sentent trop leur prose.

it would have been a hundred times easier for me [to write in alexandrines]... in as much as those are longer lines, and therefore less constrained, yet I was painfully aware that alexandrines stink of prose.[24]

---

[23] André Martinet, *Éléments de linguistique générale* (Paris: Colin, 1967), 161.
[24] Pierre de Ronsard, preface to *La Franciade*, 'Au Lecteur' (1572), in *Oeuvres Complètes*, 2 vols., ed. Gustave Cohen (Paris: Gallimard, 1950), vol. 2, p. 1011.

or again:

ils sentent trop la prose tres facile, et sont enerves et flaques, si ce n'est pas pour les traductions.

they stink of informal prose, and are nerveless and flat, except in translations.[25]

He thought the twelve-syllable line was fit only for 'tragedies and translations', by which he meant that it was a serviceable line which didn't make too many demands on a poet who already had his hands full with the task of translation, and that, for the same reason, it was OK for tragedy, where attention was not primarily on the verse. He also complained that alexandrines had 'trop de caquet' ('too much cackle') in them, unless written by a master hand, meaning, once again, that they sounded too like common-or-garden chitchat. Ronsard took this dim view of twelve-syllable couplets because he heard them in the acoustic of other forms he was used to, forms with shorter lines, whose rhymes therefore occurred more densely and audibly, often written according to complex and showy patterns of rhyming. His ear, that is, was attuned in reverse from an English ear when it first comes to Racine's couplets; incautious English listeners hear the couplets against the norm of the blank verse they are used to in tragedies, the rhymes sound more prominent to such an ear, as if they were optional extras, more or less tasteless ornaments wilfully stuck on every twelve syllables. But blank verse is not the default option for verse in every language, that's a superstition of Little Englanders; there was in French no blank verse default-setting against which alexandrine couplets could be heard as pompous and decorative.

In the hundred years between Ronsard and Racine, tastes changed and the alexandrine became the norm for non-lyrical French verse. This was not because people began hearing the alexandrine itself as glittery and tuneful, but because the appetite for poetic spangliness had declined. Racine himself disdained the 'pointes et de misérables jeux de mots' ('conceits and wretched plays on words') which had been the rage in earlier generations; and the evidence of his revisions to his own texts shows him removing rather than inserting what might earlier have been regarded as whizzo special effects, as, for instance, in *Andromaque* 863, when the Trojan widow explains to Hermione that they are not rivals because she has eyes only for the

[25] Pierre de Ronsard, 'Au Lecteur apprentif', *Oeuvres complètes*, ii. 1015.

dead Hector, and hates Pyrrhus because he is the son of the man who killed her husband. Originally, the line read: 'Par les mains de son Père, hélas! j'ai vu percer' ('By his father's hands, alas, I saw struck down').[26] But Racine revised to: 'Par une main cruelle, hélas! j'au vu percer / Le seul, où mes regards prétendaient s'adresser' ('By a cruel hand, alas!, I saw struck down the only man on whom my gaze desired to turn').[27] And what he revised out here was the play of words on 'Père' and 'percer', with its implication that a father is a person who pierces and wounds, who 'fathers' (*père-cer*-s) by piercing and wounding (*percer*). He also removed the assonantal chime 'par'/'père', 'percer'. Roland Barthes, who takes a monolithically Oedipal view of Racine's plays, would perhaps have been dismayed that this searching pun, which so encapsulates his theory of the playwright's work, had been excised; I quite regret its disappearance myself, but then I have a depraved taste for verbal lurex. But Racine was probably actuated by the conviction that people in great distress—such as Andromaque here—do not have the leisure for elegant verbal play. It is a conviction which was shared by many English people from the late seventeenth century on, who came to feel that Shakespeare's relentless jokes, even in the direst circumstances, were a blot on his copy-book. It seems to me easy and essential to defend Shakespeare's habits in this respect, but you can do so without deluding yourself that Shakespeare should be the norm for all other writers, that there is nothing to be said for a more sobered language than came to us out of Stratford. Racine was close to the devout and hyper-intellectual circle at Port-Royal, and shared their rational suspicion of verbal play:

Combien le desir de faire une pointe a-t-il fait produire de fausses pensées? Combien la rime a-t-elle engagé de gens à mentir?

How often has the desire to score a verbal point led to distorted thinking? How often has rhyme entrapped people into a lie?[28]

'How often has the desire to score a verbal point led to distorted thinking?': you need only have listened to Prime Minister's Questions to take the force of that question. So those who think Racine writes in 'a strict and limiting rhyme-scheme' are labouring under a misapprehension produced by unreflectively applying to French norms derived

---

[26] Racine, *Andromaque*, III.iv.863 (original version), *Oeuvres complètes*, vol. I, p. 228.
[27] Racine, *Andromaque*, III.iv.863–4 (revised version), *Oeuvres complètes*, vol. I, p. 1359.
[28] Antoine Arnauld and Pierre Nicole, *La logique ou L'Art de penser* (Paris: Savreux, 1668), 358.

from what they learned at home. Alexandrine couplets came into fashion because they were *less* 'limiting' as a form than what had gone before, they were, as Ronsard heard them, easy-peasy because 'moins sujets', not to mention that 'limiting' is not, as some people suppose, a synonym of 'crippling'; any purposeful human activity has and needs recognized limits. Racine is not 'limited'—in the sense of 'frustrated' or 'inhibited'—by his couplets; you might as well think fish are imprisoned by water. You find fewer instances of localized verbal play in Racine than in Shakespeare, though there *are* cases like Oreste's 'Dans sa Cour, dans son Coeur, dis-moi ce qui passe' ('In his court, in his heart, tell me what's going on')[29] where the chime of 'Cour' and 'Coeur' goes deep into the civilizing process which is so central to the play, and where the alexandrine—if you listen to it—tells you that Oreste is more interested in the 'Coeur' than in the 'Cour' (so far as they can be disintricated), because the sixth syllable, where 'Coeur' is placed, is a structurally highlighted position in the line. The rhythm of the French line adds a dimension of meaning, which you'd need to translate as 'In his court, and, what's more, in his heart, tell me...' to bring out. What you find in place of a density of local quibbles is larger-scale structures of verbal recurrence which produce tight, enmeshing semantic complexes (Shakespeare has these large-scale structures too). These may be picked out by rhymes, as 'Hermione' is given its character as a word in the play by rhyming so often with 'abandonne' (about half of the rhymes on her name), or they may be words with more than one meaning such as 'flamme', a literal or a metaphorically erotic 'flame', the flames which burned Troy down and which continue to lick away at the heart of a person who is carrying a torch for another, a word whose complexity slowly dawns over the course of a play and which changes its sense according to the dramatic situation, as a well-cut gem refracts light at different angles when you turn it in your hand.

Or, to take an example from a different, much later play, consider the way that 'réparer' changes shape depending on where you view it from in *Athalie*, Racine's last work for the theatre. In the first scene, the devout Jew, Abner, comes to the temple and falls into conversation with Joad, the high priest; Abner, though he works for the pagan queen Athalie, still practises his faith, but he has given up hope, because the

---

[29] Racine, *Andromaque*, I.i.102, *Oeuvres complètes*, vol. 1, p. 202.

hope of the Jews lay in the line of David, and Abner believes (wrongly, as it will eventually turn out) that the royal line is extinct; the Jews are therefore condemned, he thinks, to servitude under heathen rulers. He puts his despair like this: 'Le Ciel même peut-il réparer les ruines / De cet arbre séché jusque dans ses racines?' ('Can even heaven itself repair the ruins of this tree which is withered right down to its roots?')[30] This is the only time the word 'racine' appears in the theatrical work of Racine, a cute fact, but the focal word in these lines is 'réparer'. From Abner, it expresses the impossible hope of a restoration of the line of David. It comes again later in the play from the mouth of his employer, the pagan queen Athalie, daughter of Jezebel, a hate-figure for devout Jews. Athalie has had a nightmare in which the ghost of her mother appeared to her and warned her of the terrible power of the Jewish God, a power Jezebel had herself felt when her body was torn apart in the street by dogs. This is how Jezebel looked when she appeared to Athalie:

> Même elle avait encor cet éclat emprunté,
> Dont elle eut soin de peindre et d'orner son visage,
> Pour réparer des ans l'irréparable outrage.

She even still had on that borrowed glamour with which she took pains to paint and decorate her face, so as to repair the irreparable devastation of the years.[31]

Here, the restoration which can come to the Jews only through a son of David is grotesquely refigured as the make-up on which old Jezebel relies to keep herself looking glam long after she has actually lost her looks. The coincidence in the word 'réparer' of the Jewish messianic hope and the vain desires of an ageing, pagan coquette could hardly be more sardonic. And it is in convergences like this over a long span that Racine's verbal imagination specializes, as, for instance, in the patterned recurrence of 'abattre', from Hermione's 'abbatue', used of Priam, to Oreste's 'abattre', used of Pyrrhus, or in the 'autel' ('altar') which recurs with a grim symmetry ten times in the lines between 996 and 1574 of *Andromaque*. In such details, we see that the dialect of tragedy can enact a form of lexical retribution, as if the words uttered took revenge on themselves.

---

[30] Racine, *Athalie*, I.i.139–40, *Oeuvres complètes*, vol. 1, p. 1021.
[31] Racine, *Athalie*, II.v.494–6, *Oeuvres complètes*, vol. 1, p. 1033.

The alexandrine is not monumental; it is unceremonious by the standards of poetic formality of its time rather than pompous and monolithic; it is not remote from the actualities of French speech; and it does not have a fixed rhythmic shape which audibly and predictably persists throughout a Racine play. There are thirty-six possible ways of dividing up an alexandrine, and it is rare in Racine for two consecutive lines to be subdivided in the same way (the first two consecutive rhythmically isomorphic lines in *Andromaque* are 14–15, and these lines are signalled as a couple by ostentatious rhetorical paralleling). Please forget the misleading phrase 'regular alexandrine'; it trips easily off the tongue, I know, but it does so only to trip you up and stop you listening and thinking. One main reason why English ears hear Racine so stodgily and dully is that English ears are tuned in to run-on or enjambement only at the line-end, whereas French lines of verse can also run on in the middle of a line, over the structural caesura at the sixth syllable. But the caesura at the sixth syllable is only notionally 'fixed'; it may be stronger or weaker, and it can be enjambed with an effect quite as strong in the French system as a terminal run-on in English. Take Abner's lines about the withered roots of Jewish hope: 'Le Ciel même peut-il réparer les ruines / De cet arbre séché jusque dans ses racines?' Neither of these lines has a strong break after the sixth syllable: a caesura must come at the end of sense-unit because a caesura combines an accent and a notional pause, and accents in French fall at the end of sense-units. But 'peut-il' is not a sense-unit, the auxiliary verb in its inverted form shows that it is part of a question which hasn't been properly framed till we get the main verb: 'The sky itself can it?', can it *what*? can it repair? The voice, in the urgency of Abner's despair, in his self-lacerating sarcasm about pious hopes for Jewish renewal, strides over the formal division at the sixth syllable. And it does so again in the next line, because the sense-unit does not end at 'withered'—the problem with the tree of the line of David is not that it is a bit withered, trees are often a bit withered, habitually so if they are deciduous; the branches look bare and tatty and yet the tree still comes back into leaf next spring. But the tree of Jewish messianic hope, the family tree of David, is 'withered-right-down-to-its-roots', even the bits underground which you can't see have withered and died. This wonderful and wholly typical couplet is, of course, open to performance in different ways by actors of different temperaments in productions of different styles; Racine's scripts are *exactly* like Shakespeare's in this respect.

I'll end with an example from Corneille, to give a bit more general application to the point about how important it is to listen in to the middles as well as the ends of lines in French verse. Prusias, the king of Bithynia, is in a pickle, or 'dilemma' as it is called in the dialect of tragedy; he has conflicting demands to meet from several directions, from his Roman imperial masters, from his wife, and from his eldest son, Nicomède. Here are the father and son trying to sort out the mess they're in:

PRUSIAS

Mais donnons quelque chose à Rome, qui se plaint,	3+5+4
Et tâchons d'assurer la Reine qui te craint.	3+3+2+4
J'ai tendresse pour toi, j'ai passion pour elle,	3+3+4+2
Et je ne veux pas voir cette haine éternelle,	6+3+3
Ni que des sentiments, que j'aime à voir durer,	1+5+2+4
Ne règnent dans mon coeur que pour le déchirer.	2+4+6
J'y veux mettre d'accord l'Amour, et la Nature,	6+2+4
Etre père, et mari dans cette conjuncture...	3+3+6

NICOMÈDE

Seigneur, voulez-vous bien vous en fier à moi?	2+4+4+2
Ne soyez l'un, ni l'autre.	4+2

PRUSIAS

Et que dois-je être?	+5

NICOMÈDE

Roi.	+1

PRUSIAS

But let's pay some heed to Rome, which has grounds for complaint, and let's try to reassure the Queen, who's afraid of you. I'm very fond of you, but I'm infatuated with her, and I can't stand the sight of this endless hatred, nor can I bear that feelings which I'd like to see last should reign in my heart only to tear it to bits. I'm trying to harmonize love and natural affection in my heart, trying to be both father and husband in this tricky situation...

NICOMÈDE

My lord, will you be so good as to trust my advice about this? Don't be either father or husband.

PRUSIAS

What would you have me be then?

NICOMÈDE

King.[32]

---

[32] Corneille, *Nicomède* (1651), IV.iii.1903–18, in *Oeuvres complètes*, 3 vols., ed. Georges Couton (Paris: Gallimard, 1984), vol. 2, p. 691.

I list in the right-hand margin the subdivisions of twelve, as I hear them, in each of the lines. You can see at a glance that no two consecutive lines are in the same shape. Even the first two lines in the extract, which look similar because each begins 'conjunction + first person plural imperative' ('Mais donnons... Et tachons') and each ends 'relative pronoun + object pronoun + third person singular present tense verb' ('qui se plaint, qui te craint') are not identical to my ears, because I think the syntagmatic constraint which holds 'donner quelque chose a quelqu'un' together is tighter than that which joins units separated by the caesura in the second line. A sense of what the lines *mean* is what governs their rhythm, and this is why it is so drastic a mistake to hear their rhythm as uniform or predictable, because when you do that, you also flatten out all the dramatic edges and peaks of human interactive meaning which the lines carry. Rhythm is an essential element in the interpretation of the lines, because rhythm in French marks out sense-units. Disagreement is often possible—as here, someone might argue for hearing the lines as isomorphic, dividing both up 3+5+4, and such a person could argue in favour of hearing the lines as rhythmically parallel just because they are so syntactically parallel. Or take the third line: its two halves are evidently mirrors of each other syntactically:

First person pronoun + verb + noun + preposition + personal pronoun (twice)

but the two hemistichs are not rhythmically identical (3+3, 4+2), and neither could they be interchanged, putting the first second and vice versa (setting aside that 'toi' would then be the rhyme-word), because the second half of the line has a sense of augmentation or crescendo, requiring as it does that 'passion' be pronounced, according to a standard poetic licence, as having four syllables—an effect I try to bring out by translating as 'I'm very fond of you, but I'm infatuated with her'—the rhythmic shape of the second hemistich needs to be heard as implying a strong vocal emphasis. Or take the last line quoted, divided into three between the two speakers. Lines divided between speakers repay close attention because they set a tricky task for the actors, who have to rehearse thoroughly to be sure of picking up the cue smartly, even more so when the second speaker is interrupting the first. These exchanges between speakers usually occur at moments of heightened pressure in the dialogue, so they are also good places to check the emotional temperature of a scene. Because the alexandrine has a formal division at the sixth syllable, speaker-switch at that point is the smoothest in terms of versification and likely therefore to be the calmest in terms of the human dynamic. Speaker-switch at other points in the line is more likely to be an interruption or driven by strong interactive forces, and—as a general rule—the more asymmetrical the division of the line, the choppier the human waters it charts. So here, Corneille arranges the last line so that the word 'Roi', a word of the greatest political and human potency in these plays as in the world in which they were written, is thrown into maximally high relief by coming alone as the last syllable of the line, an exceptional way of subdividing twelve. Coming from a son to a father, from a prince to a king, telling him how to behave himself, it should have in our imaginations as we read it a sharp impact, and, if the actor playing Nicomède knows his business, the word will have the effect on stage which Stendhal attributed to the mention of politics in a work of art: it will come like a pistol-shot in the theatre.[33]

---

[33] Stendhal, *The Charterhouse of Parma*, trans. Margaret Mauldon (Oxford: Oxford University Press, 2009), 414.

8

Kafka's relations

Two beginnings:

Als Gregor Samsa eines Morgens aus unruhigen Träumen erwachte, fand er sich in seinem Bett zu einem ungeheueren Ungeziefer verwandelt.

When Gregor Samsa awoke one morning from troubled dreams, he found himself transformed in his bed into a verminous monster.[1]

Jemand mußte Josef K. verleumdet haben, denn ohne daß er etwas Böses getan hätte, wurde er eines Morgens verhaftet.

Someone must have slandered Josef K., for, though he had done nothing wrong, one morning he was arrested.[2]

The sentences have much in common: each names, though in a slightly different way, the male protagonist of the story which is to follow; each protagonist appears as the passive object of the verb, a verb which carries the main informational force of the sentence, its shock, and which is delayed to the end of the sentence (*verwandelt*, 'transformed'; *verhaftet*, 'arrested'); both sentences have that matter-of-fact delivery of the odd, the upsetting, or the disarrayed which is a widely recognized element of what we now call the 'Kafkaesque', though the recognition and the term for it can hardly have existed when the sentences were first published. They also share the phrase 'eines Morgens', 'one morning'.

It is extremely usual for fictional narratives to begin with some indication of their setting in space or time or both; just because it is usual, it bears thinking about. In the case of historical novels, or 'factions',

---

[1] Franz Kafka, 'Die Verwandlung' ('The Metamorphosis'), written 1912, published 1915, in *Sämtliche Erzählungen*, ed. Paul Raabe (Frankfurt am Main: Fischer, 1994), 56.
[2] Franz Kafka, *Der Proceß* (*The Trial*), written 1914–15, posthumously published 1925, ed. Malcolm Pasley (Frankfurt am Main: Fischer, 1994), 'Verhaftung' ('Arrest'), 9.

marking the time of the story has an evident point; *War and Peace* concerns Napoleon's Russian campaign, and so there is little curious about the fact that its second paragraph begins: 'It was on a July evening in 1805. . . .'[3] There are innumerably various points to such dating of a fiction. But Kafka's sentences do not 'date'; they only 'time'. That is, each begins on 'one morning', but we do not know when that morning is. It might seem otiose to signal so abstractly that a fictional narrative occurs in time, for in what else could it occur? The habit of such fictional timing perhaps compares with the schoolchild's habit of marking in his or her textbooks the where and when of the act of inscribing one's name. You recall:

Eric Griffiths, 26, Liverpool Institute, Liverpool, England, Europe, The World, The Universe, In Time, In Space.

Much here is informationally superfluous; if I was in England, I was by that token in Europe, and if in Europe . . . and so on. Perhaps I was so unsure of my own place under the sun that I needed to pass myself memos of my own address. As with the timing of fictional narratives, the fact that I wrote such things in my book is of interest because I was doing something very usual; many others did the same, and I may have done so only because many others did so too. Had I been the only one, I might rightly have been singled out for reproof as a notable vandal or sent for treatment and compassion as suffering from deficiencies in socialization. But the habit was rife at 11, as the habit of 'one morning' or its equivalents is rife in our fictions. As a habit, marking textbooks attests to a more general need among the young to register the world's mark on them and, at the same time, to make their mark on the world. I mean: when a child is handed a textbook, it receives a small slice of an extensive culture. Implicit in the book are many human practices of gathering, storing, and spreading information, and many further practices (trade, law, human tradition, conquest) which are implicit in those practices. All books, having themselves histories, are in that sense history-books. The book locates the child, because the book is part of a mesh of human skills and doings, and the child is one point in that mesh, a dot on the graph-paper the species has drawn and is drawing. On the other hand, the child holds the book, may encounter it with

---

[3] Leo Tolstoy, *War and Peace* (1869), trans. Rosemary Edmonds, 2 vols., rev. edn. (Harmondsworth: Penguin, 1978), vol. 1, p. 3.

varying degrees of blankness, intimidation, or defiance. Thus, the long address 'Eric Griffiths... In Time, In Space' says both 'I am *here*' (acculturated in this specific way rather than that, speaking this as my native language, in this school) and also '*I* am here' (you think I am merely a grid-reference on a map others have drawn but, from where I stand, the map unfolds from me, I am its scale). And such a double assertion is implicit in fictional phrases like 'eines Morgens', as they serve to locate the story they launch somewhere amid the many recountings, the mass of information, of previous culture (the phrase is a narrative formula, a sign of club-membership in the Narrators' Circle) and, at the same time, by an act of free specification, individuate that story, give it an identity of its own (the phrase is not only an instance of something more general but also its particular self, occurring here, with such and such, as yet unknown, jobs to do in this tale, for 'eines Morgens' does not mean 'any old morning' but 'one particular any old morning'): they admit that the fiction is in history and yet maintain that it is not simply of history. For 'one morning' is not a historical claim, any more than 'once upon a time' refers to a time which any clock has ever shown or will be able to show.

Kafka's sentences have something in common with the start of Gogol's 'The Nose': 'On March 25th there occurred in Petersburg an extremely strange thing.'[4] One strange thing that occurs in Gogol's story is that there dawns a March 25th which is the March 25th of no particular year. Nor is this 'March 25th' quite like, say, 'May 1st' in so far as 'May 1st' is 'May Day'—that is, the May is of no particular year because it is the May Day of any and every suitable year since the custom of observing May Day was instituted. The 'extremely strange thing' that happened is 'extremely strange' because it does not happen often, certainly not with annual regularity. And yet any real March 25th must come directly after a March 24th and just before a March 26th, and, applying this logic, must then have a unique place in a temporal series—that is, to be 'a' March 25th, it must be a specific March 25th, that is, the March 25th of this year rather than that. But Gogol's day is not on the calendar of any recorded or recordable year. If we tried to find the day by assuming that Gogol is employing here the convention

---

[4] Nikolai Gogol, 'The Nose' (1836), in *The Complete Tales of Nikolai Gogol,* trans. Constance Garnett, ed. Leonard J. Kent, 2 vols. (London: University of Chicago Press, 1985), vol. 2, p. 215 (the translation of Gogol's opening sentence differs slightly in this edition from the version given above).

of loose reference to time we ordinarily use when making arrangements for the near future or remembering the recent past, when we say 'OK, July 11th it is then' or 'But I sent the letter on March 12th', that is, the convention of assuming that the date named falls within the twelve-month period in which we find ourselves at the moment of utterance, we could give a date to his March 25th, orienting ourselves from the date of publication of the story—it is March 25th of either 1835 or 1836, depending on exactly when the story first appeared. But this solution, though it has its attractions, misses the point of Gogol's placing his story both in time, 'March 25th', and out of time, 'March 25th of no year', a point made succinctly in one entry of his 'Diary of a Madman' which is headed: 'No date. The day didn't have one.'[5]

The date on which the story was published can in principle be established; the date on which the story begins cannot. So we could not on the basis of the story have said on March 25th 1995, 'today is the 160th or 159th anniversary of an extremely strange thing happening in St Petersburg, at least so Gogol alleges'. That is, because Gogol's story floats in and out of temporal series, we too are adrift; we cannot date ourselves with regard to its events. Another example may make this clearer, a Dickensian version of 'eines Morgens':

Thirty years ago, Marseilles lay burning in the sun, one day. A blazing sun upon a fierce August day was no greater rarity in southern France then, than at any other time, before or since.[6]

If the 'now' from which *Little Dorrit* measures its 'thirty years ago' is the year in which these opening sentences were first published (1 December 1855), the novel begins in 1825; if we count back from its first publication in one volume, from its first 'finished' state, it opens in 1827. Either date is OK, and neither date is right. Because *Little Dorrit* opens thirty years before someone begins reading it, its system of dating is to some extent internal to the fiction itself, you cannot replace 'Thirty years ago' with 'In 1820-something' without altering the bearing of historical time on the fiction, the fiction's elusion of date. Dickens begins by specifying a unique spot in time, 'one day'; he then makes it more

---

[5] Nikolai Gogol, 'Diary of a Madman' (1835), in *The Complete Tales of Nikolai Gogol*, vol. 1, p. 255 (the translation of Gogol's heading differs slightly in this edition from the version given above).

[6] Charles Dickens, *Little Dorrit* (1855–7), ed. Harvey Peter Sucksmith (Oxford: Oxford University Press, 2012), 15.

definite—it is an August day; then he tells us that there is nothing special about this day he has taken the trouble to specify, it was 'no greater rarity...then, than at any other time, before or since'. No doubt, part of the impact of the novel's magnificently virtuosic opening was, for readers poring over the first instalment, that it switched on the blaze of Mediterranean sunlight amid an English December; it transported them. Yet the novel may continue to do this, even if read in Marseilles on a fierce August day. And it can continue to do this partly because 'one day' is not a date but the signal of a permanent possibility. In fiction, we signal permanent possibilities by phrases such as 'one day' or 'eines Morgens'; they mean: allow that this happened 'once' (and the point of allowing that, is that you will recognize that it could happen again). A story must begin somewhere—there must be a 'March 25th', 'eines Morgens', or suchlike—but what it begins is a parable about experience in time quite generally understood, and so the specific time named is an example of time itself and not only a date in time. Much the same applies to place. I could put my point another way: a story must begin somewhere, but when does 'story' begin? I might in principle be able to say when and where I first read 'Die Verwandlung', but when, exactly, did I first become able to read it *as a story*, when did I acquire the concept 'story' and exercise the understanding of that concept which shows when I do not, reading *Little Dorrit*, ask fretfully, as I might were *Little Dorrit* not a novel but a chronicle: 'yes, but was it 1825 or 1827?' 'Story' antedates all the stories we read, partly because almost everybody learns 'story' before he or she learns to read, by being told stories, and it is to that prehistory of story that the combined precision and imprecision of such phrases as 'eines Morgens' point. Knowing how to read a story as a story is a skill, and there is no one time or date which can be assigned to the acquisition of a skill; in this respect, understanding a story is like knowing how to count: we cannot say to a child 'Now I will read you your first story' any more than we can say 'Now I will show you how to do your first sum'. As Wittgenstein asked: 'Would it mean anything to say: "I want to shew you how 8 x 9 first made 72?"'[7] Or to say: I shall now tell you when 'eines Morgens' was. The skill of 'reading stories', like that of calculating, dawns on us; it does not occur at a specifiable time.

---

[7] Ludwig Wittgenstein, *Remarks on the Foundation of Mathematics*, trans. G. E. M. Anscombe, ed. G. H. von Wright and R. Rhees, 3rd edn. (Oxford: Basil Blackwell, 1978), 'Part VI, point 4', p. 307.

These are more than logical wrinkles such as might interest a philosopher who was trying to articulate the logic of fictional discourse. They affect the way in which we 'take' stories. When Josef K. first speaks to a court, he remarks:

Was mir geschehen ist...was mir geschehen ist, ist ja nur ein einzelner Fall und als solcher nich sehr wichtig, da ich es nicht sehr schwer nehme, aber es ist das Zeichnen eines Verfahrens wie es gegen viele geübt wird. Für diese stehe ich hier, nicht für mich.

What has happened to me...what has happened to me is, is indeed merely an isolated case and, as such, not very important, anyway I don't take it very seriously, but it is symptomatic of a procedure to which many others fall victim. And it is for those others that I stand up here, not for myself.[8]

If 'once upon a time' or 'eines Morgens' or suchlike had the logical force of specifying a unique location in time for a specific event (as when A. J. P. Taylor writes 'at 2.41 a.m. on 7 May [1945] the Germans signed an instrument of unconditional surrender on all fronts at Eisenhower's headquarters'),[9] then a story introduced by such a phrase would have the interest only of the facts that it recorded. In the case of the German surrender, such interest is considerable; many other events, however, occurred at 2.41 a.m. on 7 May 1945, most of them unrecorded and of no interest even to those who were involved in them— someone yawned, probably; someone else ate a sardine, no doubt. Such events are 'isolated case[s] and, as such, not very important'; written down and offered to others' attention, they would be at best items for a 'human interest' story in a newspaper. A case such as that of Josef K. or Gregor Samsa, though, is an 'einzelner Fall' but also, as Josef K. says, a 'Zeichen', a token, a sign, of something more general than itself, as the 'Morgen' on which their cases begin is a specific time and an example of time itself and what it can bring into being. A basic purpose of fiction, that is, is to stand as instance to an as yet unstated rule, to stand, as Josef K. stands before the court, not only for himself but for all those others whose case is relevantly similar. And this is one central sense in which we can speak of fiction as 'representative' as well as 'representational'.

---

[8] Franz Kafka, *Der Proceß.* 'Erste Untersuchung' ('First Investigation'), 52.
[9] A. J. P. Taylor, *English History, 1914–1915* (first published 1965 as vol. 15 of *The Oxford History of England*), ed. Sir George Clark, 2nd edn. (Oxford: Oxford University Press, 2001), 593.

Everything hinges on the demure qualifying phrase 'relevantly similar' in the formulation 'all those others whose case is relevantly similar'. Considered from one angle, hardly anybody has a case 'relevantly similar' to that of Gregor Samsa and his family, turning into a giant bug being an exceptionally rare occurrence. On the other hand, the very fantasticality of the tale has often been understood as licensing unbridled allegorization, so that all the specific details of the story count for nothing (or at least any detail inconvenient to an exegete can be discounted); all cases can be treated as relevantly similar to this one because it concerns a supposed 'human condition' in the extreme abstract, and Kafka's fiction can be made to yield up at will any nostrum which satisfies a reader or made to confirm any pre-existent model (Marxist, psychoanalytical, Christian-existentialist) that may have been brought to it. Yet a piece of evidence which counts equally for two or more mutually contradictory propositions counts in fact for none, and is probably not evidence at all. All fictions, I repeat, stand in some way as instances to an as yet unstated rule, but to understand and say how they stand is a question of some delicacy, a matter of which kind of story we happen to be reading; the failure of allegorical readings of Kafka's stories is not that they are mistaken, it is that they have not begun to be readings of *Kafka* because they have not asked: 'what kind of story is this?'

It is easy to be misled in such matters because different kinds of story use the same equipment to different ends (a great deal of excitement in narratology and historiography has arisen from a failure to heed this fact). Take, for instance, the word *einmal*, which serves in the classic German fairytale as collected by the Brothers Grimm the function that 'once upon a time' serves in English (such tales remained among Kafka's preferred kinds of reading throughout his life). Thus, many tales begin: 'Es war einmal ein König...' or 'Es jagte einmal ein König in einem großen Wald...' or 'Es war einmal ein armer Mann, ...' ('Once upon a time there was a king...'; 'Once upon a time a king was out hunting in an enormous wood...'; 'Once upon a time there was a poor man...').[10] The function of *einmal* at the beginning of a fairytale is not to make, nor to pretend to make, a claim about an occurrence which happened on one occasion (as when, if someone

---

[10] Jakob and Wilhelm Grimm, *Kinder- und Hausmärchen*, 2 vols., 5th edn. (Leipzig: P. Reclam, 1843); for such openings to tales, see e.g. vol. 1, pp. 55, 101, 286; vol. 2, pp. 71, 174.

asked me, 'Have you ever been to Prague?', I might reply 'Yes, once'); rather, it means: 'This tale is the kind of tale in which anything can happen' (consider the difference in terms of your guess about what might follow if I began telling you a story, 'Once upon a time, when I was in Prague' or 'Once when I was in Prague'). One sign that in fairytales we are not dealing with unique events concerning individual agents is the fact that very many tales in the Brothers Grimm's collection begin 'Es war einmal ein König…', without its ever arising as a problem whether the *König* mentioned is the same *König* as the one in the previous story, or his brother, or his enemy; nor is this *König* usually named. But how 'Die Verwandlung' would itself be transformed if its 'eines Morgens' became the fairytale 'einmal', if there were many tales beginning, 'When Gregor Samsa awoke one morning from troubled dreams' and continuing in various ways:'he found that he had won the lottery', 'he found that he had turned into a narratologist', and so on. In the fairytale, the *einmal* introduces events permutable in very numerous ways, where the specific permutations may not matter as long as they follow some rather general rules (hero or heroine will not die, evil characters will be defeated, and so on) and where, in inverse proportion to the fantasticality of event, some fundamental values will be solidly maintained—loyalty rewarded, cunning triumph over force, and so on.

Contrast this with an *einmal* from Kafka's unfinished novel *Der Verschollene* (*The Man Who Disappeared*), which tells the story of Karl Rossmann's adventures after he has been sent away from home (characteristic Grimm motif) because he was seduced by a female servant and got her pregnant (utterly uncharacteristic Grimm motif). This is part of the passage, some thirty pages in, when we hear Karl's version of the seduction which precipitates the narrative; Karl is about 16 when the event takes place, the servant twice his age. There are three sentences beginning *Manchmal* ('Sometimes'), describing skittish and puzzling behaviour on her part, from which nothing results. Then:

Einmal aber sagte sie 'Karl!' und führte ihn, der noch über die unerwartete Ansprache staunte, unter Grimassen seufzend in ihr Zimmerchen, das sie zusperrte…und legte ihn in ihr Bett, als wolle sie ihn von jetzt niemandem mehr lassen und ihn streicheln und pflegen bis zum Ende der Welt.

One time, though, she said 'Karl!' and led him, astonished as he still was at this unprecedented way of addressing him, amid sighs and odd gesticulations, to her tiny room, and locked the door…and laid him on her bed, as if she would never give him up to anyone and would stroke and tend him to the end of the world.[11]

Here, as shows in the way *einmal* breaks the anaphoric sequence at the start of four consecutive sentences—an exceptionally rare, rhetorical obviousness in Kafka—'Manchmal... Manchmal... Manchmal... Manchmal... Einmal' ('Sometimes... Sometimes... Sometimes... One time'), *einmal* really is an operator whose function is to mark a single occurrence, to emphasize how her behaviour on one occasion broke from the past as also to stress the implications of fracture this one event is to have for Karl's future. Hence the quiet poignancy with which Kafka frames this seduction between an 'Einmal' and a 'bis zum Ende der Welt' ('until the end of the world'). The 'once upon a time' of fairytale never anticipates 'the end of time' (this is one feature which distinguishes fairytale from myth), but rather an 'ever after' or 'for the rest of their lives'.

Let me give another instance of how Kafka learned to make time pass in his stories from stories like those in the great collection of the Brothers Grimm. Once again, there is a lexical identity between the fairytale and how Kafka relates events, but this lexical identity coexists with a radical divergence of purpose in the telling. Locutions such as 'In dem Augenblicke...' or 'Kaum hatte sie...' ('At the very moment when...', 'Scarcely had she...') are typical of the folktale; here is the Sleeping Beauty pricking her finger on the spindle in the Grimms' version:

Kaum hatte sie aber die Spindel angerührt, so ging der Zauberspruch in Erfüllung, und sie stach damit.
In dem Augenblicke aber, wo sie den Stich empfand, fiel sie auch nieder in einen tiefen Schlaf.

Scarcely had she touched the spindle when the spell was fulfilled, and she pricked herself with it.
And at the very moment that she pricked her finger, she fell down in a deep sleep.[12]

The narrative heavily underscores the relation here between cause and effect: by the repeated 'aber' (which I have not been able to

---

[11] Franz Kafka, *Der Verschollene* (*The Man Who Disappeared*; also known as *America*), posthumously published 1927, ed. Max Brod (Frankfurt am Main: Fischer, 1994), 'Der Heizer' ('The Stoker'), 35–6.

[12] Jakob and Wilhelm Grimm, 'Dornröschen', in *Kinder- und Hausmärchen*, vol. 1, p. 295.

translate); with the formulaic locutions 'Kaum hatte sie...' and 'In dem Augenblicke...'; by the explicit 'so ging der Zauberspruch...'. And this is a world of magical causality, where the seamless interconnection of the words of the narrative stands for the inescapable potency of the spell that has been cast. Though 'at the very moment when', evidently, orients the events in time with regard to one another (it says they happen simultaneously), simultaneity in this kind of tale betokens a logical equivalence; we might almost rewrite the informational content of the passage as: 'Enchanted spindle + injured finger = deep sleep', where '=' is the best translation of 'In dem Augenblicke'. Now take the same phrase in *Der Verschollene*. Karl is visiting a rich man's house, has been variously bewildered by what goes on there, and wants to get back to his uncle who has told him he must be home by midnight. He is caught reluctantly in the middle of a pointless conversation about interior design when:

In diesem Augenblick erklangen zwölf Glockenschläge...Karl fühlte das Wehen der großen Bewegung dieser Glocken an den Wangen. Was war das für ein Dorf, das solche Glocken hatte!

At that very moment there rang out twelve strokes of a bell...Karl could feel on his cheeks the wind which arose from the mighty motion of this bell. What sort of a village could it be which had bells like that![13]

Much here is archetypal of the fairytale—the enchanted significance invested in midnight, the dramatic intrusion of a chiming clock, even the gigantism implied by the fact that the bell which tolls is so large it stirs a breeze that can be felt across a considerable distance. Yet Kafka's very moment of midnight has none of the logico-causal quality of a fairytale's 'In dem Augenblicke'; there has been no *Zauberspruch* ('spell') uttered which is now fulfilled—and, particularly Kafkaesque, the consequences which follow for Karl from these chimes have not been foretold and, though drastic, are largely unexplained in anything which follows. Simultaneity does not here imply a logical relation between events; indeed, it is just the lack of logical relation between what immediately precedes the chiming and the chiming itself which the prose chooses to emphasize. A traditional narrative motion, 'at that very moment', has been preserved into a context where its significance, if it

---

[13] Franz Kafka, *Der Verschollene*, 'Ein Landhaus bei New York' ('A Country House in New York'), 95.

has any, reverses that which it traditionally had; 'at that very moment' now means 'the absence, the withdrawal, of the meaning which "at that very moment" used to have'. This profoundly Kafkaesque turn to storytelling, this abeyance of a traditional sense even as the traditional form persists, is even clearer in his handling of other words which perform, though less obtrusively, similar functions to 'at that very moment', words like *da* ('as') or *gerade* ('just then'). Thus, in an early tale:

Als er aufblickte, biß gerade die Krämerin in ein Stück Kuchen, das mit brauner Marmelade bedeckt war.

As he looked up, the shopwoman was just biting into a piece of cake that was spread with a dark-coloured jam.[14]

No amount of ingenuity will find a causal or logical connection between Raban's looking-up and the shopwoman's biting. And, though we cannot be sure, because the story is unfinished, it is probably safe to say that the looking-up, and the biting, and the cake, and the fact that the jam was dark rather than light in colour, have no 'special significance'; none of these details happens in fulfilment of a spell or any other schematization of the world through human words. These details are merely details, the rule of which they are instances is the extremely important, though messy, rule: 'Not all details are instances of the operation of a rule.' It is true in a way that such characteristic Kafka moments serve towards his representation of a godforsaken world—by which I mean, a world without legible, spiritual significances, significances thought of as in some sense coming from outside the world, a world in which things 'just happen' or happen 'by accident', a world of which in its entirety it makes no sense to ask the question 'why?' And in so far as that is the case, then the very abeyances of sense in the connective tissues of Kafka's fictional world can themselves be allegorized as recording the alleged death of God and the supposedly consequent dereliction of a sense of metaphysical orderliness or significance in the events of our spatio-temporal existence or 'world'. Personally, I am as unconvinced by the notion of Kafka's stories as symbolic messages about not-God (thus conceived as the supra-mundane source of the intelligibility of human life) as I am by the matching notion of his stories as symbolic messages about God (equally thus conceived as the supra-mundane source of the intelligibility of human life). It is only

---

[14] Franz Kafka, 'Hochzeitsvorbereitungen auf dem Lande' ('Wedding Preparations in the Country'), written 1907–8, posthumously published 1957, in *Sämtliche Erzählungen*, 244.

one kind of theology which conceives God in this way, though many literary intellectuals talk as if this were the only possible kind of God; from other theological points of view, God thus conceived has a striking resemblance to the devil. There are, that is, religious traditions in which an attention to the contours of this world without desire or attempt to read them as iconic of a transcendent world is itself a religious act, a mode of recognizing the transcendent rather than all that is left to us when we no longer believe in it. In such traditions, it makes sense to say 'Attention is the natural prayer of the soul', or to remark, as did a devout Hasid (a form of Judaism for which Kafka showed more than usual sympathy) when asked why he had gone to visit a famous rabbi:'I did not go to the "Maggid" of Meseritz to learn Torah [the divine law] from him but to watch him tie his bootlaces.'[15] And secondly: it is charming, in the way that superstitions are often charming, to believe that fictional practices line up in point-for-point correspondence with convictions about how the non-fictional world is constituted. But for all its charm, this is merely a superstition: human fictional worlds are all, of course, made in this world, but from this it does not follow that all such fictional worlds are pictures of this world. From the fact that Dickens's novels mostly have happy endings, you cannot infer that either he or his audience believed that things generally turn out for the best in the end.

We must go a longer, less immediately charming way to understand how details mean in Kafka's writing, how his fictions are instances of rules. Impatience with detail is a characteristic of one of Kafka's most memorable late creations, the dog who speaks the 'Forschungen eines Hundes' ('A Dog's Researches'; the title was supplied by Max Brod). This dog is a tired yet also tireless student of his own species; he sometimes wonders, though, whether his discoveries add anything to the great commandment each mother-dog teaches her young when she sends them into the world, 'Wet everything you possibly can' (which translates, for us humans, into the observation that a main purpose of many dogs' lives seems to be to piss everywhere possible):

Was hat die Forschung, von unseren Urvätern angefangen, entscheidend Wesentliches denn hinzuzufügen? Einzelheiten, Einzelheiten und wie unsicher ist alles. Diese Regel aber wird bestehen, solange wir Hunde sind.

[15] Gerson Scholem, 'Ninth Lecture: Hasidism: The Latest Phase', in *Major Trends in Jewish Mysticism* (1941), 3rd edn. (New York: Schocken, 1995), 325–50 (p. 344).

What has research, since the day when our ancestors began it, of decisive importance to add to this? Details, details, and how unreliable they all are. This rule, though, will stand fast, as long as there are dogs like us.[16]

There is a human inclination to believe that rules are more durable, firmer, harder, more crystalline than the instances they govern, instances which by comparison to the rule which governs them are ephemeral, frail, and unclear. Literary scholars, for instance, feel they have gained knowledge, secured their grasp on a piece of writing, when they can spot within it tropes or conventions or topoi, because tropes, conventions, and topoi all operate at a higher level of generality than any particular feature of a specific text; to be able to classify the less general under a more general heading is widely regarded as some sort of epistemic advance. Students of narrative feel similarly about being able to classify together characters from different texts under the heading of some 'type'—the 'repressed spinster', the 'unreliable father'—or about being able to identify certain recurrent narrative motifs—the prohibition, the giving of a magical gift—in apparently very dissimilar tales. So too, a psychological researcher might rejoice in the discovery that three distinct individuals were all suffering from the same 'basic' complex, as a social scientist might have the sensation of striding forward when he covered a domestic quarrel, a riot in the streets, and a civil war with one term such as 'conflict-situation'. It seems likely that one reason for such an inclination to prize the rule over the instance is that a model of human knowledge, developed in the physical sciences some centuries ago, has migrated to the human sciences, without having its credentials checked at the frontier. One aspect of this model of scientific knowledge is the quite rational presumption (rational for the physical sciences, I mean) that an explanatory law is deep just in proportion to the number of particular instances which it can govern—thus, if I have three laws each of which explains three phenomena, and you produce a single law which accounts for all nine phenomena, your law is to that extent 'deeper' than mine. There seems no good reason to accept this model for humane sciences such as the interpretation of literature and its history, and some good reasons not to rely on it uncritically. Humane understanding need not express itself in laws whose power

---

[16] Franz Kafka, 'Forschungen eines Hundes' ('A Dog's Researches'), written probably 1922, posthumously published 1931, in *Sämtliche Erzählungen*, 331.

or explanatory depth is measured in terms of the number of instances which they govern: on the contrary, humane understanding is expressed rather by the articulation of what Hegel called the 'concrete universal', that is, through the preserving and recognizing of the particular in the light of those greater regularities through which the individual is individuated.[17] Thus, there is certainly a narrative convention which I have described when talking about the phrase 'In dem Augenblicke', 'at that very moment', which could be called the convention that simultaneity implies either causal interrelatedness or logical equivalence or both; this convention operates even in Kafka's stories, though it operates there in a complex and individual way, is reinflected so that its significance is sometimes suspended, sometimes ironized, and so on. It is not clear that a scholar who merely tagged the passage about the chiming bells from *Der Verschollene* as '*Augenblick*-convention' would have taken a step forward in his understanding either of the passage or of the convention. Equally, there is evidently a satisfaction to be gained from 'diagnosing' Kafka—alienated intellectual, father-fixated, manic-depressive, ethnically and linguistically marginalized, what have you. There are many alienated intellectuals, though, whole herds of the father-fixated, but there is only one Kafka. This is not to deny that each or all of these terms might apply to this lovely individual soul, only to remind ourselves that if we are trying to describe his individuality, we may not be simply assisted by possessing handfuls of such terms, whose power, such as it is, resides in their ability to cancel the individual instance and bring it under a rule.

From the point of view of the researching dog, the rule is firm and, from the heights of its firmness, it relegates all that is not the rule to the status of mere 'detail', 'Einzelheiten, Einzelheiten'. So too, a scientist of the human might classify, say, me as, say, 'oral compulsive' because of various features of my behaviour, and dismiss my presentation of counter-instances as mere *Einzelheiten*. Yet it is possible to take a different line on 'details', as, for instance, Kafka did in the opening paragraph of his *Brief an den Vater* (*Letter to the Father*), the long letter he composed towards his father in 1919, his most strenuous attempt at justice, and

---

[17] Georg Wilhelm Friedrich Hegel, 'Preface: Of Scientific Cognition', in *Phenomenology of Spirit* (1807), trans. A. V. Miller (Oxford: Clarendon Press, 1977), 2–46 (p. 17).

which begins (note the fully historical, reporting use of 'einmal'; this is not a fairytale):

Liebster Vater,
Du hast mich letzthin einmal gefragt, warum ich behaupte, ich hätte Furcht vor Dir. Ich wußte Dir, wie gewöhnlich, nichts zu antworten, zum Teil eben aus der Furcht, die ich vor Dir habe, zum Teil deshalb, weil zur Begründung dieser Furcht zu viele Einzelheiten gehören, als daß ich sie im Reden halbwegs zusammenhalten könnte.

Dearest Father,
You asked me once recently what I meant by saying I was afraid of you. I had no answer to give you, partly indeed because I am afraid of you, and partly because too many individual details went to make up this fear for me to be able to talk about them even half-coherently.

Kafka's concern, as he writes—he hopes, fairly—to his father, is with those details, even though he knows this concern will make his letter—it is eighty printed pages long—'sehr unvollständig' ('very incomplete')[18]. He absolutely does not seek a rule or set of rules which will arrange those details, or enable him to gain a vantage on them from, as it were, above them, from a higher plane of generality. A higher plane of generality would be of no use to him, for it was not on that plane he met his father; this letter is written from one *Einzelwesen* ('individual') to another, and its proper language is therefore a language of *Einzelheiten*, 'individualnesses', 'details'. A rule, even or especially a rule which is guaranteed to 'stand fast', would be of no use to him or to his father, let alone to the long abrasion of their life in common.

And, anyway, it is not always the firmness but sometimes the flexibility of rules which stands us in good stead. Or perhaps it would be better to say: take it as a rule that no rule is ever firmer than its applicability to instances. Let me try to explain that gnomic maxim through an instance. Kafka wrote many stories in which the central protagonist is an animal; 'Die Verwandlung' is his first masterpiece in this vein. At least since Aesop, it has been a usual human practice to write fictions, with animals as characters, which point morals about human behaviour; making animals the protagonists seems long to have been thought to be a way of simplifying out the details, so that the rule the stories exemplify would shine forth the more clearly. Here is one of Aesop's fables in

---

[18] Franz Kafka, *Brief an den Vater* (*Letter to the Father*), written 1919, posthumously published 1953, ed. Max Brod (Frankfurt am Main: Fischer, 1990), 5.

Sir Roger L'Estrange's English, along with part of Sir Roger's attempts to comment on it:

A *Wolf* had got a Bone in's Throat, and could think of no better Instrument to ease him of it, than the Bill of a *Crane*; so he went and treated with a *Crane* to help him out with it, upon condition of a very considerable Reward for his Pains. The *Crane* did him the good Office, and then claim'd his Promise. Why how now Impudence! (says t'other) Do you put your Head into the Mouth of a *Wolf*, and then, when you've brought it out again safe and sound, do you talk of a Reward? Why Sirrah, you have your Head again, and is not that a sufficient Recompence.

Here is a Fiction of one *Crane* that scap'd, that there might not want one Instance of an Encouragement to a dangerous Act of Charity: But this one Instance is not yet sufficient to justify the making a common Practice of it, upon the same Terms... How many do we see daily, gaping and struggling with Bones in their Throats, that when they had gotten them drawn out, have attempted the Ruin of their Deliverers? The World, in short, is full of Practices and Examples to answer the Intent of this Fable.[19]

Those who believe that radical, self-conscious ambiguity in fictions was invented only quite recently should reflect on how ancient a fable this is, and on the fact that Sir Roger L'Estrange, by no means a man ahead of his time, comments on its ambiguity with such sophistication. 'Here is a Fiction of one *Crane*' notes cannily that from a story told about individuals, we should not move incautiously to more general conclusions. *One* crane got away with it, OK, but do we not need to hear about 51 per cent of cranes before we have a proper statistical basis on which to formulate a rule of conduct? (How would it be if fairytales began 'Fifty-once-percent upon a time...'?) The worldly and prudent Sir Roger knows that 'one Instance is not yet sufficient to justify the making a common Practice'. Nor is one instance sufficient to justify the drawing of any general conclusion; hence, the intellectual vacuity of many discussions nowadays of the ideology said to be implicit in fictions (think of the furore created by the fact that one sort-of transsexual appears as a serial killer in *The Silence of the Lambs*, despite Thomas Harris's painstaking efforts in the novel, repeated in the film, to emphasize that there is no known correlation between transsexualism and serial murder; dreadful to contemplate the response of the League

---

[19] Sir Roger L'Estrange, *Fables of Aesop and Other Eminent Mythologists: with Morals and Reflexions* (London: R. Sare et al., 1692), Fable 8: 'A Wolf and a Crane', pp. 7–8.

of 'Travelling-Salesmen and Proud of It' to 'Die Verwandlung', were it to catch their attention).[20]

Think how many ways there are of misunderstanding this story about the wolf and the crane. Someone might take it as an excerpt from a book by David Attenborough and say 'I don't believe any crane would ever do that'—this person has not recognized that it is a fiction. Someone else might say: 'Decent of the crane, but, as I am not a crane, of what concern is the story to me?'—this person has not recognized that the story is a fable, an example of a rule. Yet a third person might say: 'Oh I see, I should always help people in distress, whatever the risk', and start inviting all the winos in Cambridge to sleep in his room— this person has derived a rule from the instance but neglected the instantiation of the rule. And a fourth might conclude: 'Too right, the thing about winos, as you soon find out, is that most of them are absolutely untrustworthy. Cross to the other side of the road, and walk on by, that's what I say'—and this person has, equally correctly, derived a different, indeed contradictory, rule from the same story, and, equally incorrectly, not understood that a purpose of such fables is to draw attention to, to promote thought about, the permanently tricky business of knowing how to derive and apply a rule. What is the moral of this tale? Something like: 'Be kind, but also be careful'—a very good rule indeed, but one which is not more 'firm' than any of the many occasions to which it might be applied, for the rule does not itself answer the question of how it itself should be applied, does not tell me whether to do this would be to be kind or reckless, to do that to be prudent or harsh. The genius of Aesop's fable is that it teaches at the same time a rule and the fact that there may be exceptions to it, or questions of its applicability; it is a paradigm of one interrelation of rule and instance. The capacity of Aesop's fiction to do this stems from the fact that it is both exemplary and specific at the same time, that it concerns one crane and one wolf—'an isolated case, and as such not very important'—but that it offers these two creatures for our consideration in a way which makes them 'count' far other than merely numerically.

To speak of the encounter of instance and rule is to speak in a very abstract way of a conflict, a dynamic, which is at the heart of fiction. Our fictions concern individuals—this is a fact of such generality that

[20] Thomas Harris, *The Silence of the Lambs* (London: Heinemann, 1988).

it often goes as unnoticed as the air we breathe, but is no less vital than air. Most of our fictions concern spatiotemporally unique beings who have proper names, even if only so short a name as 'K.' in *Das Schloss*. Yet it is not impossible to imagine beings who never told fictions about individuals but only about collectivities; their novels would be called *The Karenin Tribe* and *The Copperfields*; there would be no 'love-scenes', as we call them, only orgies; sentences such as 'I was born on July 11th' would be systematically replaced by 'On July 11th the membership of the Griffiths clan increased by one'; there would prob-ably be a large number of wars, and certainly many, many meetings—in fact, the sentence 'I've got a meeting' would be wholly superfluous in such fictions, for people would have nothing else, there would indeed not be any 'people', as we think of them, only agglomerations. Yet our fictions now have some resemblance to such dull, not to say repulsive, imaginable stories, for in our fictions, as Proust writes, 'the individual is bathed in something more general than himself'.[21] That is, our fictional personages, events, objects, are not sheerly irreducible particulars, but intimations of what Marx called species-being, sketches of an as yet unrealized humanity, representatives.[22] The pleasure of fiction, as well as its problem, is that we move as we read between a generalized and an individualized understanding of what we read, between treating the story as instance and as rule, *einziger Fall* and *Zeichen*. This motion is the source of fiction's lifelikeness, for we make such moves daily in our dealings with other people.

Walter Benjamin has written best about rule and instance as regards Kafka:

The word 'unfolding' has a double meaning. A bud unfolds into a blossom, but the boat which one teaches children to make by folding paper unfolds into a flat sheet of paper. This second kind of 'unfolding' is really appropriate to the parable; it is the reader's pleasure to smooth it out so that he has the meaning on the palm of his hand. Kafka's parables, however, unfold in the first sense, the way a bud turns into a blossom. That is why their effect resembles poetry. This does not mean that his prose pieces belong entirely in the tradition of Western

---

[21] Marcel Proust, *Remembrance of Things Past*, trans. C. K. Scott Moncrieff and Terence Kilmartin, 3 vols. (London: Chatto & Windus, 1981), vol. 1: *Swann's Way, Within a Budding Grove, The Guermantes Way*, 970 (the translation differs slightly from that given above).

[22] Karl Marx, *Economic and Philosophical Manuscripts 1844*, in *Karl Marx: Selected Writings*, ed. David McLellan, 2nd edn. (Oxford: Oxford University Press, 2000), 'Alienated Labour', 85–94.

prose forms; they have, rather, a similar relationship to doctrine as the Haggadah [a body of stories illustrative of the Law] does to the Halakah [the body of Jewish requirements and stipulations]. They are not parables, and yet they do not want to be taken at their face value; they lend themselves to quotation and can be told for purposes of clarification. But do we have the doctrine which Kafka's parables interpret and which K.'s postures and the gestures of his animals clarify? It does not exist; all we can say is that here and there we have an allusion to it.[23]

And yet this wonderful passage is misleading about parables and doctrine. To believe that one ever 'has' a doctrine ('do we have the doctrine which Kafka's parables interpret') in a sense comparable to that in which I may or may not 'have' a CD-player is to misunderstand, as the researching dog misunderstands, the relation of rule to instance, when he thinks of the rule as firm and the 'Einzelheiten' as 'unsicher'. The rule must touch instances; only with regard to instances can understanding of the rule be shown. And it is therefore the case that one never 'has' a doctrine in the sense of 'possessing' it; one has a doctrine only in the sense in which one may 'have' a child, as something engaged in growth, not always predictable, which may wondrously inspirit or strangely disappoint. Nor does 'parable' smooth out meaning so that a reader or hearer may hold it in the palm of his hand; parable releases instance onto the apparent security of rule. As, for instance, when one of the greatest of Jewish rabbis was asked about the Law:

And behold, a certain lawyer stood up, and tempted him, saying, Master, what shall I do to inherit eternal life?

He said unto him, What is written in the law? how readest thou? And he answering said, Thou shalt love the Lord thy God with all thy heart, and with all thy soul, and with all thy strength, and with all thy mind; and thy neighbour as thyself.

And he said unto him, Thou hast answered right: this do, and thou shalt live. But he, willing to justify himself, said unto Jesus, And who is my neighbour? And Jesus answering said, A certain man went down from Jerusalem to Jericho.[24]

And then he tells the parable of the Good Samaritan. 'A certain man...' makes the same move that 'eines Morgens' makes; it starts a

---

[23] Walter Benjamin: 'Franz Kafka: On the Tenth Anniversary of his Death', in *Illuminations* (1970), trans. Harry Zohn, ed. Hannah Arendt (London: Bodley Head, 2015), 108–35 (pp. 118–19).

[24] Luke 10:25–30.

fiction. There was and is, of course, no such man; we do not understand that this is a story unless we understand that; yet one point of the fiction is that you never know when you will meet him. What the lawyer wanted when he asked 'who is my neighbour' was a rule, a super-rule which would tell him when and how to apply it, a litmus-test of neighbourship. The point of the parable is that there could be no such rule, no such test. All Jesus says in reply to the question, to the desire for a rule, is 'Einzelheiten, Einzelheiten', details, details. Extraordinary, in this respect, his resemblance to Franz Kafka: I wonder if they could be related?

There is a parable about the relation between doctrine and parable, rule and story; it is also an account of the withdrawal of significance I was talking about when comparing Kafka's relations to those of the Brothers Grimm. It comes at the end of Gerson Scholem's book on *Major Trends in Jewish Mysticism* (a book dedicated to the memory of Walter Benjamin, as it happens), and concerns the Baal Shem, the founder of Hasidism:

When the Baal Shem had a difficult task before him, he would go to a certain place in the woods, light a fire and meditate in prayer—and what he had set out to perform was done. When a generation later the 'Maggid' of Meseritz was faced with the same task he would go to the same place in the woods and say: We can no longer light the fire, but we can still speak the prayers—and what he wanted done became reality. Again a generation later Rabbi Moshe Leib of Sassov had to perform this task. And he too went into the woods and said: We can no longer light the fire, nor do we know the secret meditations belonging to the prayer, but we do know the place in the woods to which it all belongs—and that must be sufficient; and sufficient it was. But when another generation had passed and Rabbi Israel of Rishin was called upon to perform the task, he sat down on his golden chair in his castle and said: We cannot light the fire, we cannot speak the prayers, we do not know the place, but we can tell the story of how it was done. And, the story-teller adds, the story which he told had the same effect as the actions of the other three.[25]

In the church of Sant'Anastasia in Verona, Kafka's eye was caught by a detail near the door, a detail easily overlooked on first entering the building, whose decorated rib-vaults invite the eye upward, while the church's shape and purpose take attention east to the altar. It was one of two (we do not know which) small, polychrome grotesques

---

[25] Gerson Scholem, *Major Trends in Jewish Mysticism*, 349–50.

at ground level.[26] He wrote a postcard about the dwarf he saw to
Felice Bauer:

In der Kirche S. Anastasia in Verona, wo ich müde in einer Kirchenbank
sitze, gegenüber einem lebensgroßen Marmorzwerg, der mit glücklichem
Gesichtsandruck ein Weihwasserbecken trägt.—Von der Post bin ich ganz
abgeschnitten, bekomme sie erst übermorgen in Riva, bin dadurch wie auf der
andern Welt, sonst aber hier in allem Elend. F[ranz.]

In Saint Anastasia's in Verona, where I'm sitting worn-out in a pew, facing a
life-size marble dwarf; he has a happy look on his face and is carrying a holy-
water stoup.—I'm completely cut off from the mails, won't be able to pick up
any letters until at the earliest the day after tomorrow in Riva, and so I feel as
if I were in the next world, but otherwise I'm here in all my wretchedness.
F[ranz.][27]

The patched and worn figure in Verona looks cheerier in person than
in a black-and-white reproduction, partly because he is in fact surrounded by those pinkish marbles common in the churches of the
Veneto, and their reflected lustres tinge him with a slight blush, not
exactly rosy but more healthful than in a photocopy. Even allowing for
that difference, Kafka's description is peculiar: 'he has a happy look on
his face' (even more peculiar in the standard English translation, which
has him looking 'blissful'). There are things about the marble dwarf
which alleviate his lot: he may be permanently bowed down under the
holy-water stoup, but he has a seat, and even a stool to take the weight
off his feet; this sixteenth-century figure is more humanely treated
than the writhing lions and suchlike of the Romanesque who bear
the whole weight of cathedral porches such as those of Modena and
Cremona. And yet he doesn't look exactly happy to me. Why did Kafka
see happiness on his face?

The dwarf's happiness to Kafka's eyes may be another instance of
that tendency in his prose to record even series of disasters calmly,
without fuss or protest, a tendency which is a source of his stories'
power both to scare and to comfort or placate, another instance, then,
of Kafka's equanimity. On the other hand, the postcard notes several
times of Kafka himself that he is not especially cheery: he is 'müde'

---

[26] The two figures are reproduced on the cover of this book.
[27] Postcard to Felice Bauer, 20 Sept. 1913; posthumously published 1967. Franz Kafka,
Briefe an Felice und andere Korrespondenz aus der Verlobungszeit (*Letters to Felice and Other
Correspondence during their Engagement*), ed. Erich Heller and Jürgen Born (Frankfurt am
Main: Fischer, 1993), 466.

('worn out') and 'hier in allem Elend' ('here in all my wretchedness'). Perhaps we should understand the dwarf in contrast to Kafka himself, the implication then being that Kafka is worse off than a life-sized marble dwarf; the fact that Kafka noticed the dwarf might show not his comic resilience but his capacity for self-pity (if we can distinguish strictly between these two aspects of this writer).

It also needs considering what Kafka meant by sending such a card to Felice Bauer. He had met her just over a year before he wrote it; in fact, it was sent on the first anniversary of his first postal communication to her, 20 September 1912, though whether he was marking that anniversary we do not know. It is impossible briefly to describe the intensity of the torment to which he subjected her and himself in that year, and in the next four years during which they became engaged and then disengaged more than once: suffice it to say, as some indication of the weight of their relation with each other on both of them, that this card, sent one year after his first letter to her, appears on page 466 of the German edition of what remains of his letters to her (all her letters to him are believed lost). As a card sent by a holidaymaker, it leaves something to be desired: it does not tell her how the weather is, nor does it wish that she was here; its laconic force might, of course, be reproachful of her (she ought to be there, for then he would be less wretched) or of himself (he ought not to have put himself out of the reach of even postal communications from her). Yet this very laconic quality—he mentions exhaustion and wretchedness in the same breath, as it were, as the dwarf and his travel plans for Riva—could equally be taken to mean, 'as you see, nothing much special is happening', an implication that there is 'no news' he wishes to tell, a tiredness with his own story. The card begins 'In der Kirche S. Anastasia' and ends symmetrically 'in allem Elend', as if wretchedness were a place too, somewhere Kafka could be 'in' as he was in Verona, so that the fact that he is miserable had no more and no less importance than a postmark.

The card turns in a way that Kafka's stories often turn:

. . . bin dadurch wie auf der andern Welt, sonst aber hier in allem Elend.

. . . and so I feel as if I were in the next world, but otherwise I'm here in all my wretchedness.

He tells her he is beyond the reach of human communication, and so feels as if he were in the next world—if we stop reading there, we have the sense that to be in another world than this one is a deprivation, would entail loneliness; at 'sonst aber' ('but otherwise'), though, the alternative to being in that elsewhere turns out to be being 'here in all my misery', and so the prospect of an 'andern Welt' can become more inviting. The phrase pivots and swivels, the fulcrum on which it does so is the 'sonst aber'. Kafka's prose is studded with such 'aber's and other words which perform the same turn (and in this too, it derives from the narratives of the Brothers Grimm). Sweet are the uses of adversatives like 'but', 'yet', 'however', 'on the other hand'; they are often, for example, the media of Kafka's extreme fair-mindedness, as in the *Letter to the Father*, which no sooner mentions an injustice or a cruelty of the father than it acknowledges the strain he was under or how provoking Kafka realizes he was and is (from the first two paragraphs: 'doch', 'wenigstens', 'aber doch wenigstens', 'auch sonst', 'mit Ausnahme vielleicht': 'still', 'at least', 'but yet at least', 'but not even', 'with the possible exception of'). In the stories, such equanimity between opposed considerations may become a more flickeringly dramatic oscillation of a protagonist's mind, as he turns now this way now that, between futile hope and equally futile despondency, as in the opening passage of 'Die Verwandlung': 'How would it be, he thought, if I had a bit more of a lie-in, but that was quite impossible... But when after similar struggles he lay there sighing... But then he said to himself... But Sir, Gregor cried, beside himself... But now Gregor had become much calmer'—and so on, the 'aber's wriggling away in the narrative, as pitiably beyond Gregor's control as his many new little legs.

Such adversatives work in Kafka's writing as, on the one hand, tranquil bearers of intellectual poise and, on the other, the harried scene-shifters of his swerving narratives, the stops and starts of a fictionally agonized mind. The truly Kafkaesque aspect of these hardworking words is that they often do both these kinds of work at once, as indeed the 'sonst aber' of his postcard may be heard to do, according to whether we hear the last clause as making a wry, self-knowing joke or lapsing into despondency or as desponding about how incessantly wryly self-knowing he is or arising out of despondency to an achieved wryness. For Kafka's world is one in which you cannot sustain such antitheses, set the maddening or maddened over against the meticulous, for instance; it is rather a world whose very accuracies perplex, and where the more you are told the less you know (in this respect, he is evidently close to the torturing precisions of Samuel Beckett).

Take this passage from *Das Schloß*, in which Olga tries to make 'absolutely clear' (as politicians will not stop saying nowadays) the terms of her brother Barnabas's employment in the castle:

Er kommt in Kanzleien, aber es ist doch nur ein Teil aller, dann sind Barrièren und hinter ihnen sind noch andere Kanzleien. Man verbietet ihm nicht geradezu weiterzugehn, aber er kann doch nicht weitergehn, wenn er seine Vorgesetzen schon gefunden hat, sie ihn abgefertigt haben und wegschicken. Man ist dort überdies immer beobachtet, wenigstens glaubt man es. Und selbst wenn er weiterginge, was würde es helfen…

He's allowed into some offices, but they are still only a fraction of this total, for there are partitions and behind them are yet more offices. He is not exactly forbidden to go on further, but still he can't just carry on further if he's already seen his superiors, been dealt with by them and sent on his way. And what's more they keep a watch on you all the time there, at least we think they do. And even if he could get further in, what good would that do…[28]

The first two sentences I quote are both wound around the doubled, insistent adversative phrase 'aber…doch' ('but…still'); the extra, semantically needless but colloquially familiar, emphasis perhaps conveys how hard Olga tries to excuse the fact that Barnabas can't be of more help to K. This double insistence is then overtopped by the 'überdies' of the next sentence ('And what's more…'). At this point, the castle grows to resemble one of those palaces of surveillance, with heat-sensitized corridors, laser-alarms, and all-seeing cameras, through which a hero in a movie has to make his way armed only with indomitable human cunning and perhaps the love of a good woman. But then Olga's and Kafka's unremitting honesty deprives us of this fantasy; she makes a concession: 'And what's more they keep a watch on you all the time there, at least we think they do'—the excitement of 'überdies' ('what's more') is cooled by the admission of 'wenigstens' ('at least'). Perhaps one is not fighting a super-equipped evil empire at all, heartening though it is to picture oneself in such a role; perhaps everybody has just gone for an extended lunch, and it would be easy to waltz through to the inner sanctum, if one could pick one's moment. And then yet again, the next sentence takes even this thought away, because even if one could get through, one has no idea where one might get through to, and so no idea of the good one's penetration

---

[28] Franz Kafka, *Das Schloß* (*The Castle*), written Jan.–Sept. 1922, posthumously published 1926, ed. Malcolm Pasley (Frankfurt am Main: Fischer, 1994), ch. 16, pp. 213–14.

might be supposed to do. Information flows and ebbs about us, on the turn of each concessive or adversative, as hypotheses are offered and withdrawn.

In the slow light of exegesis, when the detailed life of the passage is made laboriously explicit, writing like this can seem tiresome. When such passages are then allegorized into large statements of existential angst or permanent epistemological scepticism or what have you, it is the kind of thing that puts people off Kafka, and rightly so. But Olga speaks very quickly, the twists and turns of her remarks, as of the possible responses to them, are intensely dramatic, sparking unpredictably in the way that quite ordinary conversations between human beings leap and curve from promise through qualification to retraction, as hopes get started, pass through suspicion, surmise, doubt whether one has understood quite what the other person was on about or is after, to eventuate at any of the many places we can occupy on the scale between confidently getting the drift or feeling queasily at sea. The triumph of the writing in its agile representation of these fairly usual lurches between two people talking to one another—lies, that is, in the absolute realism of Kafka's art.

How vital the asymmetries of the sentences here can be seen if we contrast Olga with the exceptionally rhetorical and studied passage of late Kafka, from 'Der Bau', in which a subterranean carnivore tells someone, perhaps us, perhaps itself, about its habits and its dwelling-place. This is the passage in which the burrower imagines what it might do if the hostile forces it feels itself beset by were at last concentrated into one other living creature, a palpable enemy, and what it would like to do to that enemy:

Wenn er doch jetzt käme, wenn er doch mit seiner schmutzigen Gier den Eingang entdeckte, wenn er doch daran zu arbeiten begänne, das Moos zu heben, wenn es ihm doch gelänge, wenn er sich doch für mich hinein-zwängte und schon darin soweit wäre, daß mir sein Hinterer für einen Augenblick gerade noch auftauchte, wenn das alles doch geschähe, damit ich endlich in einem Rasen hinter ihm her, frei von allen Bedenken, ihn aufspringen könnte, ihn zerbeißen, zerfleischen, zerreißen und austrinken and seinen Kadaver gleich zur anderen Beute stopfen könnte, vor allem aber, das wäre die Hauptsache, endlich wieder in meinem Bau wäre, gern diesmal sogar das Labyrinth bewundern wollte, zunächst aber die Moosdecke über mich ziehen und ruhen wollte, ich glaube, den ganzen, noch übrigen Rest meines Lebens. Aber es kommt niemand und ich bleibe auf mich allein angewiesen.

If he were to turn up now though, if in his filthy curiosity he were to uncover the entrance though, if he set to work to move away the moss from over it though, if he managed it though, if he forced his way in instead of me though, and even got so far in that I just caught for one last moment a glimpse of his rear, if all this were to happen though, and I could at last pounce on him from behind without a second thought, and bite him to bits, flay him to tatters, rip him to shreds and drain him dry and chuck his body in with all my other trophies, but above all (and this is the main thing) get back at last into my burrow, how gladly then would I for once gaze at my labyrinth, but not before I'd pulled the lid of moss back over me, and I'd be at peace, I really think, at peace for the whole of the rest of my life. But actually nobody ever turns up and I'm left alone to my own devices.[29]

Six successive clauses are built around a 'wenn...doch' ('if...though'), an oratorical self-display rare in Kafka's stories; this show of structured eloquence continues in the triply alliterating and rhyming 'zerbeißen, zerfleischen, zerreißen'. I think it indicates Kafka's distaste for such special effects that he deploys them here in the manufacture of so bloodthirsty a fantasy (Kafka in his equanimous loneliness is a prophetic writer: Hitler had organized the failed Munich putsch about the time this story was written and was in prison composing his own imaginary burrow, *Mein Kampf*, not that Hitler is anything more than one instance of the general rule of terror depicted in Kafka's tale).

This wet dream of carnage detumesces through a series of 'aber's in the course of which the symmetries of the prose evaporate away ('but above all'... 'but not before'... 'But actually'); the algebra of such a disappointment, such a withdrawal of satisfaction and hyperbole, is just that of the 'sonst aber' of the postcard from Verona; the creature imagines another—to it, better—world, and yet has to admit that it is still just in actuality, 'hier in allem Elend', 'But actually nobody ever turns up and I'm left alone to my own devices'. We should admit that we too feel some of the disappointment which seeps through these 'aber's and, admitting that, detect in ourselves an element of ourselves which is susceptible to the creature's vision, a hunger for narrative, for event, however atrocious, a hunger which may be refined in comparison with what the creature wants but which is not wholly alien to those wants, as if the creature were, if not us, then at least inside us.

---

[29] Franz Kafka, 'Der Bau' ('The Burrow'), written 1923–4, posthumously published 1931, in *Sämtliche Erzählungen*, 369–70.

Walter Benjamin had not seen the postcard Kafka sent from Verona about the marble dwarf, known to the Veronese as 'Il gobbo', the hunchback, but he fastened with great insight on the centrality of such a figure to the writer's work:

> ... the prototype of distortion, the hunch-back. Among the images in Kafka's stories, none is more frequent than that of the man who bows his head far down on his chest: the fatigue of the court officials, the noise affecting the doormen in the hotel, the low ceiling facing the visitors in the gallery ... The same symbol occurs in the folksong "The Little Hunchback" ... :
>
> > When I kneel upon my stool
> > And I want to pray,
> > A hunchbacked man is in the room
> > And he starts to say:
> > My dear child, I beg of you,
> > Pray for the little hunchback too.
>
> So ends the folksong. In his depth Kafka touched the ground which neither 'mythical divination' nor 'existential theology' supplied him with. It is the core of folk tradition, the German as well as the Jewish. Even if Kafka did not pray—and this we do not know—he still possessed in the highest degree what Malebranche called 'the natural prayer of the soul': attentiveness. And in this attentiveness he included all living creatures, as saints include them in their prayers.[30]

We might add to the list of men who bow their heads far down on their chests Georg Bendemann's white-haired father, who performs the gesture, or Gregor Samsa as he dies: 'Dann sank sein Kopf ohne seinen Willen gänzlich nieder' ('Then of its own accord his head bowed completely down'); we might add too the Franz Kafka who wrote the forty-second aphorism in the Zürau notebook: 'Den ekel- und haßerfüllten Kopf auf die Brust senken' ('To lower your head, full of disgust and hatred, to your chest').[31] This bowed head, to which Benjamin draws our attention, may be bowed in prayer, or shame, or with, as it were, the weight of this world's atmosphere on its skull, an atmosphere we ignore daily but which these stories enable us for a while to scent, even to sustain.

---

[30] Walter Benjamin, *Illuminations*, 129–30.
[31] Franz Kafka, 'Die Verwandlung', in *Sämtliche Erzählungen*, 96; Zürau notebook, aphorism 42, in Franz Kafka, *Beim Bau der chinesischen Mauer und andere Schriften aus dem Nachlaß* (*The Great Wall of China and Other Unpublished Writings*), ed. Hans-Gerd Koch (Frankfurt am Main: Fischer, 1994), 235.

Such an atmosphere, such a consciousness of what kind of creatures we are, of our species-being, is something hard consistently to grasp, because it is so general a fact about our world that to see it is like seeing one's own eyes, or rather seeing one's own faculty of sight. Wittgenstein comments on this in his *Remarks on the Philosophy of Psychology*:

Die Fakten der menschlichen Naturgeschichte, die auf unser Problem Licht werfen, sind uns schwer zu finden, denn unsere Rede *geht an ihnen vorbei*,—sie ist mit andern Dingen beschäftigt. (So sagen wir Einem 'Geh ins Geschäft und kauf. . . ' und nicht 'Setz den linken Fuß vor der rechten Fuß etc. etc., dann lag Geld auf den Schalter, etc. etc.')

The facts of human natural history which throw light on our problem are hard to detect, for our way of speaking *passes them by*, it is concerned with other things. (Thus we tell someone 'Go to the shop and buy . . . '—not 'Put your left foot in front of your right foot etc. etc., then put the money on the counter etc. etc.')[32]

Wittgenstein had a genius for examples, but perhaps the instance here is so brilliantly condensed that it would be useful to spell it out a bit. His point is that an order like 'Go to the shop and buy' employs several concepts; a person who understands and follows the order possesses several skills—he knows how to move his body in desired directions, he recognizes shops as contrasted with, say, public lavatories, he understands the exchange of money for goods. All these are complex skills, rich concepts, as we can see if we imagine how much we would have to say to someone who replied to the order 'Go? What do you mean "go"?' or 'Shop? What do you mean "shop"?', and so on. Suppose you said to someone 'Read this Kafka story by next Wednesday' and they said 'Story? What do you mean "story"?' To make explicit what is involved in our exercise of these skills would be a long business, rather like Josef K.'s account of his whole life in all its details; it would require a form of 'menschlichen Naturgeschichte' ('human natural history') as Wittgenstein calls it. Considering what it is to obey the order 'Go', for instance, we find that to be able to walk at will entails our having proprocentricity, that is, an individual's sense of his own body as his own and to a very considerable degree under his own control. It is in fact

---

[32] Ludwig Wittgenstein, *Remarks on the Philosophy of Psychology*, written late 1940s, posthumously published 1980, 2 vols., trans. G. E. M. Anscombe, ed. G. E. M. Anscombe and G. H. von Wright (Oxford: Basil Blackwell, 1980), vol. 1, Point 78, p. 18.

possible to lose this practical sense of one's own corporeal self, as Oliver
Sacks records in his case-history of 'The Man Who Fell Out of Bed'
(in *The Man Who Mistook his Wife for a Hat*), or as, indeed, Franz Kafka
had related in 'Die Verwandlung' and on the many other occasions in
his fictions when people experience desperate separations from their
own physical selves. And yet so constant is propriocentricity for most
of us that we scarcely know we possess it—even the word for it is
strange and learned. The concepts of our ordinary language, our *Rede*,
'pass by', as Wittgenstein says, such elemental realities of our being
the creatures that we are, as Kafka stories 'pass by' unexplained and
momentarily spotlit details like the gilt caryatids above the captain's
door in *Der Verschollene*. And so it is that our *Rede*, how we talk, which
is one of the distinctive realities of our being the creatures we are, is
constituted as such by its overlooking these very general facts of human
natural history, these equally distinctive realities of our being the creatures we are, as if we were doomed always to be merely passers-by in
our own lives, glimpsing the process of our being in the world as cows
in a field are glimpsed from a train.

One thing that such intent writing as Kafka's can do for us is to slow
our transit through our selves. The attentiveness which Benjamin
praises him for is a form of patience and asks a patience in return—the
kind of patience it took to invent Olga's speech about the castle, and
the answering patience to follow that invention in its details. One fact
of human natural history Kafka brings to light is the 'aber'-ness of our
experience, the world's recalcitrance and our persistences against its
obduracy. For it is not impossible to imagine creatures, like us in most
ways, who would not experience 'aber'-ness as we do; these creatures
would have, say, pre-set timers inside themselves which always switched
off in advance any desire which was not in fact to be fulfilled, or, at
least, they would lose interest very quickly in something which was
not going quite according to their plans—such creatures would not be
distinguished by long-term or collaborative purpose, it is true; by our
standards they would be under-achievers; they would have their form
of contentment, though, and have it more securely than we do ours
(we might think of them as a kind of dolphin). They would not have
equanimity because equanimity is built around 'aber's. Imagining these
easily switched-off beings, how they would differ from us, we realize
that 'aber' is structural to our desiring as we desire, rather than merely
an impediment to desire which meets it from outside. (This argument
has some resemblance to Konrad Lorenz's account of the intertwining

of intra-species aggression and personal bonding between individuals in his classic *On Aggression*, which I read only after thinking up the argument; I mention this to indicate another sense in which Kafka might be considered a prophetic writer, for some of his tales anticipate by a generation the ethological revolution in zoology.)[33]

Realistic fiction, such as Flaubert's or Kafka's, is a form of human natural history, and human natural history in the Wittgensteinian sense is something distinct from social or psychological science. The realism of such writing consists in attention to overlooked general facts of human nature—to such things as our experience of time, our capacity to draw rules from instances as also to know when instances do not suggest rules, our abilities to aspire and to concede, our thwartedness. To claim this for these writers is also to claim something for my own way of reading them: the attention I pay to time-markers or conjunctions is not critical miniaturism or myopia. On the contrary. To observe the connective tissues of realistic story, its 'he said's and 'then's, 'at just the moment when's, is to pay attention to elemental constituents of the fictional worlds and the world outside fiction. In novels, for example, we distinguish between 'dialogue' (the things the characters say) and 'narrative frame' (the things said by the fiction about the characters); there are innumerable ways in which novelists may stitch together these two parts of a story, all of them variants on the fundamental 'he said', 'she said'. 'He said' and 'she said' and their many possible elaborations are often overlooked by readers of novels, and indeed, part of their function is to be neglected; they support the continuance of story as the marble hunchback in Sant'Anastasia's supports the holy-water stoup (someone who thought the stoup was a funny hat the hunchback was wearing would misunderstand, as someone who thought that the story was there only to fill in gaps between the speech-markers would misunderstand). These speech-markers are structural conventions of our storytelling, but just because they are conventions it does not follow that they are 'mere conventions'. On the contrary, again. To the real artist no convention is 'mere'; convention is rather just where artistry is likely to be most challenged, most at work.

For what are the grounds of our assent to this convention of the novel, this partitioning of dialogue and frame? Certain very general facts of

[33] Konrad Lorenz was a founding father of ethnology, the study of animal behaviour, best known for his discovery of the principle of attachment, or 'imprinting', through which a bond is established between a newborn creature and its caregiver.

human natural history are involved here too. Imagine, as Wittgenstein does at one point in the *Philosophical Investigations*, a species of beings like us except that they could only think aloud, as children when they begin to read can often not read unless they also vocalize what they are reading.[34] It seems likely that in the novels of such creatures the conventional distinction dialogue/narrative frame would either not operate or operate with a meaning different from the meaning it has for us. So, facing this convention of 'he said', 'she said', we encounter something basic, bypassed, about ourselves, as also, when we consider an artist's work with that convention, we discover what a being like ourselves can make of beings like us.

The kinds of thing our talking passes by but which our fictions can give us pause over are not always as abstract as this. In Flaubert's *L'Éducation sentimentale*, for example, a great deal of attention is drawn to encirclement: I mean, to occasions on which Frédéric notices another human being surrounded (*entouré*) by attentive beings of the same species. This predilection for circlings is also expressed by a fondness for the preposition *autour* ('round'). The many instances of this, considered singly, do not amount to much, but they mount up, they build an ethos, which can then crystallize out in ecstatic moments such as his vision of the beloved Mme Arnoux one day—'le soleil l'entourait' ('the sun encircled her'), as if the sun itself stood all around her, hanging on her words and gestures—or, a rare moment when Frédéric is himself at the centre of a circle rather than looking on longingly from outside it—his contentment with his mistress, Rosanette, taking breakfast on their balcony of a morn-ing, when in her nightgown and her slippers 'elle allait et venait autour de lui' ('she went back and forth all round him').[35] The simultaneous weight and lightness of 'autour de lui' there seems to me wonderful, created from the fact that Flaubert has throughout his novel taken care of such a small and easily overlooked phrase; it shows us something of what we are, of how much we can invest in details, such as the being 'surrounded'. In the preposition *autour*, we glimpse one aspect of what it is for man to be, as Aristotle said he was, a *zoon politikon*, a social animal.

In the case of Kafka, for example, consider the range of the word *Ruhe* ('peace') and its cognates in his stories. The range of the word and

---

[34] Ludwig Wittgenstein, *Philosophical Investigations*, trans. G. E. M. Anscombe, 2nd edn. (Oxford: Blackwell, 1958), Part I: 331, p. 108.

[35] Gustave Flaubert, *L'Éducation sentimentale*, (1869), ed. S. de Sacy (Paris: Gallimard, 2015), Part 2, ch. 6 and Part 3, ch. 3 (pp. 347, 465).

its cognates—*beruhigen, unruhig,* and so on—is inherent in the German language itself, which can mean so many things by it, from metaphysical quietude to daily peace and quiet. Kafka did not invent the range, he just grants us time to feel its width. 'Die Verwandlung' begins, 'Als Gregor Samsa eines Morgens aus unruhigen Träumen erwachte' ('When Gregor Samsa awoke one morning from troubled dreams'); we may pass by 'unruhigen' here, it is so common a locution in our way of talking, so common a phenomenon to have had a troubled night, but the story will bring to light an *Unruhe* and a corresponding desire for *Ruhe* of extraordinary proportions. Yet because the word is given us in all its dailiness, and what Kafka makes out of it is made *from* that dailiness, all the more abstract understandings of this *Unruhe*—Pascalian 'fallenness', say, or Marxist alienation, or existential angst, or a Freudian 'Unbehagen in der Kultur' ('unease with being "civilized"')[36]—are seen instantiated in the particulars of local upset and vexation, and, by a converse motion, small irritations and let-downs may be exfoliated out into more sweeping theoretical concepts. This double move of instantiation and exfoliation may help us better see the place of *Rede* in 'menschlichen Naturgeschichte', focus the role of thought in our life, the life in our thoughts.

   There are points of view from which my adoption of Wittgenstein's word 'menschlich', the 'human', and my consequent tendency to say 'we', might be reprehensible, indeed untenable. It is, indeed, true that human beings regrettably often mistake things they are familiar with from their own cultures or portions of culture for the essentially human, and that such mistaking can give rise to unpleasantnesses or evil (sexism, racism, New Labour, and so on). Yet those who, from this observation of the sad propensity human creatures have to narrow and superficial views about their world, extend a critique of the very concept of the 'human', a critique which claims that such a concept is no more than a transient historical phenomenon whose time has passed, or has never been more than a mystification of the drive for domination of particular cultures, are making a big mistake, or rather several big mistakes. The ethical and political dangers of such an argument should be obvious: if there is no coherent sense to the notion of a transcultural humanness, there can be no 'human rights'; if there are no

---

[36] Sigmund Freud, *Das Unbehagen in der Kultur* (Vienna: Internationaler Psychoanalystischer Verlag, 1930). Freud's title means something like 'The Uneasiness in Civilization'; it was first translated into English, by James Strachey, as *Civilization and its Discontents.*

human rights, there is no appeal against the powers to exploit and to destroy which any particular group of people may happen to possess; there is only the struggle between contending forces, none of which has any legitimacy or rationale beyond itself. I remind you of the profundity and vehemence of Hitler's contempt for humanistic ethics, and his striking resemblance to some recent idols of advanced thought, Michel Foucault, for instance. But the denial of humanness is also philosophically unsustainable; it is not true that all the attributes of human creatures are 'socially constructed': there is no society in the world in which human beings are not spatio-temporally individuated, mortal, capable of feeling physical pain, and endowed with language; such unconstructed elements of human nature are indeed the basis of any social construction we can imagine or have achieved. These are the '*facts* of human natural history'.

People are so impressed by our variance from each other they neglect what we have in common. We have, or think we have, such a number of opinions about so many things, all different and all, as the short-sighted delight to say, equally valid, that we become fogged about our substantial unanimities. One reason why this is so is that the depth of our agreement with one another shows in some ways less in what we say about things that in what we agree is not worth talking about, or just in what we omit to mention, in what we concur to overlook. As a figure in the early Kafka story 'Beschreibung eines Kampfes' ('Description of a Struggle') says:

Wir bauen eigentlich unbrauchbare Kriegsmachinen, Türme, Mauern, Vorhänge aus Seide und wir könnten uns viel darüber wundern, wenn wir Zeit dazu hätten. Und erhalten uns in Schwebe, wir fallen nicht, wir flattern, wenn wir auch häßlicher sind als Fledermäuse. Und schon kann uns kaum jemand an einem schönen Tage hindern zu sagen: 'Ach Gott, heute ist ein schöner Tag.' Denn schon sind wir auf unserer Erde eingerichtet und leben auf Grund unseres Einverständisses.

And indeed we construct unemployable armaments, towers, walls, silk curtains, and well might we puzzle ourselves greatly about this, if we had the time. Put us in the balance, we do not sink, we are poised, even if we are uglier than bats. And in fact on a lovely day hardly anyone can stop us saying: 'Good Lord, it's a lovely day today.' For in fact the earth on which we are installed is ours and we live on the basis that we are of one mind.[37]

---

[37] Franz Kafka, 'Beschreibung eines Kampfes' ('Description of a Struggle'), written 1903–4, published posthumously 1935, in *Sämtliche Erzählungen*, 227.

Clearly, the list with which this extract begins—'unemployable armaments, towers, walls, silk curtains'—in its ill-assortment acknowledges the disparity of human purpose, how widely we diverge from each other as we pursue our specialisms, warmongers remote from silk-weavers. It would be rash to argue from such diversity that the category 'human' is empty, for all the items in the list are governed by 'wir bauen' ('we construct'; 'we make'); each of these varying human products is a sign of an ability to plan beyond the moment, each requires the collaboration of other creatures such as ourselves for its construction or in its use. The very heterogeneity of the items in the list confirms rather than casts doubt on the existence of beings identifiably human, for 'we' are 'builders'. What Kafka depicts through these words of his imagined character is human self-contentment; this self-contentment has no conception of a possible place outside the human, as it were, from which it might be blamed or in any way judged. Man is the measure of all things, as the human saying goes— put him in the scales of justice, he sustains himself; nobody but he judges whether days are lovely or not, for the earth is his, he thinks. The very intensity with which Kafka conceives of this world entirely full of the human and empty of all else beside might begin to suggest to us, even to us as humans and humanists, a certain suffocation in these notions of our selves with which we entertain ourselves.

This line of thought comes out more clearly when Kafka puts a similar species-self-confidence into the mouth of a dog:

Denn was gibt es außer den Hunden? Wen kann man sonst anrufen in der weiten, leeren Welt? Alles Wissen, die Gesamtheit aller Fragen und aller Antworten ist in den Hunden enthalten.

For what exists apart from dogs? To whom else in all the wide, empty world should we call? All knowledge, the whole repertoire of questions and answers, is summed up in dogs.[38]

How subtle here the verb 'anrufen' ('call to'), for in German one may 'anrufen' a dog or a friend on the other side of the street, but the word has also a more upmarket usage in 'Gott anrufen', to invoke or implore God. In one respect, the question 'To whom else in all the wide empty world should we call?' comically reverses the role of dogs in our world, so pleasantly and obediently at our beck and call; in another respect,

---

[38] Franz Kafka, 'Forschungen eines Hundes', in *Sämtliche Erzählungen*, 333.

these dogs who encapsulate all that is known are us, and it is we who have no masters on whom to call. According to dog-science in the story, food comes from above, though there are many hypotheses as to how quite it is thus provided; these dogs, that is, have not noticed that human beings who are taller than they are exist and feed them. How do we feel, then, when we ourselves, the taller ones, are overlooked? One response may be that these dogs are foolish animals, whose science knows nothing even of the fundamental things (that is, as far as we are concerned, about us). We could be charmed or vexed by such foolishness. Kafka chose wisely when he chose dogs to be so completely neglectful of the existence of humans, for we think of dogs as our best friends—how sharper than a serpent's tooth it is to have a thankless dog. Yet in the story, the reader is addressed as a dog, 'a dog such as you or me', and there are several broad jokes to this effect, as with Kafkaesque neologisms such as 'Mithund', a fellow-dog formed on the analogy of 'Mitmensch', fellow-human being, or 'Durchschnittshund', formed on the analogy of 'Durchschnittsmensch', the 'average man', as who should say 'the dog in the street', or 'the dog on the Clapham omnibus'. But if we are dogs, or can recognize ourselves in this dog, of what are we comparably ignorant with all our knowledge when we fail to know what is above us, the above from which our food comes, when we think we have nothing on which or no one on whom but ourselves, to call?

Kafka has an aphoristic fable on the subject:

Die Krähen behaupten, eine einzige Krähe könnte den Himmel zerstören. Das ist zweifellos, beweist aber nichts gegen den Himmel, denn Himmel bedeutet eben: Unmöglichkeit von Krähen.

Crows maintain that one crow by itself could destroy the heavens. No doubt, no doubt, but this shows nothing against the heavens, for 'the heavens' just means: the impossibility of crows.[39]

These thoughts concern only what it is to have a species-bound conceptual horizon: I mention this in case some of you should fear that Kafka and I have designs on your religious convictions or lack thereof. All I say does no more than mark out, as a dog with its urine, the boundaries within which we think; nothing I say points beyond those boundaries, even were such pointing possible. The subtlety of Kafka's

---

[39] Zuräu notebook, aphorism 32, in *Beim Bau der chinesischen Mauer*, 233.

animal stories lies in his investigation of species-being, something which classic animal fables such as those of Aesop rarely engage in. You recall, perhaps, the fable of the fox and the crow: the crow had a piece of cheese in its beak; the fox saw the cheese and wanted it, so he begged the crow to sing him a song because he had heard how fabulous a singer the crow was; flattered, the crow opens his beak to perform, drops the cheese, and gets jeered at by the fox. Sir Roger L'Estrange comments in his version of the *Fables*:

The Flatterer first counsels his Patron to his Loss, and then betrays him into the making himself ridiculous; as what can be more so, than for a *Raven* to value himself upon his *croaking*, or an *Ass* upon his *braying*?[40]

But to a raven's ears, what sweeter music than the croaking of its own kind? Here the fable lends only human ears to ravens and asses, reinstates the human creature as we figure in 'Description of a Struggle': 'the earth on which we are installed is ours and we live on the basis that we are of one mind', and that, as with the dogs in Kafka's story, there is no other mind to be of. Being 'of one mind' is often achieved only at the cost of being also 'of one eye', in the sense that the force of our concurrence with each other crowds out our ability to see the world in any way but ours, as the character in 'Description of a Struggle' fails to conceive of what it might be like to be a bat, dismissing them in the bypassing insult 'uglier than bats'. But what if a mouse called Josefine thought she was a *prima donna* and the other mice were never sure whether what she came out with was coloratura or squeaking? In his last completed story, which imagines this to be the case, and which is spoken by a reasonable but musically challenged mouse, Kafka achieved his sweetest and subtlest inquiry into species, and particularly into the species that we are, a species of individuals.

Whatever Darwin thought he had explained in *The Origin of Species*, it was not his intention to account for what might sketchily be termed the 'individual soul'.[41] The title of his celebrated work tells you this: it is about how classes of creatures come into being, how it came to be that there are dogs, mice, cats, humans, but not how it came to be that there is an Eric Griffiths or a cat called Aberdeen. In the case of all other species on this planet, Darwin's failure to explain individuality might

[40] Sir Roger L'Estrange, *Fables of Aesop*, Fable 14: 'A Fox and a Raven', p. 14.
[41] Charles Darwin, *On the Origin of Species* (London: John Murray, 1859).

not matter much, for, though mutual recognition of individuals is present in some species (the greylag goose of Konrad Lorenz),[42] this recognition does not approach that self-conscious and constitutive sense of individuals as individuals which typifies human beings. No other species, so far as we yet know, names its own individual members, for example. But 'considering oneself an individual' is another distinctive, trans-cultural feature of humanness (though the manner and content of such individuality vary over time and across cultures, the fact of the individuatedness of human self-consciousness does not). Darwin assisted in the creation of Kafka's animal stories to the extent that he encouraged human beings to recognize their own species as just one among many species, and so loosened the hold on us of that self-preoccupation which the dog voices when he asks what else there is in the wide, empty world but dogs. Yet Kafka's stories are also set against not Darwin, but against those vicious offshoots of Darwinism such as 'scientific' racism, the readiness to treat other human individuals as mere dispensable instances of a species whose interests and drives must always override the frail claims of the single person. Hence, the foreboding in his last stories as the word *Volk*, of which the world was shortly to hear so much so loudly, comes into prominence, a foreboding evident at the very heart of the charm in such imaginings as that of the researching dog, who remarks that variations between individual dogs make a 'persönlich sehr großer, volklich bedeutungsloser Unterschied' ('a big difference to each dog personally, but one which is insignificant from the point of view of the *Volk*'), with its broad, humorous phrasing which allows each dog to be 'persönlich' ('personally') rather than 'hundlich' ('individual-dog-ily') concerned, a word which does not exist and whose non-existence attests to another fact about the natural history of human concepts. So, when the dog speaks of:

... die Sehnsucht nach dem größten Glück, dessen wir fähig sind, dem warmen Beisammensein.

... longing for the greatest happiness of which we are capable, for warm togetherness.[43]

---

[42] In *Der Kumpan in der Umwelt des Vogels* (*The Companion in the Environment of Birds*) (1935) Lorenz described *Prägung* ('imprinting') in birds such as the greylag goose.

[43] Franz Kafka, 'Forschungen eines Hundes', in *Sämtliche Erzählungen*, 325.

or the nice mouse mentions the joy of conjointness, all the mice feeling together with each other 'im großen warmen Bett des Volkes' ('in the huge, warm bed of the species'), we humans reading these remarks should shudder at them even as they attract us. For though, as God observed, it is not good that man should be alone, there are forms of being-together, of collectivity, whose warmth is purchased only at the cost of eradicating what is human about us, because we are that unique creation (unique on this planet anyway), a species of individuals. In our time, the cost which some humans have exacted as the price of their own 'warmen Beisammensein', of a solidarity of some humans with each other in a *Volk*, has included the exclusion, the excision, of many human creatures from the category of the human, a nullification of fellow-creatures even more drastic than literature's neglect of the seamstresses whom Kafka saw as creatures left behind by the Ark, pressing their faces against a porthole, a faintly discerned 'something dark' ('etwas Dunkles').[44] I refer to the millions exterminated by Hitler's Germany, by that evil, partial imagination of species-solidarity against which it is part of Kafka's distinction to be a witness, a witness whose strength is entirely in its own renunciation of strength, its frailty.

His last completed story is called 'Josefine, die Sängerin, oder Das Volk der Mäuse' ('Josefine the Diva, or We Mice'), pivoting on its 'oder' ('or') between a named individual and a collectivity. 'Das Volk der Mäuse' would less freely be translated as 'The Mouse-People', but this does not convey the warm terror in the German word 'Volk', nor the nearness of the 'Volk der Mäuse' to 'Rattenvolk', the rat-people, a preferred anti-Semitic term for the Jews, Kafka's people, if he had a people. We mice, we humans, we Germans: how retchworthy these 'we's, and how attractive. The opera-singing mouse is the only one of the animals in his late stories who has a name (the ape in 'Ein Bericht' has been given a name, 'Rotpeter', which he repudiates); in having a name, she has strayed away from species-solidarity, become an 'Einzelwesen', an individual being. She is called 'Josefine' because that is the feminine of 'Josef', a name which matters to Kafka because it feminizes the 'Josef K.' of *Der Proceß*, a name which in turn mattered because of the story of Joseph and his brothers, the greatest story in Jewish tradition of fratricidal hatred for a specially gifted individual.

[44] Diary entry, 16 Dec. 1910, in Franz Kafka, *Tagebücher 1910–1923* (Frankfurt am Main: Fischer, 1992), 23.

'Josefine, die Sängerin' faces Kafka's own quirkiness, his passionate devotion to an art which he can scarcely account for to himself, let alone others. The nice mouse, the voice of species which talks to us in the story, puzzles over this so individual a case, a case so individual it is no longer a case, just an exception to a non-existent rule:

Was treibt das Volk dazu, sich für Josefine so zu bemühen? Eine Frage, nicht leichter zu beantworten als die nach Josefinens Gesang, mit der sie ja auch zusammenhängt...Manchmal habe ich den Eindruck, das Volk fasse sein Verhältnis zu Josefine derart auf, daß sie, dieses zerbrechliche, schonungs- bedürftige, irgendwie ausgezeichnete, ihrer Meinung nach durch Gesang ausgezeichnete Wesen ihm anvertraut sei und es müsse für sie sorgen; der Grund dessen ist niemandem klar, nur die Tatsache scheint festzustehn.

What drives us mice to take such trouble over Josefine? Good question, and one no easier to answer than the question about Josefine's singing, with which it is indeed intimately bound up...Sometimes I have the impression that we mice conceive our relationship to Josefine as follows: she, this fragile creature for whom such allowances have to be made, who is somehow distinguished, in her opinion distinguished because of her singing, has been entrusted to us and we have to look after her; why this should be so nobody knows, but there it is, that's how things seem to be.[45]

It seems to me that something like this is true of our relation to Kafka himself; it is as if he had been entrusted to us, and that if there came a day when we betrayed that trust, by overlooking, absent-mindedness, or inattention, or any other offshoot of our self-contented reliance on our current 'warmes Beisammensein' ('warm togetherness'), then we would find ourselves in the position of the spokesmouse who says— whether regretfully, Kafka does not tell us—'in den alten Zeiten unseres Volkes gab es Gesang; Sagen erzählen Davon und sogar Lieder sind erhalten, die freilich niemand mehr singen kann' ('in the prehis- tory of our species singing existed; there are proverbs about it, and even musical notations have been preserved, though of course nobody knows how to sing them any more').[46] Speaking of forgetfulness, I should mention that although I have been concerned with Franz Kafka, we ought not to forget that he had five siblings. Two brothers died in infancy; three sisters survived Dr Kafka. None was a writer of fictions. Their names were Ottla, Elli, and Valli; all three were murdered

---

[45] Franz Kafka, 'Josefine die Sängerin, oder Das Volk der Mäuse', written March 1924, published April 1924. *Sämtliche Erzählungen*, 176. Kafka died on 3 June 1924.

[46] 'Josefine die Sängerin', in *Sämtliche Erzählungen*, 172.

by the Nazis. It seems only justice, justice such as he pursued and which pursued him, that we should remember the three sisters, who went down into something dark, whenever we concern ourselves with him, the odd, the reluctant even, survivor (though he predeceased them).[47]

[47] Franz Kafka's two younger brothers, Georg (1885–87) and Heinrich (1887–88), died before he was seven; his three sisters were Gabriele ('Elli') (1889–1944), Valerie ('Valli') (1890–1942), and Ottilie ('Ottla') (1892–1943). Elli and Valli were probably both killed in the Chelmo (Kulmhof) extermination camp; Ottla died in Auschwitz-Birkenau, having volunteered to accompany a group of Jewish children there.

9

Primo Levi

Nietzsche and his mind parted company in January 1889 on the via Po, which runs in the heart of Turin from Piazza Castello down to the river. Legend gives several specific locations for the onset of his madness; according to one version, it happened on the corner where the via Carlo Alberto meets the via Po. Nietzsche had arrived in Turin in April 1888, and completed *Twilight of the Idols* there as well as writing much of *The Anti-Christ, Ecce Homo,* and *Nietzsche contra Wagner.* He was in a fever over his own greatness, as he had been for years, but was now clearly winding up for a smash: 'I am not a human being I am dynamite... I am by far the most terrible human being there has ever been; this does not exclude the possibility that I may be the most beneficent;'[1] he thought a new calendar should be inaugurated, and declared the day he finished *Götzen-Dämmering (Twilight of the Idols),* 30 September 1888, 'the Day of Well-Being, the first day of Year One'.[2] 'On 30th September, a great victory; the seventh day; a god takes a relaxing stroll along the banks of the Po.'[3] Just over thirty years later, Italians were to hear, and this time from real rather than delusional megaphones, as the Fascist Era was inaugurated that they were now in Year One. What caused Nietzsche to think himself so great were states of his brain probably symptomatic of advanced syphilis or of some other irreparable organic perdition, brain-states which within six

---

[1] 'Ich bin kein Mensch, ich bin Dynamit...Ich bin bei weitem der furchtbarste Mensch, den es bisher gegeben hat; dies schließt nicht aus, daß ich der wohltätigste sein werde.' Friedrich Nietzsche, *Ecce Homo* [1888], in *Werke,* vol. 2, pp. 1152–3.

[2] Friedrich Nietzsche, quoted in Lesley Chamberlain, *Nietzsche in Turin: The End of the Future* (London: Quartet Books, 1996), 200.

[3] 'Am 30. September großer Sieg; siebenter Tag; Müsiggang eines Gottes am Po entlang.' Friedrich Nietzsche, *Ecce Homo,* in *Werke,* vol. 2, p. 1145.

months had swallowed him. The reason he gave for thinking himself great was his overthrow of Christianity as he understood it, his 'transvaluation of all values', which he celebrated in a one-man liturgy of paeans to noble, self-affirming, remorseless, artistic types such as himself and diatribes against tender-heartedness. One of the last such incantations he wrote comes at the end of *Ecce Homo*:

in the concept of the *good* human being, there banded together all the weak, the sick, the botched at birth, those who suffer from their own selves, all that *which ought to perish*—the law of *selection* thwarted / hybridized, an ideal made of opposition to the proud and well-born, to the person who says Yes, who knows the future, who answers for the future.[4]

He found Turin a city after his own heart, in his own image, and would indeed have had difficulty in finding it anything else, for he was extremely short-sighted and also because, though he had lived on and off in Italy for a decade, he spoke little Italian and no Piedmontese. Nonetheless, within a day of arrival, he was sure about Turin:

This is really the town which can be useful to me *now*! Just the sort of place I can get hold of...But what a dignified and serious city it is! Nothing of the capital city about it, and nothing modern either, as I had feared: it is rather a town where a seventeenth-century court might take up residence, with a single dominant taste in everything, courtliness, *noblesse*. Aristocratic calm is maintained in every detail: there are no shabby little suburbs; a unity of taste, which extends even to the colour (the whole city is yellow or reddish brown). And for the feet as for the eyes it is a classical place! What safety, what pavements, not to speak of the buses and trams, the organization of which is absolutely marvellous![5]

---

[4] 'im Begriff des *guten* Menschen die Partei alles Schwachen, Kranken, Mißratnen, An-sich-selber-Leidenden genommen, alles dessen, *was zugrunde gehen soll*—, das Gesetz der *Selektion* gekreuzt, ein Ideal aus dem Widerspruch gegen den stolzen und wohlgeratenen, gegen den jasagenden, gegen den zukunftsgewissen, zukunftverbürgenden Menschen gemacht.' Nietzsche, *Ecce Homo*, in *Werke*, vol. 2, p. 145.

[5] 'Das ist wirklich die Stadt, die ich jetzt brauchen kann! Dies ist handgreiflich für mich...Aber was für eine würdige und ernste Stadt! Gar nicht Großstadt, gar nicht modern, wie ich gefürchtet hatte: sondern eine Residenz des 17. Jahrhunderts, welche nur einen kommandiereden Geschmack in allem hatte, den Hof und die *noblesse*. Es ist die aristokratische Ruhe in allem festgehalten: es gibt keine mesquinen Vorstädte; eine Einheit des Geschmacks, die bis auf die Farbe geht (die ganze Stadt ist gelb oder rotbraun). Und für die Füße wie für die Augen ein klassischer Ort! Was für Sicherheit, was für Pflaster, gar nicht zu reden von den Omnibus und Trams, deren Einrichtung hier bis ins Wunderbare gesteigert ist!' Nietzsche to Peter Gast, 7 Apr. 1888, in Friedrich Nietzsche, *Briefe* (Frankfurt am Main and Leipzig: Insel Verlag, 1993), 342–3.

He got the trams right, anyway. Though Nietzsche was a great walker, he had not walked far in Turin, for the city's industrial expansion had already begun before 1888 (though its most famous factory, Fiat, didn't arrive until 1899) and Nietzsche could have found plenty of 'shabby little suburbs' if he had wanted to. The city had been the capital of the Dukes of Savoy for centuries, and signs of its courtly past were indeed all round him, including the via Po itself, driven in a straight, haughty line through old quarters of the city to give a grand prospect down which the Duke could ride from his palace in Piazza Castello to the river and the mountains, so beloved of his dynasty, beyond.

And yet the via Po is not evidence of 'a single dominant taste in everything' but rather of the changing tastes and exigencies which faced a boss-class Nietzsche liked to fancy as 'calm', for the via Po runs from a central square (Piazza Castello) which encompasses a thirteenth-century castle, and palaces of various epochs (Renaissance, Baroque), down to the pseudo-classical Piazza Vittorio Veneto, whose very name attaches the square to the nineteenth-century Italian state. Turin had indeed once been the courtly city Nietzsche delighted in, but it had also been a more bourgeois capital quite recently; from 1861 to 1864 it was capital of the newly unified Kingdom of Italy and housed the country's first parliament in Palazzo Carignano, within sight of Nietzsche's third-floor room. (There were riots, during which dozens of Turinese were shot, in September 1864 when news spread that the capital was to be transferred, first to Florence and then to Rome.) Nor was Nietzsche right about there being 'nothing modern' in Turin. The year he arrived there the architect of the city's most famous landmark/eyesore died just as his ultra-extravagant building, the Mole Antonelliano, was being completed; by far the tallest building in Turin then, a grotesque marvel of late nineteenth-century engineering which, when he eventually noticed it, Nietzsche vastly admired. This vaulting structure was originally planned as a new synagogue for the Jews of Turin, but it was many times larger than the 2,000 or so of them could possibly need and they wisely passed it on, while it was still on the drawing-board, to grander purposes; it is now a museum of cinema.

And just as Nietzsche self-contradictorily admired the Mole while loathing the 'modern', so his last act before he lost his wits was, according to legend, a self-contradictory act of that compassion and solidarity with the weak and incompetent which he had so torrentially denounced as the slave-morality of Christianity. It is said that, on the street-corner I have mentioned, he saw a man maltreating a horse (it might have been a driver of one of the trams he rejoiced in); he embraced the horse and tried to halt the blows, shouting—according to one Italian account—'Tu disumano, tu bastonatore, tu massacratore di questo destriero' ('You inhuman brute, you cudgeller, you murderer of this steed'—the Italian is stilted enough to have been picked up from libretti, and Nietzsche was a lover of operetta, but it is too natty an irony that Nietzsche, who so looked down on the 'human all-too human', should have resorted in this final moment of lucidity to the ethical standard—'disumano'—he rejected).

After this he collapsed and was taken back to his room, where he passed several days playing the piano in the nude; he wrote letters to his remaining contacts signed sometimes 'Dionysos' and sometimes 'The Crucified One' and claiming to be not only God but also King Carlo Alberto, who had died forty years previously, unlike God, whose death Nietzsche had announced more recently. A week later, he was returned to Switzerland and then for the remaining years of his life to his mother's care and his sister's attentions. He lost his fondness for animals, it seems, for he was unkind to dogs and spoke little in his last decade, but when he did, his favourite word was 'elegant'.

I tell the story of Nietzsche's collapse in Turin as a puppet-play version of the drama that was to be played out on a more spectacular scale in the life of Primo Levi. Nietzsche's case touches on Levi's life-work in many ways, most harshly in Nietzsche's reliance on a Darwinian principle of 'natural selection' as a key element in his attack on a Judaeo-Christian ethic of compassion. The German phrase from *Ecce Homo*, 'das Gesetz der *Selektion* gekreuzt', which I translated as 'the law of *selection* thwarted / hybridized', shows its twisted roots in Social Darwinism because the word *Selektion* is a specialized use in German, whose more usual words for a 'selection' are *Auswahl* or *Auslese*; *Selektion* is mostly confined to such terms as *Selektionstheorie*, the 'theory of natural selection'. Nietzsche chose his words with care in order to insinuate that members of our species have no duty of care towards other individuals of the same species, for his word *gekreuzt* means not only 'thwarted' or 'transgressed', nor only 'hybridized' or 'cross-bred', but also 'marked with a cross'. This play with *gekreuzt* is sardonic but not as fierce or terrible as the pun on *Gesetz*, 'law', a pun which was not Nietzsche's invention but, more or less unwittingly, the brainchild of many scientists and enthusiasts for half-understood science in the nineteenth century, of those Social Darwinists who thought that the laws of evolution Darwin had discovered could easily be translated into laws of society, governmental policy, and moral rules, by adopting which human beings could speed up the process which had produced themselves and direct it to higher ends which they imagined themselves competent to assess. Evolution had taken millions of years to produce a being capable of understanding evolution, but it would not be long before that being could harness evolution and drive it, like a horse pulling a tram down foreseen grooves, to the evident perfection of the species. Thus, in one such version of Darwin, *Selektion*, a law of nature, became the inhuman rule of the death-camps, as Levi slowly learns in *Se questo è un uomo*, until he asks in the book's fourth chapter the dread question, set apart as a paragraph of just one sentence:

È dunque vero quello che si sente dire, di selezioni, di gas, di crematorio?

Is it true then what you hear said, about selections, about gas, about the crematorium?[6]

Nietzsche had contradictory attitudes to Darwin, sometimes calling him a Messiah and sometimes criticizing his work for attaching too much evolutionary importance to the role of adaptation to environment— not that Nietzsche had any observational evidence to contradict this essential element in Darwin's account; Nietzsche was a philosopher and just knew Darwin had to be wrong because the importance he assigned to adaptation didn't suit Nietzsche's conception of the self-determining individual. (Whereas for Levi the process of adaptation to a new environment and what such adaptation can do to the self is a principal object of study.) The topic of observational evidence as contrasted with metaphysical or quasi-religious frame-beliefs will also prove central to Levi's work. By a 'frame-belief', I mean something like a 'world-picture' or *Weltanschauung*, as the swankier among us might put it, an 'ideology' if you like. A religious belief in the existence of God, for example, is not the same kind of belief as an empirical belief in the existence of Turin, though some superstitious people think evidence can be marshalled for the former belief as for the latter. As the example of Nietzsche's letter about Turin shows, Nietzsche was not a careful observer, unlike Levi; he lacked Levi's patience before and

[6] Primo Levi, *Se questo è un uomo* (*If This is a Man*) [1958] (Turin: Einaudi, 2014), 45.

deference to the hard intricacies of fact. This difference between them shows in the styles they thought appropriate to write in: Nietzsche has the emphasis and conviction of a prophet (six of the seven italicizations in the two brief quotations from him are gestures of stress, of his sense of the importance of what he says and, it could be added, of his self-importance in saying it). You might have thought that, God having died, prophecy would have become extinct too, but far from it. Nietzsche is only one lurid instance of how discursive habits apt to the world of religious frame-beliefs persist in the absence of those frame-beliefs which might have given them sense. I shall refer to this persistence as 'positivism', by which I'll mean nothing more precise than 'a quasi-religious faith in scientific methods and discoveries'. Levi, by contrast, who was trained as a scientist and earned his living for years as an industrial chemist, writes quite differently, writes what he called in a 1976 interview 'il linguaggio pacato e sobrio del testimone ...' ('the calmed and sober language of a witness ...').[7] One way of distinguishing between an empirical belief, such as belief in the existence of Turin, and a frame-belief, such as belief in the existence of God or belief that evolution has been fully understood and is now manageable by us, would be to ask whether there is a style of writing appropriate to the belief: there are ways of writing characteristic of those who think God has spoken to them, as there are ways of writing apt for those who believe there is no such speaking God, but there is no style apt to belief in the existence of Turin.

Take Nietzsche's enthusiasm for the 'single dominant taste in everything' which his myopic glance discovered in Turin. Even if he had not been wrong about the evidence, there would still be a question about his predilections, about his schematic preference for uniformity over variety, perhaps even about his unreflecting tendency to cry up mastery wherever he thought he found it (the word I translate as 'dominant' is *kommandierenden*). Consider by way of contrast this description of a townscape:

innumerevoli tetri edifici quadrati di mattoni nudi, a tre piani, tutti eguali fra loro; fra questi correvano strade lastricate, rettilinee e perpendicolari, a perdita d'occhio ...

[7] Primo Levi, *Se questo è un uomo*, Appendix I, p. 174.

countless gloomy buildings, squared off with bare bricks, three storeys high, all identical one with another, between which ran paved streets in straight lines and at right angles to each other, as far as the eye could see...[8]

The buildings here were monochrome too, not with the ochre Nietzsche admired in Turin, but grey. The urban symmetry, the ease of traffic through-put which many have observed in Turin were here too, but they conduce not to proportions restful for the eye but to what the common Italian idiom acutely calls 'perdita d'occhio', literally, 'loss of eye'—a blinding monotony, a homogenization which defeats all sense of salience and which Levi underlines in the calmed, observant accuracy so typical of his writing as it weighs the facts, underlines by a run of seven, unvaried terminations in 'i'—'innumerevoli tetri edifici quadrati di mattoni nudi'. Such unbroken runs of the same termination occur, of course, more frequently in Italian than in English as a banal result of simple facts about Italian phonology, but a run of like terminations is usually avoided by a meticulous expert in materials, including language, such as Levi, except when, as here, the effect is to the point. A single, dominant taste was operative in these countless gloomy buildings too, though this description encourages us to recognize that such a single, dominant taste has a double aspect: it can conduce equally to a crushing tyranny as to the uplifting aesthetic harmony which enchanted Nietzsche. These straight lines, paved streets, and uniform buildings might have made the camp a home from home for the Turinese Levi, but this is not how he felt about Buna-Monowitz, the suburb of Auschwitz he is describing. Levi lived the first two decades of his life in a long, thin, oblong segment of Turin: two rectilinear parallel roads one block apart—the Corso Re Umberto, on which he was born, at number 75, where he also died, and the much smaller via Massena, up which he walked to his primary and then, a bit further, his secondary school—mark out his territory for much of his youth. There were, of course, also trips to the park and to the mountains; his territory as a child was not specially cramped. Perhaps his familiarity with this repeatedly trodden and retrodden rectangle, as well as his chemist's skill in recognizing the same element in different compounds, alerted him to the fact that concentration camps were not so distinct from civilized society as some more eloquent than thoughtful accounts of the camps suggest. In Levi, the *Lager* is not an 'unimaginable horror' or

---

[8] Primo Levi, *La tregua* (*The Truce*) [1958] (Turin: Einaudi, 2014), 10.

an 'unspeakable monstrosity', as it is convenient for those who have lazy imaginations and slovenly speech to make out, but rather its horror consists in the fact that we find there too: 'molti lineamenti della società in cui viviamo, in una forma che io direi caricaturale' ('many features of the society in which we ourselves live, in the form of what I might call a caricature').[9]

Had it occurred to the passers-by who stopped to help Nietzsche when he collapsed at the corner of via Carlo Alberto and via Po that he needed not only a medical doctor but perhaps also an expert in personality disorders, a diagnostician of aberrance and immoralism, they could have found one two minutes' walk away, at 18 via Po, where the world-famous criminologist Cesare Lombroso had his laboratory. Lombroso is not much heard of nowadays, because most of his theories have been discarded, but he was an authority in his day—a professor at the University of Turin since 1878, he was often called in as an 'expert witness' at criminal trials and, indeed, people were hanged on his supposed evidence just as more recently women have been imprisoned on the supposed evidence of a presumed expert in the likelihood of cot-deaths. And here again, a feature of the via Po correlates with the path Levi's life was to take, for 'expertise' is in varying ways another of his principal subjects and methods: there was his expert training as a chemist which saved his life in the *Lager* and from which he earned a living for many years, but also, more broadly, his admiration for other people's skills as shown in *L'altrui mestiere* (*Other People's Trades*) and in *La chiave a stella* (*The Wrench*). Lombroso's special knack was cranial measurement; he thought he had established correlations between size and shape of the head and criminal tendencies.[10] He had, that is, confused in an exceptionally crass way the 'mind' and the 'brain', and so conveniently simplified for himself inferences from physical measurement of the brain to the dispositions and character of the mind. It may be that one day an identity will be established between the mind and the brain, but we are still a long way from any such achievement; we do not know how consciousness arises from matter, and before we arrive at any such knowledge our own consciousness

[9] Primo Levi, *Conversazioni e interviste* (*Conversations and Interviews, 1963–1987*), ed. Marco Belpoliti (Turin: Einaudi, 1997), 48.

[10] Cesare Lombroso, *Criminal Man* (1876), trans. Mary Gibson and Nicole Hahn Rafter (London: Duke University Press, 2006).

may need to develop its capacity for understanding in ways we cannot
at present foresee.

It was, though, characteristic of nineteenth-century positivism to
think that such psycho-physical correlations were easily made (they
were basic to that 'scientific racism' so ably and dismayingly charted in
Stephen Jay Gould's *The Mismeasure of Man*): the man who discovered
fingerprints, Francis Galton, was sad not to be able to distinguish
between Asian, Caucasian, and Negro fingers; he also conducted not
only a statistical enquiry into the efficacy of prayer but also a research
project whose purpose was to determine in which geographical
regions the prettiest girls were to be found.[11] There were reputable
experts who believed that intelligence was correlated with the distance
between the root of the penis and the navel. It would be a great mistake to think that only the uneducated identified virtue with blond
hair and blue eyes and vice with big noses and greasy complexions; it
would be an equally great mistake to think that it is scientific knowledge
which of itself guards us against superstition.

Primo Levi's father had known Lombroso and similar figures of
enlightened opinion in turn-of-the-century Turin:

> in giovinezza aveva frequentato i circoli positivisti della Torino di allora:
> Lombroso, Herlitzka, Angelo Mosso, scienziati scettici ma facilmente illusi,
> che si ipnotizzavano a vicenda, leggevano Fontenelle, Flammarion e Annie
> Besant, e facevano ballare i tavolini.

> in his youth, he used to hang around in positivist circles of which there were
> many in Turin then: Lombroso, Herlitzka, Angelo Mosso—all sceptical experts
> who were easily taken in, who took it in turns to hypnotize one another, read
> Fontenelle, Flammarion, and Annie Besant, and were into table-tapping.[12]

I haven't been able to find out who Herlitzka was, but Angelo Mosso
was a psycho-physiologist like Lombroso, a generation older, and also
a professor at the University of Turin. You should not be surprised at
Levi's association of spiritualism and scientific inquiry, for 'psychic
research' was a common pastime among positivists: the first Italian
spiritualist society was founded at Turin in 1865; the great Cavour, first
prime minister of a unified Italy, appeared after his death to several
people there, including Massimo d'Azeglio, man of letters, liberal

---

[11] Stephen Jay Gould, *The Mismeasure of Man* (London: Norton, 1981).
[12] Primo Levi, 'Il mondo invisible', in *L'altrui mestiere* (*Other People's Trades*) [1985] (Turin:
Einaudi, 2002), 187.

progressive, the statesman who promoted the civil liberties of Piedmont's Jews, after whom Levi's grammar-school was named. Nietzsche himself is said by some to have attended a seance in Turin (whether this is so or not, he was a fascinated student of some of Galton's more absurd works). Turin has for centuries been a city noted both for its rationality— Erasmus studied there, the great mathematician Lagrange was born there—and also for rationalist excesses such as freemasonry (the masons founded a Temple of Virtue there as early as 1765) and magic, the bastard offspring of an immoderate zeal for technology. So too the reading which Levi mentions as common knowledge among positivists of his father's acquaintance is a product of that fertile area where tatters of shaky, empirical evidence and shreds of decayed religious belief combine to breed odd notions: Flammarion, for example, was a serious astronomer and also a popularizer of astronomy, one of whose most popular notions was that the canals on Mars just *had to be* the work of an advanced civilization; Annie Besant was a secularist, an advocate of birth control, a founder member of the Fabian Society, and at the same time a fervent disciple of Madame Blavatsky and her 'theosophy', a murky pool of garbled ancient wisdom and modern psycho-babble into which W. B. Yeats also dipped his credulous toes (though he would have been appalled to be otherwise associated with Annie Besant and her socio-political views).

In 1955 Levi spoke of the twentieth century as 'quel secolo in cui la scienza è stata curvata' ('this century in which science has been twisted').[13] He was no doubt thinking primarily of Nazi pseudo-science, but he would not have wished to encourage the belief that only wicked Germans had bent science from its true methods and goals: eugenics, which the Nazis practised with such lopsided fervour was widely believed in throughout the liberal-democratic world as well as in totalitarian regimes, and indeed is still being practised on a small scale, as in screening for Down's syndrome, cleft palate, and other minor deviations from what is considered the desirable norm. Positivistic pseudo-science mushroomed in the totalitarian regimes of the twentieth century, but the spores of those nightmares were themselves at least a century old; they go back to the callow materialism, the unreflective translation of Darwinism into the ethical and political

---

[13] Primo Levi, *L'asimmetria e la vita* (*Asymmetry and Life*) [1955], ed. Marco Belpoliti (Turin: Einaudi, 2002), 7.

sphere which Levi's father would have encountered in the enlightened salons of Turin and which can also be found in the pages of Nietzsche. It is, in fact, more difficult to be an atheist than some people suppose; belief in God may be abandoned, but great intellectual and emotional vigilance is necessary if such a belief is not to be replaced by a worse credulity, a malign irrationalism or hyper-rationalism—by, in short, belief in an idol. True atheism requires what Levi said an industrial chemist needed when he started his career in that discipline and the instruments with which a modern chemist works had not yet been invented; it requires 'una pazienza da non credere' ('patience beyond belief'), which we might, leaning on the phrase a little, also translate as 'the patience of unbelief, the patience not to believe', a patience such as many positivists—'scienziati scettici ma facilmente illusi'—lacked.[14]

Another way of distinguishing between an empirical belief, such as belief in the existence of Turin, and a frame-belief is that it is often much harder to tell when frame-beliefs contradict each other. The scientific spiritualists of Turin, for example, probably believed, as good scientists, the injunction: 'do not accept that anything exists unless you have empirical evidence of its existence', but they also believed something like: 'the soul is immortal.' They therefore sought for empirical evidence of the existence of an immortal soul, or rather, deluded themselves into believing that evidence of survival after death (such as might be provided by psychic research) was evidence of immortality, which it is not. Turin's credulous sceptics are just one example of the general truth which the anthropologist Clifford Geertz points to when he emphasizes how important it is for a theorist of religion (and of other cultural formations, it might be added) 'to see man as moving more or less easily, and very frequently, between radically contrasting ways of looking at the world, ways which are not continuous with one another but separated by cultural gaps'.[15] Geertz could have found a demonstration of his truth a few doors further down the via Po, at number 28 in fact, where Primo Levi's paternal grandmother lived; Levi reports of her that she attended devoutly and on alternate days the synagogue and the parish church of Sant'Ottavio. So energetic was her religious syncretism or hedging of her bets, depending on how you look at it, that 'pare che andasse addirittura sacrilegamente a

---

[14] Primo Levi, *La chiave a stella* (*The Wrench*) [1978] (Turin: Einaudi, 2014), 148.
[15] Clifford Geertz, *The Interpretation of Cultures* [1973] (London: Fontana, 1993), 120.

confessarsi' ('it seems she may even have gone, downright sacrilegiously, to confession').[16] This extreme assimilation by a Jew of Catholic practice mattered to Levi because he himself felt, and not with shame, that he was an 'assimilated' Jew, to the extent that he would sometimes demur at being called a 'Jewish writer', though he never denied that he was a Jew; it was simply that the culture in and out of which he wrote was Piedmontese—call it Italian if you must—much more signally than it was Jewish. Nor was this assimilation for Levi a matter of only individual concern; he thought (and rightly) that it was typical of the Jewish diaspora in Italy to have been profoundly assimilated in a way which is not, for instance, true of Spanish Jews, and this in turn mattered to him after his return from Auschwitz when he had to come to terms with, and for, the complicity of Italians in Nazi anti-Semitism, as also when he gauged his own distance from the Zionism of the Israeli government. There is a lot of evidence that Levi was right about this assimilation of Italian Jews; one especially charming anecdote is told by a Jewish woman from the ghetto in Rome, the most ancient of Jewish settlements in the peninsula:

There were Christians living in the neighborhood with us, and they were just like us. They even spoke like us—most of them had picked up the Roman Jewish dialect. There was a woman next door who said she was Christian—but no one believed her because she was always using Jewish expressions and oaths: 'I swear on the sepherim that I go to mass', she used to say, 'I swear on a scroll of the Torah'.[17]

Here is Levi on visits to this grandmother's flat on via Po:

Non ricordo quasi nulla di lei, che mio padre chiamava Maman (anche in terza persona)... Mio padre, ogni domenica mattina, mi conduceva a piedi in visita a Nona Màlia: percorrevamo lentamente via Po, e lui si fermava ad accarezzare tutti i gatti, ad annusare tutti i tartufi ed a sfogliare tutti i libri usati... piuttosto superstizioso che religioso, provava disagio nell'infrangere le regole del Kasherút, ma il prosciutto gli piaceva talmente che, davanti alla tentazione delle vetrine, cedeva ogni volta, sospirando, imprecando sotto voce... Quando arrivavamo sul pianerottolo tenebroso dell'alloggio di via Po, mio padre suonava il campanello, ed alla nonna che veniva ad aprire gridava in un orecchio: 'A l'è 'l prim 'd la scòla!', è il primo della classe.

---

[16] Primo Levi, *Il sistema periodico* (*The Periodic Table*) [1975] (Turin: Einaudi, 2014), 18.
[17] Alexander Stille, *Benevolence and Betrayal: Five Jewish Families under Fascism* (London: Jonathan Cape, 1992), 179.

I remember almost nothing about the woman my father called 'Maman' (even when referring to her in the third person)...Every Sunday morning, my father took me on a walk to visit Granny Màlia: we used to go slowly right down via Po, and he would stop to stroke every cat we met, to sniff all the truffles, and flick through all the second-hand books...He was superstitious rather than religious and breaking the rules of kosher made him uneasy, but he liked ham so much that, when he was faced with temptation from a shop-window, he would give in to it every time, sighing and cursing under his breath...When we reached the dark landing of her flat on via Po, my father would ring the bell, and when she came to open the door he would shout in my grandmother's ear: 'A l'è 'l prim 'd la scòla!', he's top of his class.[18]

I draw your attention to several points in this memory: first, to the fact that Levi's father called his mother and spoke of her not as 'Mamma' but as 'Maman', that is to say: in French. Pretentious, *lui*? Not at all. Turin is only 150 or so kilometres further from Paris than it is from Rome, and so closer geographically to Paris than to Naples and anywhere further south in Italy. More importantly, the House of Savoy had for centuries held possessions in what is now France or Switzerland as far north as Geneva and west beyond Nice into Provence. Levi's story is in part the story of another nineteenth-century -ism with effects perhaps even more drastic than positivism, I mean, nationalism, and we will not tell that story properly, or understand it fully, if we allow flimsy borders drawn by the recent ambitions of states to cloud our sense of the cultural and social realities in which people live. Levi, like his father before him and like many educated Turinese today, uses French words quite unselfconsciously, as when he drew a distinction between the individualism of literary authorship and the collaborative nature of a chemist's work: 'nel lavoro di un chimico raramente ciò che si fa è firmato, o, se lo è, è firmato da un'équipe' ('in a chemist's work, the results are rarely signed, or, if they are signed, they bear the signature of an équipe').[19] 'Équipe' came to him as naturally as 'Maman' to his father. Natalia Ginzburg, another Turinese Jewish writer of Levi's generation, often notes of someone in her memoir, *Lessico famigliare*, that he or she 'parlava con l'erre'—that is to say, spoke with the French rather than the Italian 'r'; she even records that her father was frenchified to the extent that he counted money in francs rather than lire.[20]

---

[18] Levi, *Il sistema periodico*, 18–19.   [19] Primo Levi, *Conversazioni e interviste*, 23.
[20] Natalia Ginzburg, *Lessico famigliare* (*Family Sayings*) [1963] (Turin: Einaudi, 2010), 7.

Levi hints at the political importance of this ancient Franco-Italianate quality in Piedmontese culture when, in *Il sistema periodico*, he tells a story about how he was offered work by a certain 'Dottor Martini' (an evident alias) during the period when Mussolini's racial laws were in force; Levi recognizes the man is a friend and not a Fascist sympathizer because he fixes a meeting at the 'Hotel Suisse di Torino' and not at the 'Albergo Svizzera', 'come avrebbe dovuto fare un cittadino ligio' ('as a loyal citizen ought to have done').[21] With regard to language as to architectural style, it is wise to be more sceptical than Nietzsche about those who seek to impose 'a single dominant taste in everything'.

My extract from Levi's memoir of visits to his grandmother begins with a bit of French and ends in Piedmontese dialect—'A l'è 'l prim 'd la scòla.' Though Levi himself did not speak fluent Piedmontese, he wrote about it often and the variety of tongues is a central feature of his writing, from the harsh polyglot words of the *Lager* to the amiable idiom of *La chiave a stella*. In particular, the dialect of Piedmontese Jews mattered to him in ways which show how diversity of speech was for him not only an aspect of style, but also an emblem, a focus of loyalty, an object of as it were ecological tenderness:

I nostri padri, e soprattutto le nostre madri, si servivano quotidianamente e con naturalezza del giudeo-piemontese: era la lingua della famiglia e della casa. Erano tuttavia consapevoli della sua intrinseca forza comica, che scaturiva dal contraste fra il tessuto del discorso, che era il dialetto piemontese, rustico e laconico, e l'incastro ebraico, ricavato dalla lingua dei patriarchi, remota ma ravvivata ogni giorno dalla preghiera pubblica e privata e dalla lettura dei Testi, levigata dai millenni come l'alveo dei ghiacciai.

Our fathers, and especially our mothers, made use every day and quite unself-consciously of Judaeo-Piedmontese: it was the idiom for family and domestic matters. They were, though, aware of its intrinsically comic power, which sprang from a contrast between the fibre of the discourse, which was the clipped, peasant dialect of Piedmont, and its Hebrew frame, drawn from the speech of the patriarchs, a distant speech but one brought back to life every day through public or private prayer, through the reading of the Scriptures, a speech polished over millenia like the bed of glaciers.[22]

There is no better description of some aspects of Levi's own style, in *Se questo*... and thereafter, than this sublime moment in which he conjoins a sense of the comic and the thought of vast trans-temporal

---

[21] Primo Levi, *Il sistema periodico*, 102.   [22] Levi, *L'asimmetria e la vita*, 216.

processes such as are evident in glaciation, in which he thinks of a patriarchal Hebrew as both 'remota'—as it was for an assimilated, atheistic Jew such as himself—but also 'ravvivata ogni giorno', just as, early in *Se questo*, he thinks of the deported Jews in terms of the exodus from Egypt, or later, when noting that lack of a spoon compelled you to lap up your ration of soup like a dog, he recalls Judges 7.5 and how there Gideon discriminated between those he would and those he wouldn't take on as soldiers on the basis of how they drank from a river, whether like men or like dogs. This Judaeo-Piedmontese matrix is the matrix of his writing, the fibre of whose discourse is also contrastive: measured and calmed, as befits the speech of a witness, a trained observer like the chemist, Levi; comic, even in circumstances which were far from amusing, but also capable (and capable partly because comic) of a millenial eloquence like that of a psalm, as here when the prose leaps up to the thought of mountains (Levi was a keen mountaineer). It is, I think, particularly worth noting how deep and keen a sense of long process Levi can instil into his writing as he does through this reference to glaciation, worth noting because it is this patience with long process which makes Levi's writing truly Darwinian, apt as a style for someone who takes, as Levi took, evolution as a frame-belief. It is an odd thing that in the nineteenth century human beings learned for the first time how long a time their own evolution had taken; geology, palaeontology, astronomy, and the biological sciences all greatly expanded the time-scale relevant to their subjects. It is sometimes claimed that the discoveries of these sciences were what put paid to God, at least God as previously conceived by many. But you might have thought that, though 'eternity' would have to disappear along with God, the vast histories and pre-histories opened up by these sciences could have to some extent taken eternity's place, and kept human beings sensible about the real dimensions of time in which they live. This has not been the case; on the contrary, history has shrunk in the wash, as if the human mind recoiled from what it had discovered about the protraction of its own history. Nietzsche, nothing if not symptomatic as usual, for example incessantly contrasts past notions with a present conceived as suddenly and absolutely different from the past: 'Shall we still speak thus today ?'; 'Today...we see ourselves as it were entangled in error'; 'this itself seems to us today merely an acute form of folly'; 'Today we do not believe a word of it'; 'We no longer have any sympathy today with the concept of "free will"'; 'we have found the exit out of whole millennia of labyrinth'.[23] The tone of that last remark, its inane positivistic unrealism about cultural process, is remarkably similar to Marx and Engels's claim in their *Manifesto* that the Communist Party knows the answer to the riddle of history and knows that it, the Communist Party, is that answer.[24] Nietzsche writes as if a frame-belief like Judaeo-Christianity were an empirical belief which can, if evidence and circumstances require, be changed as quickly and with as little trouble as a pair of underpants. But people's minds don't change frames like that (although, of course, Nietzsche was not interested in people, having set his heart on the superman—'what do the *rest* matter?—The rest are merely mankind.—One must be superior to mankind in force, in *loftiness* of soul—in contempt....'[25] A related phenomenon occurs when you hear, as I did recently, two people on the radio discussing the fact, which astonished and shocked them, that thirty years after sex discrimination had been outlawed, men and women were still not treated equally in the workplace. Thirty years, what an age! Attitudes like this show that some people who have given up belief in God have adopted in its place a dreamy, childish belief in the State and how quick its fixes are likely to be. It is no doubt merely journalism and its distorted perception of temporal process which leads a sensible woman like Victoria Derbyshire on Radio 5 to say something like, 'well, this is the age-old problem of where to site a new runway, isn't it?', where 'age-old' cannot mean more than 'fifty years old'.

Levi was alert to these perspectival distortions of time, the real time of cultural change rather than the sham time of cultural commentators or politicians and their bogus pronouncements that the world has completely altered in the last five years or five minutes, like President

[23] 'Werden wir heute noch so reden?'; 'Heute... sehen wir... uns gewissermaßen verstrickt in den Irrtum'; 'erscheint uns heute selbst bloß als eine akute Form der Dummheit'; 'Wir glauben heute kein Wort mehr von dem allen'; 'Wir haben heute kein Mitleid mehr mit dem Begriff "freier Wille"'; 'wir fanden den Ausgang aus ganzen Jahrtausenden des Labyrinths'. Friedrich Nietzsche, *Götzen-Dämmerung (Twilight of the Idols)* in *Werke,* vol. 2, p. 951, 959, 966, 973, 976; *Der Antichrist (The Anti-Christ)* [1895] in *Werke*, vol. 2, p. 1166.

[24] Karl Marx and Friedrich Engels, *Manifesto of the Communist Party* (1848), in *The Red Republican*, trans. Helen Macfarlane, ed. G. Julian Harney (London: S.Y. Collins, 1850); Karl Marx, 'Private Property and Communism', from *Economic and Philosophical Manuscripts 1844*, in *Karl Marx: Selected Writings*, 95–103 (p. 97).

[25] 'was liegt am *Rest*?—Der Rest ist bloß die Menschheit.—Man muß der Menschheit überlegen sein durch Kraft, durch *Höhe* der Seele—durch Verachtung...'. Friedrich Nietzsche, *Der Antichrist*, in *Werke*, vol. 2, p. 1163.

Bush, who said on 11 September 2001 that nothing would ever be the same again, and then, on 13 September 2001, advised his fellow Americans to return to work, almost, you might say, as if nothing had happened. You would expect Levi to be sharp about such things; after all, the burned child fears the fire and, as he rightly observed: 'Del resto, l'intera storia del breve "Reich Millenario" può essere riletta come guerra contro la memoria' ('What's more, the entire history of the short-lived "Thousand Year Reich" can be reinterpreted as a war against memory').[26]

It may seem strained to link the habits of our mass media, their fast-and-loose play with historical perspective, to Nazism, but we should exercise our memories and recall how great a role control of the mass media played in the rise to power of dictators—Mussolini, after all, was a newspaperman. Whatever the rights and wrong of this matter, one reason why Levi's work deserves attention is that he takes up his pen on behalf of memory rather than against it, for the sake of small hybrid communities, such as the Jews of Piedmont, who rarely figure in the slogans of the state or in the sweeping projections of epoch-mongers like Nietzsche. And for those who have patience like Levi's with the all-too long, all-too various history of our species, he gives good reason why they should concern themselves with these instances in which cultural process can really be seen at work, reasons why they too should be, as he was, 'incuriosito, ed anche intenerito, da questa patetica sopravvivenza della lingua biblica nel linguaggio familiare e dialettale' ('fascinated, and indeed touched, by this pathetic survival of the Bible's language within the everyday language of dialect').[27] Unsurprisingly, given what happened to him, 'sopravvivenza' was Levi's deepest and most urgent subject, and this too makes him a profoundly Darwinian writer, for 'survival' is a Darwinian theme, though Levi would ask, as positivists eager for the solution to everything did not pause to ask, 'survival as what?'; 'survival of the fittest', fine and dandy, but 'fittest for what?'

---

[26] Primo Levi, *I sommersi e i salvati* (*The Drowned and the Saved*) [1986] (Turin: Einaudi, 2014), 20.

[27] Levi, *L'asimmetria e la vita*, 219.

IO

Godforsakenness

Samuel Beckett had many troubles in the theatre. One in particular, with the following prayer-sequence from *Endgame*: a father, Nagg, his son, Hamm, and a third person, Clov (who may be the grandson or just a quasi-adopted quasi-member of the family) try addressing God:

> HAMM: Let us pray to God.
> CLOV: Again!
> NAGG: Me sugar-plum!
> HAMM: God first! [*Pause.*] Are you right?
> CLOV: [*Resigned.*] Off we go.
> HAMM: [*To* NAGG.] And you?
> NAGG: [*Clasping his hands, closing his eyes, in a gabble.*] Our Father which art—
> HAMM: Silence! In silence! Where are your manners? [*Pause.*] Off we go. [*Attitudes of prayer. Silence. Abandoning his attitude, discouraged.*] Well?
> CLOV: [*Abandoning his attitude.*] What a hope! And you?
> HAMM: Sweet damn all! [*To* NAGG.] And you?
> NAGG: Wait! [*Pause. Abandoning his attitude.*] Nothing doing!
> HAMM: The bastard! He doesn't exist!
> CLOV: Not yet.[1]

The Lord Chamberlain, who was then the censor of the English stage, declined to permit God to be referred to as a bastard, though he was prepared to allow 'swine'. Such is the theological acumen and delicacy of English authorities. Beckett first refused to accept any changes in the script, and wrote to the director: 'I am afraid I simply cannot accept omission or modification of the prayer passage which appears to me indispensable as it stands . . . I think this does call for a firm stand. It is

---

[1] Samuel Beckett, *Endgame* [1958] (London: Faber & Faber, 2009), 34.

no more blasphemous than "My God, my God, why hast Thou forsaken me?" [2]

Those words are reported in two of the Gospels, St Mark's and St Matthew's, to have been Christ's last words from the cross. St Mark's is the earlier version, from which St Matthew's differs in no substantial detail:

And at the ninth hour Jesus cried with a loud voice [*phōnē megalē*], saying Eloi, Eloi, lama sabachtani, which is, being interpreted, My God, my God, why hast thou forsaken me?

And some of them that stood by, when they heard it, said, Behold, he calleth Elias [Elijah]. [3]

Beckett, who was brought up as a protestant and had a verbal memory which relinquished nothing that matters, quotes verbatim the King James Version. In the Gospel according to St Luke, Christ dies saying, also in a great voice, 'Father into your hands I will commit my spirit (23.46); St John's Christ is more softly spoken, he just says '*tetelestai*', 'it is finished' (19.30).

As verse 35 of the fifteenth chapter of St Mark's Gospel shows, these last words were misunderstood from the first moment they were spoken: 'And some of the bystanders, hearing this, said, "Look, he is calling Elijah".' Many were the humiliations which surrounded our Lord in His passion—a show-trial, mockery, flagellation, being spat upon, nakedness, having his death turned into a public spectacle, indeed a lottery-draw as the soldiers diced for the prize of his clothing—but this final mistaking had a particular bitterness. The person who said, according to St John, 'To this end I was born, and for this cause came I into the world, that I should bear witness unto the truth' (18.37), dies hearing the last words he said bent out of true. He might be imagined, as His eyes turn up and in onto the extinguishing of all light and as the aftertaste of vinegar fades from His lips, thinking of those He came to save, His audience: 'They *never* listen.'

People have followed the precedent set by these first hearers, and have been mishearing the words for two millennia. They are not, admittedly, easy to hear. A popular rendition in recent times of what He meant by them goes like this: 'In a final moment of lucidity, the poor deluded

[2] Beckett to George Devine, 26 December 1957, in *The Letters of Samuel Beckett*, ed. Martha Dow Fehsenfeld, Lois More Overbeck, George Craig, and Daniel Gunn, 4 vols. (Cambridge: Cambridge University Press, 2009–16), vol. 3: *1957–65* (2014), p. 81.

[3] Gospel according to St Mark, 15:34–5.

carpenter's son, who was an exceptionally nice guy but very mixed up by the superstitions of his day, realized that all this "god" stuff had been a big mistake. He died, as we all must die, being only human, a wholly lonely death.' Christ, that is, at the moment of His death, prefigured Nietzsche by realizing that God is dead, or is a bastard who doesn't exist. He is therefore the prime atheist, the archetypal godforsaken man; as such—these are the curious thought-processes of our day—he is all the more worthy to be worshipped, or at least vehemently admired. Poor dear, so sad, so sweet. This is not how at least some of the first audience misheard His exit-line. They misheard 'Eloi', a form of 'Elohim', a cosmopolitan name for 'God' (as contrasted with the name of the God of Israel, Jehovah), as 'Elijah', the name of the prophet, who was one of those beings God had favoured by assuming bodily into heaven. They didn't hear Him as complaining that God did not exist, but rather as asking a special favour of God via Elijah, *the* special favour which God alone can grant, avoidance of death, the ultimate in body-swerves. But this too was not what He was saying. For to say that he was 'saying' any-thing may be to say too much, because he may have been quoting, and 'to quote' is not quite 'to say'. He was quoting Hebrew scripture, His last words being the first verse of a psalm, number 22:

My God, my God, why hast thou forsaken me?
     why art thou so far from helping me?
     and from the words of my roaring?
O my God, I cry in the day time,
     but thou hearest not;
and in the night season,
     and am not silent.
But thou art holy,
     O thou that inhabitest the praises of Israel.
Our fathers trusted in thee:
     they trusted and thou didst deliver them.
They cried unto thee,
     and were delivered:
thy trusted in thee,
    and were not confounded.
But I am a worm, and no man:
     a reproach of men, and despised of the people.
All they that see me laugh me to scorn:
     they shoot out the lip, they shake the head saying,
He trusted on the LORD that he would deliver him:
     let him deliver him, seeing he delighted in him.

But thou are he that took me out of the womb:
  thou didst make me hope when I was upon my mother's breasts.
I was cast upon thee from the womb:
  thou art my God from my mother's belly.
Be not far from me:
  for trouble is near;
  for there is none to help.
Many bulls have compassed me:
  strong bulls of Bashan have beset me round.
They gaped upon me with their mouths,
  as a ravening and a roaring lion.
I am poured out like water,
  and all my bones are out of joint:
my heart is like wax;
  it is melted in the midst of my bowels.[4]

Whatever individual psalms were at first—*otototoi*, lyric poems raised up from outcry—the psalms collectively had become by the time of Christ's dying the psalter, a collection of sacred writings, ritually aimed at God. No psalm could deny the existence of God, or complain of misbehaviour on His part. Or better: a psalm could never be more blasphemous than Hamm's 'The bastard! He doesn't exist!', a human reproach whose self-contradiction (someone who doesn't exist can't be blamed for not existing) in fact unfolds relatedness to what it speaks against, as a child's 'I hate you' to a parent speaks most of their interanimation though this is not what the child's words say. Psalm 22 begins like this, and then goes on to express trust in God, for whatever experience of bereftness the speaker may be in as he speaks his anguished words, his words and his anguish in this kind of sacred poem, eventuate in comfort, in the rediscovery of the lost, the silent, even the errant, beloved, God. Some commentators have found the split in psalm 22 between its piercing account of godforsakenness and its reassured coda so extreme that they have been driven to believe the psalm not one but two poems, cobbled together by some pious DIY cowboy, just as some commentators have thought the Book of Job not a single work because its prose frame sounds in their ears maladapted to its verse core.

Beckett said that his line was no more blasphemous than 'My God, my God, why...'. He may have meant that Christ's last words were blasphemous, but this is not likely, given Beckett's deep and disbelieving

---

[4] Psalm 22.1–14.

relation to the Gospels. More likely, Beckett knew that Christ's last words were a quotation, from a poem which formalizes the experience of godforsakenness, and from a form of poetry which had itself become scripture, god-addressed even through the '*Silence*' of God which Beckett so mildly marks in his stage directions. Perhaps Beckett knew also that psalm 22 has in its headnote the phrase: 'To the "Doe of the Dawn".' This phrase is usually understood to mean that the psalm should be sung to a tune, a tune which pre-existed the poem and whose name was 'The Doe of the Dawn', as in the game when we say 'Sing Emily Dickinson's "Because I could not stop for death" to the tune of "The Yellow Roses of Texas" ' or 'Sing Blake's "Tiger, tiger" to the tune of the Supremes' "Baby Love"'. (Both can be done.) Not only was Christ quoting an old poem but the old poem went to an older tune.

To speak of your pain as the innocent victim of judicial torture and execution through such an allusion is to manage to think there is nothing special about your self, even as you are being crucified. A remarkable achievement. I personally think my own slight back-pain the centre of the universe. It was perhaps this achievement of not-putting-one's-self-at-the-centre-of-the-stage, this un-tragedianly quality, in Christ's last utterance which impressed Simone Weil so sharply that she wrote:

'My God, my God, why hast thou forsaken me?'
There we have the real proof that Christianity is something divine.[5]

She had trained as a geometrician and was more eager for 'real proof' than is apt or sensible in these matters. What she heard in these last words was not blasphemy, nor the whimper of humanity coming to its senses, its sense of self, and realizing there is no God, nor a self-seeking desire to be excused death, but rather the sound of death itself, the taking-into the human individual of death as radically unspecializing, and the recognition that, if God did contrive to become incarnate in Christ, to become 'Emmanuel', God-with-us, then He must have taken at least on Himself death. Simone Weil puts it this way:

Adam and Eve sought for divinity in vital energy—a tree, fruit. But it is prepared for us on dead wood, geometrically squared, where a corpse is hanging. We must look for the secret of our kinship with God in our mortality . . . God gives himself to men either as powerful or as perfect—it is for them to choose.[6]

---

[5] Simone Weil, *Gravity and Grace*, trans. Gustave Thibon (London: Routledge, 1952), 79.
[6] Simone Weil, *Gravity and Grace*, 80, 83.

I doubt if we are free just to 'choose' a powerful or a perfect God, as between brands of toothpaste, any more than it is a matter of choice what 'My God, my God, why...' means. Though we have indeed a leeway in between these words and what we might take them to mean, what they might take us as meaning. The Christian church spent about 500 years wondering about them. What those who came after Christ and called themselves Christians had to ponder was how it could be true that the same being could have been God and man at the same time, in the same place, the place of His body. This is the distinctively Christian claim, shared by no other religion as yet though aped by most fan-clubs, the claim of the Incarnation, God in one spatio-temporally unique being became man. It is extremely difficult to see or hear what might be meant by such a claim, but if the meaning of the Incarnation can be seen or heard it is to be seen and heard in the words 'My God, my God, why...' because, dying, each individual's life falls into place, and the Incarnation is just this, the falling of the divine life into time and place. Indeed, I shall suggest that Christian theology as it strove and strives to explain the sense in which Christ was both human and divine has been essentially a protracted effort to account for the divergent ways in which these last words, and other such sayings of Our Lord's, can simultaneously be heard. And this is necessarily so, because Christian theology is not a free exercise of the speculative mind but rather bound to the textual exegesis of Scripture; it is, we might put it in our parochial terms, simply literary criticism.

Let me be a little drier. It is possible to conceive that when Christ on the cross said 'My God, my God, why hast thou forsaken me?', he meant:'I shall now quote you an old saying, which, if you think about it (as you won't), will make clear to you that I am not forsaken but rather fulfilling. Like the speaker of the psalm, I appear to experience absolute dereliction, but please remember how psalm 22 ends. I accomplish past Scripture; I am now the living truth of what was said of old. It is not my death you should be concentrating on but rather how what I am now doing revivifies what you thought, however reverently, to be past and done with, the divine writings.' Or it is possible to think that He happened to say, in His unique agony, the same words as had been said by some other, now dead, speaker from the same finite tradition. He may not have been quoting or alluding; that He said the same words could be a coincidence. After all, these words are not the only

allusion to psalm 22 in the Marcan passion narrative; before Christ's
last outcry, we read this:

And they that passed by railed on him, wagging their heads, and saying, Ah
thou that destroyest the temple, and buildest it in three days,
    Save thyself, and come down from the cross.
    Likewise also the chief priests mocking said among themselves with the
scribes, He saved others; himself he cannot save.[7]

The passers-by, the priests, and scribes behave just as psalm 22 said they
would: 'All that see me laugh me to scorn: they shoot out the lip, they
shake the head, saying, He trusted on the LORD that would deliver
him: let him deliver him, seeing he delighted in him.' They cannot
themselves be thought of as alluding to the psalm, as if they had suddenly decided to form one of those clubs which delight to re-enact
the past, battles of the Civil War and suchlike. Such a 'fulfilment' of Old
Testament scripture in New Testament occurrence has long been
employed by Christian apologists to demonstrate the divine economy
in Christ's life; He really is what the prophets foretold, the history of
Israel foreshadowed. By exactly the same token, these coherences
between Old and New Testament have been mistrusted by the unconvinced. They are not very impressive as predictions of the future; all
psalm 22 says is that some people behave cruelly to those who are suffering, gloat over the misfortunes of their fellow-beings; they were like
that in the past and so are likely to be like that again. This is a sad truth
but not one which requires clairvoyance or supernatural powers to
divine, quite ordinary and bitter repetitive experience is sufficient.
What impresses me is just this lack of striking forecast; something
more 'marvellous' would be showy, and God, whatever His faults, is
not showy. Scholars are pleased to tell us that such correspondences
were written into the narrative by the evangelist, as 'proofs' of the divine nature of Christ's mission. Fair enough, but the scholars have often
a trivializing idea of what the creation or discovery of such correspondences meant for the writer. Do they mean that Mark invented
Christ's last words as they are reported? Perhaps he did, but this would
show only that St Mark was even more exceptional a writer than we
had previously thought, for the structure of possibilities in those words
and their relation to the psalm remains quite as complex, their theological

[7] Mark 15:29–31.

implications retain the same reach, whether Christ said them or Mark thought it appropriate to make out that Christ said them. It seems to me more likely that Mark is reporting in the case of Christ's words, and reporting again *but in the light of his understanding of Christ's words* when he recognizes the similarity between the mockery attending of these events and the mockery recorded in the psalm. Which is to say that the Gospel is written, at least here, 'in the spirit of Christ', and that is the impressive, the noteworthy fact.

It sounds ridiculous to claim that the same being can be simultaneously God and man. The concepts 'God' and 'man' exclude one another, their spheres diverge; try to bring them together, hold them conjoined, and you feel a push which holds them apart, as you do when trying to bring the north pole of one magnet near to another north. There is a little, insuperable swerve. Over and through the swerve, there comes the claim: these poles cannot be brought together, *because they are like poles*; what, conceptually, we cannot conjoin—the infinite and the finite, God and man—have somehow come together. St Cyril of Alexandria was firm: everything said about Christ as man must be understood as said about and by Christ as God, for the 'as-man' and the 'as-God' are here yoked together by a violence, at once stupefying and graceful:

If anyone distributes between two persons or *hypostases* the terms used in the evangelical and apostolic writings, whether spoken of Christ by the saints or by him about himself, and attaches some to a man thought of separately from the Word of God, and others as befitting God to the Word of God the Father alone, let him be anathema.[8]

Take 'My God, my God, why has thou forsaken me?', for instance. Heard one way, not as an allusion or quotation but as a coincidence, the words are a naked utterance of purely human anguish; heard in their full relation to the psalm, they could be taken as serenely, impassively content with the perfection of their 'fit'. The first 'hearing' receives them as from 'a man thought of separately from the word of God', the second 'hearing' finds in them 'the Word of God the Father alone'. Their intonational ambiguity is the sound of the mystery of the Incarnation.

---

[8] St Cyril of Alexandria, Third Letter to Nestorius, in *The Library of Christian Classics*, ed. John Baillie, John T. McNeill and Henry P. Van Dusen, 26 vols. (London: SCM Press; Philadelphia: Westminster Press, 1953–69), vol. 3: *Christology of the Later Fathers*, ed. Edward Rochie Hardy with Cyril C. Richardson (1954), p. 353.

Just this ambiguity of voice, between unprecedented utterance of pain and composed achievement of pattern, this simultaneity which bespeaks the pain of pattern itself, is also the element of tragic expression, as we know it from those works of literary art which more usually occupy us in thinking about tragedy. The usual banal reason given for denying that there can be a Judaeo-Christian tragedy (or indeed any 'really tragic' work which affirms the existence of a benign and omnipotent deity) is that Judaeo-Christianity is committed to the notion that 'everything will come out right in the end', and one thing tragedy cannot have is a happy ending. Set aside that this argument ignores the many tragedies which have endings which, though not exactly happy, are felt as 'resigned', acquiescent in the eliciting of some order; set aside the comfortable but unfounded notion that the accomplishment of the divine plan will be anything like what we in our present state would regard as 'happy'; set aside the groundless belief that how affairs end in some way cancels how they seemed while they were going on, as if the interim did not have a reality of its own—the 'moments of agony / ... are likewise permanent / With such permanence as time has'.[9] In the long run, either God becomes all in all or all becomes nothing, dust and ashes as this earth falls into the sun. Tragedy is quite indifferent to either of these conclusions, not being an art of the 'long run' but rather of the 'from time to time' realities of human experience and what we believe we can find through or within that experience. It is in any case not clear why believing that our world will ultimately peter out, incinerated, more accords with tragic practice and its cravings for significance than a belief in the world as to be completed in a way for the moment beyond us.

It is not in any views about human life which may or may not be inferable from tragic art that the particular quality of the tragic resides. Art, in this respect similar to religious faith, is a wholly practical matter, though, like any human practice, it can be conceptualized and is indeed human just in so far as it self-consciously conceptualizes itself. Conceptualizations come and go, the same practice may be variously conceptualized, and it is to the practice that we are always returned. As in the case of tragic weaving. By 'weaving', I mean just the composition of the tragic spectacle as patterned, the kind of pattern which

    [9] T. S. Eliot, *Four Quartets*, 'The Dry Salvages' II, ll. 56, 59–60, in *The Poems of T. S. Eliot*, vol. 1, p. 196.

can be exemplified in the arrival of the monster in *Phèdre* or in the
varieties of web, textile, and snare in *Othello*. Events too can be woven,
of course, and I concentrate on verbal weaving largely because this is
the sort of thing I happen to notice, and because verbal texture can be
precisely described (not that I think it an accident that tragedies have
exact linguistic shape, on the contrary). Tragic weaving takes place in
the Gospels, too, though it is often wrongly conceptualized by experts
in the sacred writings. As when Professor Evans, a distinguished New
Testament scholar, comments as follows on the tissue of allusions in the
passion narratives, allusions such as that to psalm 22:

Almost all the main constituents of the passion story...either have attached to
them explicit O[ld] T[estament] citations or have OT vocabulary woven into
the narrative. In this way it was precluded that the events, and hence the total
event which they made up, were either haphazard or accidental. They were
removed from the sphere of the contingent, which is what we particularly
associate with the historical. They were removed also from the sphere of fate,
which for the Greeks brooded over the life of man, and in the last analysis
operated even behind the lives of the gods... They were also removed from
the sphere of tragedy... This result was achieved all the more forcibly when
the chief protagonist in the story, Jesus himself, not only is made to use scripture to express the character of the events and the participation of his own will
in what is decreed, but also to use it alongside and in support of what he inde-
pendently initiates and predicts.[10]

The reasoning about, the conceptualization of, the Gospel practice is
all wrong. The presence of an older text in a younger one may be more
variously accounted for than is recognized here: self-conscious, purposeful allusion (and for a variety of purposes, not just for the fabrication of an apologetically motivated illusion of 'prophetic fulfilment');
reminiscence within an individual of his or her process of acculturation
(why is it the psalms and not the *Bhagavad-Gita* that Jesus recalls on the
cross?); trans-individual persistence of sayings, the terms of a community's coming to self-understanding; haunting and shadowing by the
past; coincidence. Take, for instance, the loud voice, *phōnē megalē*, with
which Jesus cries out his last words in St Mark and St Matthew, in
which he also cries out in St Luke, though in different words. We have
heard this loud voice before. In St Luke, for example, he begins the
passion narrative in chapter 19, as Jesus rides into Jerusalem to the

---

[10] C. F. Evans, *Explorations in Theology 2* (London: SCM, 1977), 13–14.

accompaniment of loud, acclaiming voices: 'all the multitude of the disciples began to praise God with rejoicings in a loud voice *phōnē megalē*.' The crowd shouts aloud greetings to Christ as a king; He is though left at the last hanging under a notice derisively styling him 'King of the Jews' to cry alone in his single loud voice, acclamation deserts him, turns to lament. Luke had begun his Gospel with many rejoicings at the birth of Christ and of John the Baptist (see 1:14; 1:28; 1:57; 2:10). In the light of what later happens to these two men—beheading, crucifixion—the celebrations at the births of John and Jesus have a human poignancy: how little parents can foresee what is to become of their children. The verbal weave of the text does not lift the events out of the contingent and historical; on the contrary, it creates a web of retrospection, through which we can now see the past as composed, but composed of the consciousnesses of people who could not then see the shape they would acquire. The 'loud voice' with which Jesus is greeted on His entry into Jerusalem is the same loud voice with which He was first greeted, before His birth, by Elizabeth when she cried out in a loud voice to greet the pregnant Mary (1:42)—the first welcome into the human community, the climactic moment of human triumph, the loneliness at the moment of death: all three are marked with this '*phōnē megalē*'. Now the Gospel is accomplished, we can hear that voice trans-temporally, with all its accrued ironies, its dismay, its stamina. But no person processively within the Gospel can hear it thus on any particular occasion. Jesus is the special case, because as the Divine Word he can and does hear it trans-temporally while at the same time, as fully human, he hears only through time. Metaphysically speaking, it is difficult to conceptualize this double hearing, but practically it occurs to anyone who learns to read a text thus organized, for each of us can hear both over and through time, recognize a drama in its process of coming-to-be and in its patterned completion.

Tragic dramas are organized like this too. Sophocles's *Women of Trachis*, for instance, at least in the version produced by Ezra Pound. When the chorus first hears of the fate which has befallen Herakles, they lament as follows:

> TORN between griefs, which grief shall I lament,
> which first? Which last, in heavy argument?
> One wretchedness to me in double load.
> DEATH's in the house,
> and death comes by the road.

> THAT WIND might bear away my grief and me,
> Sprung from the hearth-stone, let it bear me away
> God's Son is dead
>   that was so brave and strong,
> And I am craven to behold such death
>   Swift on the eye
> Pain hard to uproot,
>   and this so vast
> A splendor of ruin.[11]

Pound is fabricating a trans-temporal weave in this passage. He has no real warrant for the great phrase 'A splendor of ruin', with all this implies about tragic catastrophe as both a plight and a mark of prestige. He wanted the word 'splendor' at this point because he was convinced that a later passage of the play, in which Herakles comes to recognize the shape of his own agony, contained a key phrase, the pivot for the entire play, and, in order to highlight that pivotal quality, he had to create a foregoing pattern for it which in fact is not in Sophocles. The later passage is as follows:

> Time lives, and it's going on now.
> I am released from trouble.
> I thought it meant life in comfort.
> It doesn't. It means that I die.
> For amid the dead there is no work in service.
> Come at it that way, my boy, what
> SPLENDOR,
>   IT ALL COHERES.[12]

Two words in the Greek provide the basis for Pound's ecstatic capitals, two words which nothing in the earlier lines on the 'splendor of ruin' resembles—'*lampra sumbainei*', which might be less ardently translated as 'splendidly comes together', for the verb *sumbainei* less definitely rejoices in coherence than Pound's translation admits, meaning basically 'to stand with both feet together', to 'happen', to 'coincide', as well as to 'agree' or 'cohere'. That is, the Greek word admits a greater range of significances to Herakles' sense of possible pattern in these events than Pound's great-voiced paean to coherence. Pound here demonstrably works in the way some scholars presume the evangelists work,

---

[11] Ezra Pound, after Sophocles, *Women of Trachis* [1954], ed. Denis Goacher and Peter Whigham (New York: New Directions, 1985), 41.

[12] *Women of Trachis*, 49–50.

writing contour into and through occurrences; he has contributed to Sophocles a coming-together of the choric lament and the protagonist's revaluation of that lament into self-discovery. Some may want to complain of this, as Beckett complained about the novels of T. F. Powys, in which he disliked their 'fabricated darkness and painfully organised unified tragic completeness',[13] though it is radiance Pound fabricates. Whatever attitude we might take up, it needs remembering that Herakles' ecstasy comes to him through the agony of Nessus's poisoned shirt, the transcendent utterance surges up in him under the pressure of physical torment from his 'intolerable shirt of flame'.

If we wish to consider what Christ's death on the cross has meant in the imagination of the West, we do better to start from the liturgy of the Church than from its theological productions; theology was and is no more than the conceptual practice of a few Christians, whereas liturgy is communally experienced by many. The Catholic service for Good Friday contains a sequence known as the 'reproaches'; in this ancient passage (it is recorded from the fourth century AD), Christ is imagined as speaking to the congregation from the cross. It opens like this:

Cantors. Popule meus, quid feci tibi? aut in quo constristavi te? responde mihi. Quia eduxi te de terra Ægypti: parasti Crucem Salvatori tuo.

Response. Agios o Theos. Sanctus Deus. Agios Ischyros. Sanctus Fortis. Agios Athanatos, eleison hymas. Sanctus Immortalis, miserere nobis.

O my people, what have I done to thee? For I led thee out of the land of Egypt, and thou hast prepared a cross for thy Saviour. O holy God, O holy God, O holy strong one, O holy strong one. O holy immortal one, have mercy on us, O holy immortal one, have mercy on us.[14]

There are eleven more such reproaches, each time responded to in the same manner. (That the response is made bilingually in Greek and Latin indicates the antiquity of the sequence, pre-dating as it does the split between Eastern and Western Christendom.) In the verset, the people are addressed as those who are guilty of the passion, and as its beneficiaries; it is as if at the end of each response, they had come to full acknowledgement of Christ's divinity, only then to slide back into disbelief and hatred, to re-crucify Him, and need then to be again addressed as the 'O my people' who pierced His side, scourged Him,

---

[13] Beckett to Tom MacGreevy, 8 November 1931, in *The Letters of Samuel Beckett*, vol. 1: *1929–1940* (2009), p. 94.

[14] *The Gregorian Missal for Sundays* (Solesmes: Abbaye Saint-Pierre, 1990), 311–12.

gave Him gall and vinegar to drink. The liturgy here acutely feels the phenomenological ebb and flow of devotion, and preserves the fluctuant rhythm of piety and its intermittences even as it turns that rhythm into a serenely maintained symmetry. George Herbert's 'The Sacrifice' is a long dramatic monologue, elaborated out of this liturgical sequence; once again Christ is speaking from the cross; this is the moment at which he cries 'Eloi, Eloi, lama sabachthani':

> Lo, here I hang, charg'd with a world of sinne,
> The greater world o'th'two; for that came in
> By words, but this by sorrow I must win:
>   Was ever grief like mine?
>
> Such sorrow as, if sinfull man could feel,
> Or feel his part, he would not cease to kneel,
> Till all were melted, though he were all steel:
>   Was ever grief like mine?
>
> But, *O my God, my God!* why leav'st thou me,
> The sonne, in whom thou dost delight to be?
> *My God, my God—*
>   Never was grief like mine.[15]

Herbert breaks his verse-line and his rhyme-scheme for the moment of godforsakenness. He has dramatized and humanized Christ effusively, in a way unthinkable to the Gospels with their sublime reticence of affect or to the liturgical sequence; this Christ is closer to the humanistic Christ who realizes in these words that he has made a mistake and dies alone. Yet even in these lines of novel psychological portraiture, formalities are maintained, though '*My God, my God*' breaks off and 'Never was grief like mine' comes in, as it were, 'too early', the two phrases together make up the ten-syllable line which is Herbert's point of departure and to which he always returns. Christ speaks turbulently and urgently, like a man in pain though one struggling to argue his way through the pain—the marked contrastive emphases, 'that...this', in the first stanza quoted, the concessive, self-revising iteration of 'feel' in 'if sinfull man could feel, / Or feel his part'; this verse is built for vocalization as well as any play-script, for us to hear and act through, in contrast to the Gospel saying of 'My God, my God...', which has as expressive stage direction only 'in a loud voice'. We could compare the

---

[15] George Herbert, 'The Sacrifice', in *The English Poems of George Herbert*, ed. Helen Wilcox, 3rd edn (Cambridge: Cambridge University Press, 2013), ll. 205–16 (p. 102).

line from the Gospel text through the liturgical sequence to Herbert's
poem with the way pictorial representations of the crucifixion developed. There are no known representations of Christ's death on the cross
before the fifth century; until about the ninth century Christ is usually
depicted alive, with eyes wide open, and with no trace of suffering (that
is, he appears as the 'quoting' Christ, the Christ of fulfilment, not of
dereliction). Only in ninth-century Byzantium do we begin to find
representations of a physically afflicted and dying Christ, the Christ of
blood and wounds familiar to us now. (Those like William Empson
who think of Christianity as essentially a religion of torture-worship
should reflect on the fact that it took nearly a thousand years before
Christian art started to concentrate on these aspects of the crucifixion.)
For Herbert, the crucifixion has begun to sound more like a 'human
interest' story. We re-encounter an art closer to the incarnational ambiguity of the Gospels in Eliot, *Ash-Wednesday*:

> O my people, what have I done unto thee.
>
> Will the veiled sister between the slender
> Yew trees pray for those who offend her
> And are terrified and cannot surrender
> And affirm before the world and deny between the rocks
> In the last desert between the last blue rocks
> The desert in the garden the garden in the desert
> Of drouth, spitting from the mouth the withered apple-seed.
>
> O my people.[16]

Where Herbert took the skeleton of the liturgical sequence and
fleshed it out with what Christ may have been supposed to be feeling,
Eliot has broken even that skeletal structure, made it barer still. As he
does in other sections of *Ash-Wednesday*, he takes a repetitive formula
from the tradition of worship (the *Ave Maria*, the *Domine non sum dig-
nus*, the *Salve Regina*) and fractures it, positions it in his lines so that we
cannot say how much of its original context it summons allusively
back or how much of it is to be heard as bereft of that original content,
re-creating then exactly the relation between Christ's last words and
their source in psalm 22. Are the words 'O my people...' here to be
imagined as part of a ritual, or as reminisced about quite personally by
someone whose vis-à-vis with ritual we are not told (perhaps because

---

[16] T. S. Eliot, *Ash-Wednesday* (1930), 5, ll. 28–36, in *The Poems of T. S. Eliot*, vol. 1, p. 95.

he does not know it)? Herbert breaks his formal scheme for obviously dramatic purposes, but do we know what is happening when, after the triplet of rhymes 'slender / offend her / surrender', we come up with a shock against the brute iteration of 'rocks / rocks'? Why does the poem 'go wrong' there? He leaves us with a last skewed rhyme: 'apple(-seed) / people'. At one level, this rhyme is monumentally orthodox: it intimates that by His death on the cross Christ as redeemed the sin of Adam, has made of fallen human beings, the seed of the apple, with all their disparities between each other and within themselves one redeemed people. This is the primary understanding of the crucifixion in the early church—as a triumphant act of unification, not as the diremption it later became. Apple / people: Adam / Christ—such are the elements of, for example, Irenaeus's account of Christ's life as the 'recapitulation' of all preceding human history; He lived again in Himself all history and showed that it could be lived as congruent with God rather than as godforsaken: 'and that is why He came to His own in a visible manner, and was made flesh, and hung upon the tree, that He might sum up all things in Himself, in such a way that His own creation bore Him... which itself is borne by Him.'[17] Or as St Athanasius boldly and vividly puts it: 'how would he have called us to him, had he not been crucified? for it is only on the cross that a man dies with his arms wide open.'[18]

All this may be in the closing words of *Ash-Wednesday*, 5, but it has to be carefully listened for, so under the breath is it said. It is a world away from Pound's blazing capitals, his splendour of coherence. Across the page, the possible rhyme 'apple / people' is splayed, only momentarily caught, a hint, fugitive as the beginning of a smile or sudden light in the eyes; it hangs in the white space which also separates writing which is markedly Eliot's 'own' from a liturgical saying which he may or may not have made his own. Such coherence as there may be here is only nascent, but then that was true of the Gospels too when they were being written.

De Quincey describes a moment of cohering that struck someone at the point of death; this is his version of the old legend that, when

---

[17] St Irenaeus, *Against Heresies*, ed. Alexander Roberts and James Donaldson ([n. p.]: Ex Fontibus, 2010), Book 5, 18.3–19.1 (pp. 553–4). The translation differs slightly from that given above.

[18] St Athanasius, *On the Incarnation of the Word*, in *The Library of Christian Classics*, vol. 8, p. 79 (the translation differs slightly from that given above).

dying, especially it is sometimes said when drowning, your whole past life passes before your mind:

a blow seemed to strike her, phosphoric radiance sprang forth from her eye-balls; and immediately a mighty theatre expanded within her brain. In a moment, in the twinkling of an eye, every act, every design of her past life, lived again, arraying themselves not as a succession, but as parts of a coexistence . . . so that her consciousness became omnipresent at one moment to every feature in the infinite review.[19]

De Quincey's excitable prose makes it sound as if, for a moment, this woman saw her life exactly as God is said to see His universe—not bittily successive but cohered, simultaneously co-present, 'so that her consciousness became omnipresent at one moment to every feature in the infinite review'. Indeed, via an allusion, he says as much. Compare 1 Corinthians 15:52:

Behold, I shew you a mystery; we shall not all sleep, but we shall all be changed.

In a moment, in the twinkling of an eye, at the last trump: for the trumpet shall sound, and the dead shall be raised incorruptible, and we shall be changed.

For this corruptible must put on incorruption, and this mortal must put on immortality.

Now, whether De Quincey thought that the psychological experience of the woman was to be understood in the light of St Paul's account of the Last Judgement, or whether he thought that St Paul's account was rather to be regarded as a cosmically aggrandized version of this psychological experience, I neither know nor care. Allusive relation between any two points can usually be read in either direction, psalm 22 understood through Mark 15:34 or vice versa. My concern is to indicate the centrality of this phenomenon of lightning cohesion, its relation to the imminence of death, and its entire neutrality between any religious faith or absence of religious faith. Tragic weave is an artistic practice which yields such coherences; this practice is identical with the compositional practice of the Gospels. Therefore, there is no incompatibility in practice between tragic art and the expression of religious faith in a benign and omnipotent deity. That is all I need to show. I add as a free gift the assertion that not only is there no such

---

[19] Thomas De Quincey, *Suspiria de Profundis* (1845), in *Confessions of an English Opium-Eater and Other Writings*, ed. Robert Morrison, 2nd edn (Oxford: Oxford University Press, 2013), 136–7.

incompatibility, but that God is essential to tragedy because He is its supreme audience, and it is a fundamental process of tragic art to enable its human audience for a time and from time to time to guess what it might be like to be such a God.

Antony and Cleopatra is, as far as I can recall, the only play by Shakespeare in which we see, or rather hear, a god forsaking someone: Act 4, scene 3:

> *Enter a Company of Soldiours.*
> *1.Sol.* Brother, goodnight: to morrow is the day.
> *2.Sol.* It will determine one way: Fare you well.
> Heard you of nothing strange about the streets.
> *1* Nothing: what newes?
> *2* Belike 'tis but a Rumour, good night to you.
> *1* Well sir, good night.
> > *They meete other Soldiers.*
> *2* Souldiers, have carefull Watch.
> *1* And you: Goodnight, goodnight.
> > *They place themselves in every corner of the Stage.*
> *2* Heere we: and if to morrow
> Our Nauie thrive, I have an absolute hope
> Our Landmen will stand up.
> *1* 'Tis a brave Army, and full of purpose.
> > *Musicke of the Hoboyes is under the Stage.*
> *2* Peace, what noise?
> *1* List, list.
> *2* Hearke.
> *1* Musicke I'th' Ayre.
> *3* Vnder the earth.
> *4* It signes well, do's it not?
> *3* No.
> *1* Peace I say: What should this meane?
> *2* 'Tis the God *Hercules*, whom *Anthony* loved,
> Now leaves him.
> *1* Walke, let's see if other Watchmen
> Do heare what we do?
> *2* How now Maisters?   *Speak together.*
> *Omnes.* How now? how now? do you heare this?
> *1* I, is't not strange?
> *3* Do you heare Masters? Do you heare?
> *1* Follow the noyse so farre as we haue quarter.
> Let's see how it will give off.
> *Omnes.* Content: 'Tis strange.   *Exeunt.*

Enter Anthony and Cleopatra, with others.
Ant. *Eros*, mine Armour *Eros*.[20]

Even as things fall apart, they fall apart on cue; this is another 'splendor of ruin'. It is as the first and second soldiers express their confidences in how well the human arrangements for the next day's battle have been made—'I have an absolute hope...', ''Tis a brave Army, and full of purpose'—that the *'Musicke of the Hoboyes'* makes itself heard, the plaintive but attuned sound of Hercules withdrawing, music as sounding-forth a 'purpose' beyond what creatures such as these can intend. That intimation of musical purpose beyond the envisaging of any individual agent is one reason why the scene begins to sound like *The Tempest*, like Ferdinand who also doesn't know whether the music he hears is in the air or the earth. Like onlookers at the crucifixion, the soldiers give diverse significances to what they witness—a good omen, 'It signes well, do's it not?', an ill portent, 'No'. Their very uncertainties, their stabs at conclusion, their plans, their hubbub are themselves composed by Shakespeare into lightly woven verse.

Modern editors are troubled by the scene, partly because there are so many leave-takings in it, yet no one seems to go; particularly, they often reassign First Soldier's 'And you: Goodnight, goodnight', because it seems that this should be said by one of the *'other Soldiers'* they have just met. People keep on saying goodbye but nobody goes. It is a Beckettian scene—Let's go. Yes, let's go. *They do not move*—and Beckett may have alluded to it in *Footfalls*: compare 'Heard you of nothing strange about the streets' with 'Mrs W: You yourself observed nothing... strange?'[21] We should not be worried by these repeated leave-takings after which nobody leaves, certainly not by Act 4 of *Antony and Cleopatra*, because the play has been filled with delayed departures from the start. Is has the word 'farewell' more times than any other play by Shakespeare, often in spates all together as in this scene. Nor is it only the separation of Antony and Cleopatra which is so often fussed and teazled over, but that between Caesar and Antony too:

> Ant. Come Sir, come,
> Ile wrastle with you in my strength of love,

[20] *Antony and Cleopatra*, IV.iii.2467–503.
[21] Samuel Beckett, *Footfalls* (1976), in *Krapp's Last Tape and Other Shorter Plays* (London: Faber and Faber, 2009), 113.

> Looke heere I have you, thus I let you go,
> And give you to the Gods.
> *Caesar.* Adieu, be happy.
> *Lep[idus].* Let all the number of the Starres give light
> To thy faire way.
> *Caesar.* Farewell, farewell.   *Kisses Octauia.*
> *Ant.* Farewell.[22]

There is something comic about these clusters of farewells, like the behaviour of those nervous people who say they're going and then hover for ages in the doorway, thinking of something more to say, or like an actor outrageously milking an exit-line. But in these postponements of separation, we can also hear deeper, more pierced reluctance to be forsaken and to forsake. As Cole Porter has it, 'every time we say goodbye / I die a little', and these little delayings by flurries of adieux are also delays of the final separation to come on them and us all.[23] They play out the compliments, the well-wishing, like the child Freud observed in his game with the bobbin on a thread; he threw it from his cot, so he could see it no more, and staged a dismay, '*Fort!*', 'Gone!', then amused and calmed himself by drawing it back into view, '*Da!*', 'Back again!'.[24] High tragic art rehearses with its spooling eloquence prospects of larger abandonment:

> *Eros.* My deere Master,
> My Captaine, and my Emperor. Let me say
> Before I strike this bloody stroke, Farewell.
> *Ant.* 'Tis said man, and farewell.
> *Eros.* Farewell great Chiefe. Shall I strike now?
>   *Ant.* Now *Eros.*   *Killes himselfe.*
> Why there then:
> Thus I do escape the sorrow of *Anthonies* death.[25]

'Let me say...Farewell.' / ''Tis said man, and farewell.' / 'Farewell great Chiefe...': it is the *Eros*, Antony's, now leaving him, as Antony will leave Cleopatra at last, though Enobarbus had denied that he could—'Now

---

[22] *Antony and Cleopatra*, III.ii.1611–19.

[23] Cole Porter, 'Ev'ry Time We Say Goodbye', in *Music and Lyrics by Cole Porter: A Treasury of Cole Porter*, 2nd edn (New York: Chappell & Co., 1991), 202.

[24] Sigmund Freud, *Beyond the Pleasure Principle* [1920], in *Beyond the Pleasure Principle and Other Writings*, trans. John Reddick (London: Penguin, 2003), 53.

[25] *Antony and Cleopatra*, IV.xiv.2929–36.

Antony must leave her utterly.' / 'Never. He will not.' As he had an unreliable servant at his death, so she has one at hers, the Clown who will not leave the stage:

> *Clow[n]*. [...] but this is most falliable, the Worme's an odde Worme.
> *Cleo*. Get thee hence, farewell.
> *Clow*. I wish you all joy of the Worme.
> *Cleo*. Farewell.
> *Clow*. You must thinke this (looke you,) that the
> Worme will do his kinde.
> *Cleo*. I, I, farewell.[26]

It takes her another fourteen lines to get rid of him, before she can say her farewells:

> Farewell kinde *Charmian*, *Iras*, long farewell.
> Have I the Aspicke in my lippes? Dost fall?
> If thou, and Nature can so gently part,
> The stroke of death is as a Lovers pinch,
> Which hurts, and is desir'd. Dost thou lye still?
> If thus thou vanishest, thou tell'st the world,
> It is not worth leave-taking.[27]

As Cleopatra dies, she acquires that 'phosphoric radiance' which De Quincey attributes to the woman who saw her whole life in the twinkling of an eye. Shakespeare arranges things, arranges words, so that much of the play seems spoken again through her mouth, so many allusions focusing on and through her that she becomes an image of 'the soul who gathered in herself' (*synethroismene hautes eis heauten*), as Socrates about to die in the *Phaedo* describes the philosopher's soul at the edge of death.[28] Her recollections crowd in on her, and there is a pathos in this for they are all that she does not want to but will lose, her life in sum. On the other hand, her power of recollection here, her ability to concentrate the past in herself as she dies, has a mysterious serenity to it that diffuses itself through the nursery-quiet of this suicide which arranges itself to look not like a severance but a marriage. The sublimity of her dying is not unlike Christ's as he dies, however unlike her

---

[26] *Antony and Cleopatra*, V.ii.3509–15.
[27] *Antony and Cleopatra*, V.ii.3543–49.
[28] Plato, *Phaedo*, trans. and ed. David Gallop, 3rd edn (Oxford: Oxford University Press, 2009), 32.

prettified circumstances are to His stripped and spectacular victimhood (and I am not saying Cleopatra is Christlike. On the contrary, it is her unlikeness to Christ which makes the congruence in their dyings of weight). For she acquires as she prepares herself for the asp the temperate smoothness of the well-rehearsed actress. Now, as she is about to lose it, she knows her part. Tragedies themselves rehearse their protagonists and audience for leave-taking, though no amount of rehearsal can guarantee the lines will at the crucial moment come out right, let alone how the performance will be received when this mortal puts on immortality. It is a strange business, tragedy, with which we are somehow content, like the soldiers as they listen to the music with which the god Hercules forsakes Antony's and their cause: 'Content: 'Tis strange.' The strangeness, as I hear it, is like that of Christ on the cross:

he who was begotten from God the Father as Son and God only-begotten, though being by his own nature impassible, suffered in the flesh for us, according to the Scriptures, and he was in the crucified flesh[29].

I take my leave of you in lines from the *Purgatorio*, where Dante, astoundingly but not incomprehensibly, thinks of Christ as happy, '*lieto*', as he cried out 'My God, my God . . .'. Forese Donati explains why the intemperate in life circle for their purgation constantly around a fruit-tree and a fountain they cannot reach:

> 'Tutta esta gente che piagendo canta
>   per seguitar la gola oltra misura
>   in fame e 'sete qui si rifà snata.
> Di bere e di mangier n'accende cura
>   l'odor ch'esce del pomo e dello sprazzo
>   che si distende su per sua verdura.
> E non pur una volta, questo spazzo
>   girando, si rinfresca nostra pena:
>   io dico pena, e dovrà dir sollazzo
> chè qualla voglia all'abore ci mena
>   che menò Cristo lieto a dire 'Elì',
>   quando ne liberò con la sua vena.'

'All these people whose song is weeping, whose tears are attuned, followed craving beyond all bounds, and here they make themselves holy again

---

[29] St Cyril of Alexandria, Third Letter to Nestorius, in *The Library of Christian Classics*, vol. 3, p. 351.

through hunger and thirst. The scent of the fruit-tree rekindles the longing to eat and the fountain's spray which mists the foliage revives thirst in them. And not only as we go our rounds upon this level does the painful craving for refreshment comes freshly on us. I call it 'pain' we suffer but the word is 'relief', for this desire in us for the tree of satisfaction leads us there where Christ was led when he cried in gladness '*Elì*' and freed us from desire with his blood.'[30]

[30] Dante, *The Divine Comedy: Inferno, Purgatorio, Paradiso*, trans. and ed. Robin Kirkpatrick (London: Penguin, 2012), *Purgatorio*, 23, ll. 64–75, (p. 267).

II

Translations

Overnighting

The room is widowed
Each to his own
No pets allowed
Payment down

The owner looks twice
at our travellers' cheques
my head is spinning
my clothes are a wreck

Sounds of revving up
From next door
The scent of Seven-Up
Pervades the floor

All the guests
In this hotel
Speak excellent English
As spoken in hell

Let the doors close
and be put on the chain
you carry your case
I carry mine

Apollinaire: 'Hôtels'
(omitting, as the vicar says, verse four)

The line to Finistère

The stags were ill at ease beneath the rain
in Brittany as like unflighted arrows
your eyelashes came down at twilight and then
were raised to inquire about the dawn on stucco,
from where and why it tossed up branches of shade,
bicycle-wheels and spindles and distress-flares.
It could be said I have no other proof
that God still has me in his eye and that
your eyes are looking out for him as always
recessively blue like a coast-line.

Montale: 'Verso Finistère'

I love you for your body alone

It's true that we two make
an intriguing couple:
my heart's delight is pigeon-toed;
I'm not notably supple.

The one on the left has cat-'flu,
the one the right has rabies;
no halfway-decent health inspector
would permit us to have babies.

We swear we're as close as can be
but keep our hips apart.
We are prudent. Our unanimity
centres on Romanesque art.

You see yourself as a jasmine
at risk on a shaky stem.
I'm a bloodless specimen—
a moon in a veil of dilemma.

The jasmine shrinks in the light of the moon
while the moon retreats from the jasmine.
Nothing is born from their inbetween
but this line but this line but this line.

Heine: 'Lotosblume'

About to leave

It's all gone out in my heart:
frolic, disappointment, and partisanship. I've stopped hating
my colleagues and the sounds of mating.
I don't know what I need, or care what
others might need. Perhaps I have died.
The play played out, the public wends its way
home. Such dears, I love them, yawns
and all, whether fetching or forlorn
or both. How very right they are—
a take-away, a spouse, a jar
or two or three (at week-ends), is
the best that this life has to send us.
He too was right, the wretched hero
who cried aloud in Homer first, the sero-
positive Achilles: the prissiest
Philistine in Ashton-under-Lyme
is better off than I am
with my divine blood, my deeds, my curls,
lording it over a shadowy world.

Heine: 'Der Scheidende'

All for the Seraphic

1

A single white seagull
catches my eye
over the ink and the shapelessness;
the moon is on another high.

The shark and his colleagues with smaller teeth
sieve the liquid spirals of prey;
the gull is lofted and let down;
the moon is on another high.

And, O my acquiescing heart,
your love is a refugee;
you mustn't go too near the water.
The moon is on another high.

2

The seagull gives us long, hard looks
and, evidently, we look queer—
you with your heart in a book,
me with my lips at your ear.

The poor bird is dying to know
just what you pour from your lips,
whether it is caresses
or axioms they let drop.

I too would dearly like to say
what scrabbles at my heart.
Words and kisses are
with difficulty told apart.

3

And on this rock we two shall build
the church we always wanted,
based on an Improved Testament
which takes our pains for granted.

Our doubts shall all be put to sleep,
they'll give us no more anguish.
The long bêtise of love and stuff
becomes a dead language.

God has been strolling on the waves,
gently rebuking the pedalos.
He mentioned something I didn't catch
concerning us and haloes.

The Lord God holds His court in light
as also in darknesses,
and He is all that is the case.
Look at Him, there, in our kisses.

4
Evening gray on the upset tides;
the merest of stars seething
to itself; and sometimes you hear
voices. The water breathing.

Down over there the north wind plays
with the tip of a wave alone;
the flux and reflux have a way
with them, chatter and organ-tones.

Pagan waters but also priestly,
they hum and engage in debate;
their tunings reach the stratosphere
and make the stars feel great.

And so the stars collectively
are lit up with delight;
they are inflated into suns and
skeeter about the night.

In time with music way beneath them,
they wink and hesitate and gurgle.
They're interstitial nightingales;
the universe is their social circle.

And hubbub on its rounds
resounds within me mightily.
I feel a disproportionate
longing to get fucked once nightly.

5
Shade of a kiss and love in shade,
shadowy life, wonderful world.

You had supposed that all would stay
the same. You've the brains and the arms of a girl.

In fact, our darling hopes
go out with dreamless bother,
while our hearts forget themselves
the way one eyelid meets an other.

6
Sailing, sailing with very black sails
across the tiresome sea;
you're well aware that you're my rack
yet you apply yourself to me.

You've a heart like summer wind,
a dip and a current which drive me
sailing, sailing with very black sails
across the tiresome sea.

7
My room overlooks the sea.
I sit there dreaming.
The wind is a harmonica.
The waves are scheming.

I've often been in love before.
I've had lots of chums.
Where are they now? The tuneful wind
counterpoints the water's schemes.

8
The sea is laid out in sunlight,
an oily, reverberant skin.
Brothers and sisters, when I die,
let me down gently therein.

I've always been fond of the sea—
its edges, depth, and lather
have often stood me in good stead.
A couple of swells together.

Heine: 'Zu "Seraphine"'

Index